Greece in the 21st Century

For most of the first part of the 21st century Greece has been seen as a critical battlefield for the survival of the powerful and the adjustment or extinction of the weak, as if all the historical contradictions of the global financial crisis and the eurozone crisis were concentrated in that tiny part of the world, with a population of just 11 million people and a GDP of less than 2% of that of the European Union as a whole. While the country has been overpowered by the disciplinarian and deeply authoritarian policy mix of neoliberal/ordoliberal rules, as this book attempts to show, there is hope. Defeat does not end the crisis, and crisis means constant opportunity. In this state of affairs, all types of agencies try to take advantage of the conditions and opportunities in order to advance towards positions of power and provide the best of solutions for the class interests they represent. Thus, harsh conflict is inevitable and if history provides a yardstick, it is that in periods of conflict and crisis, the winner, usually, is the one who manages to strike the right political and social alliances at the right time.

The editors have assembled in this volume a number of interdisciplinary chapters and arguments which, despite their differences, share the strategic aim of a critique of both neoliberalism/ordoliberalism and new authoritarianism. Chapters examine the eurozone crisis from a variety of angles with reference to Greece, Greek politics and society. With this collection of heterodox and scholarly essays, the authors and editors aim to offer a progressive understanding of current historical circumstances.

Vassilis K. Fouskas is Professor of international politics and economics at the University of East London, UK, and the founding editor of the *Journal of Balkan and Near Eastern Studies* (Routledge/Taylor & Francis).

Constantine Dimoulas is an Assistant Professor in social administration and evaluation of social programmes at Panteion University, Greece.

Europa Country Perspectives

The *Europa Country Perspectives* series, from Routledge, examines a wide range of contemporary political, economic, developmental and social issues from areas around the world. Complementing the *Europa Regional Surveys of the World series, Europa Country Perspectives* is a valuable resource for academics, students, researchers, policymakers, business people and anyone with an interest in current world affairs.

While the *Europa World Year Book* and its associated Regional Surveys inform on and analyse contemporary economic, political and social developments at the national and regional level, Country Perspectives provide in-depth, country-specific volumes written or edited by specialists in their field, delving into a country's particular situation. Volumes in the series are not constrained by any particular template, but may explore a country's recent political, economic, international relations, social, defence, or other issues in order to increase understanding.

Catalonia: A New Independent State in Europe? A Debate over Secession within the European Union
Edited by Xavier Cuadras-Morató

Contesting Spain? The Dynamics of Nationalist Movements in Catalonia and the Basque Country
Edited by Richard Gillespie and Caroline Gray

Political Change in Switzerland: From Stability to Uncertainty
Clive H. Church

Russian Nationalism and Ethnic Violence: Symbolic Violence, Lynching, Pogrom, and Massacre
Richard Arnold

Beyond the Drug War in Mexico: Human rights, the public sphere and justice
Wil G. Pansters, Benjamin T. Smith, Peter Watt

Greece in the 21st Century

The Politics and Economics of a Crisis

Edited by
Vassilis K. Fouskas and
Constantine Dimoulas

Routledge
Taylor & Francis Group
LONDON AND NEW YORK

First published 2018
by Routledge
2 Park Square, Milton Park, Abingdon, Oxon OX14 4RN

and by Routledge
711 Third Avenue, New York, NY 10017

Routledge is an imprint of the Taylor & Francis Group, an informa business

First edition published 2018

Europa Commissioning Editor: Cathy Hartley

Editorial Assistant: Eleanor Simmons

British Library Cataloguing in Publication Data
A catalogue record for this book is available from the British Library

Library of Congress Cataloging in Publication Data
A catalog record has been requested for this book

ISBN: 9781857438673 (hbk)
ISBN: 9781351047524 (ebk)

Typeset in Times New Roman
by Taylor & Francis Books

Contents

List of illustrations vii
List of contributors ix
Abbreviations x

Introduction and Acknowledgments: What's in the Greek Cauldron? 1
VASSILIS K. FOUSKAS AND CONSTANTINE DIMOULAS

1 Eurozone Authoritarianism and the Neoliberal Project in Greece and Southern Europe 13
KEES VAN DER PIJL

2 Sovereign Debt or Balance-of-Payments Crisis?: Exploring the Structural Logic of Adjustment in the Eurozone 40
MATTHIAS KAELBERER

3 Greece and the Crisis of the Eurozone: A Structural Analysis 64
LEILA SIMONA TALANI

4 Is There Really a Eurozone Crisis? 84
TURAN SUBASAT

5 Competing Explanations and Strategies for the Greek Crisis and the Question of the Productive Model 105
STAVROS MAVROUDEAS

6 Internal Devaluation and Hegemonic Crisis (2010–16) 121
ELIAS IOAKIMOGLOU

7 The 'Politics of Fulfilment' as Preliminary for the Making of a Precarious State in Greece 142
MARIA MARKANTONATOU

8 The Political Effects of the Greek Economic Crisis: The Collapse of the Old Two-Party System 163
ALEXANDER KAZAMIAS

9 Blaming the Other: An Enquiry into the Cultural and Political Preconditions of the Greek Crisis 187
TOLIS MALAKOS

Index 203

List of illustrations

Figures

3.1 General government consolidated gross debt, 1999–2010 67
3.2 Real GDP loss 2007–2010 68
3.3 Harmonized inflation rates, % changes: PIIGS and Germany 70
3.4 Balance on current account transactions with the rest of the world: PIIGS and Germany, 1999–2010 70
3.5 Net exports of goods and services at current prices: PIIGS and Germany, 1999–2010 71
3.6 Adjusted wage share: total economy as a % of GDP, 1999–2017 72
3.7 Italy: nominal ULC breakdown (2010 = 100) 73
3.8 Germany: nominal ULC breakdown (2010 = 100) 73
3.9 Portugal: nominal ULC breakdown (2010 = 100) 74
3.10 Spain: nominal ULC breakdown (2010 = 100) 74
3.11 Greece: nominal ULC breakdown (2010 = 100) 75
3.12 Ireland: nominal ULC breakdown (2010 = 100) 75
3.13 PIIGS real exchange rates: 2000–12 77
4.1 Current account balances in selected countries 91
4.2 The components of the current account balance in the Eurozone Periphery 93

Tables

2.1 EMU Bond Yields 42
2.2 Consumer Price Index: HICP (1996 = 100) 44
2.3 Real GDP Growth (% change compared with previous year) 45
2.4 General Government deficit/surplus as % of GDP 47
2.5 Government Gross Debt as % of GDP 48
2.6 Current account balance with the rest of the world ('000m. euros) 49
2.7 rent Account Balance as % of GDP 51

4.1 The determinants of the current account disequilibrium in the Eurozone periphery 95
4.2 The share of the eurozone core countries in the trade deficits of the eurozone periphery 98
4.3 Recap—Any support for the *eurozone crisis* thesis? 100

Contributors

Constantine Dimoulas is an Assistant Professor in social administration and evaluation of social programmes at Panteion University, Greece.

Vassilis K. Fouskas is Professor of international politics and economics at the University of East London, UK, and the founding editor of the *Journal of Balkan and Near Eastern Studies* (Routledge, six issues a year since 1999).

Elias Ioakimoglou is Economic Adviser to the Institute of Labour, the think-tank of the Greek General Confederation of Workers (GGCW), Greece.

Matthias Kaelberer is Professor of political science and Chair of the Political Science Department at the University of Memphis, Tennessee, USA.

Alexander Kazamias is Senior Lecturer in politics at Coventry University, UK.

Tolis Malakos is Research Fellow in the Centre for Contemporary Aristotelian Studies in Ethics and Politics, London Metropolitan University, UK.

Maria Markantonatou is Lecturer in political sociology, University of the Aegean, Greece.

Stavros Mavroudeas is Professor of political economy at the University of Macedonia, Greece.

Kees van der Pijl is Professor Emeritus of international relations at the University of Sussex, UK.

Turan Subasat is Professor of economics at Muğla Sitki Koçman University, Turkey.

Leila Simona Talani is Professor of international political economy at King's College London, UK.

Abbreviations

ECB	European Central Bank
EEC	European Economic Community
EMS	European Monetary System
EMU	Economic and Monetary Union
EU	European Union
GDP	gross domestic product
GNP	gross national product
IMF	International Monetary Fund
NATO	North Atlantic Treaty Organization
OECD	Organisation for Economic Co-operation and Development
PASOK	Panellínio Socialistiko Kinima (Panhellenic Socialist Movement)
Syriza/SYRIZA	Synaspismos Rizospastikis Aristeras (Coalition of the Radical Left)
UK	United Kingdom
US(A)	United States (of America)
USSR	Union of Soviet Socialist Republics

Introduction and Acknowledgments: What's in the Greek Cauldron?

Vassilis K. Fouskas and Constantine Dimoulas

I

The Greek crisis is not as straightforward as many people think. From a scholarly perspective, at least, interpretations vary and even contradict each other. This book does not claim coherence in terms of consistency concerning the argument developed. Economics and politics, after all, are social sciences and, as such, are discursive undertakings: differing arguments and points of view should be welcome. However, what unites all the authors here is that they take issue with neoliberal explanations of the crisis and its neoliberal solutions. In addition, most contributors find that there is an authoritarian/undemocratic core in the eurozone project and the management of its crisis. But let us take matters from the beginning.

Both of us have, on more than one occasion (Fouskas & Dimoulas, 2012; Fouskas & Dimoulas, 2013), argued that the origins of the present crisis in Greece go as far back as the very foundation of the Greek state in 1830. This act laid out some structural and macro-sociological principles that have remained unaltered to the present day, connecting political, cultural and economic instances, internal as well as external factors, in an inextricable way. Thus, the crisis may not just be seen as solely financial, political or economic. As Tolis Malakos sketches out in his contribution, it is deeply moral and cultural, in fact, an identity crisis. In addition, throughout Greece's history, geopolitical and economic developments, ramified with domineering imperial factors, witnessed a unique symbiosis unparalleled for a 'Western European' country: as if Greece was more of a 'Balkan' and 'Near Eastern' social formation in which geopolitics trump economics in determining policy and welfare considerations and issues of war and peace. In such a calculation what matters is the perceived geostrategic value of the country by imperial powers, rather than the market value of the country as such; or, to put it differently, what matters is the Aegean Sea and the air lanes above it as an international passage, rather than the gross domestic product (GDP) and the consumer market of the country as such. In this context, the discourse of domestic 'bourgeois' élites in Greece was being dominated by the 'catch-up' story, that is how to catch up with the 'developed' Western core, whereas the core itself is more interested in power-politics than the sustainable and independent economic development of the peripheral state. We have advanced this line of argument in our joint account on the Greek crisis (Fouskas and Dimoulas, 2013). We have indeed found out that, historically, the creation of the Greek debt is consubstantial with the formation of the Greek state and is thus directly connected to (mainly Western) imperial geopolitical advances in the Ottoman space of the Balkans and the Near/Middle East in 19th century.

Founded in 1830 in the very southern cone of the Balkan Peninsula encompassing the Peloponnese, Southern Rumelia, Euboea and the complex of Cyclades islands, the Greek state resulted from an imperial geopolitical accident rather than from an economically-expanding, national industrial bourgeoisie. Instead of reflecting national revolutionary processes led by industrial capital against a feudal mode of production—as was the case, for example, with Prussia's Junkers or Italy's Piedmont—a limited Greek state was perceived by Western imperial powers as a geostrategic asset, as part of an effort to deter Russia and Egypt's territorial expansion in the Eastern Mediterranean. Geopolitical factors were paramount to Greece's founding, and today geopolitical/geostrategic questions are of crucial importance in understanding the historical origin of the Greek debt crisis. Since the founding of modern Greece, the important geographical position of the country has been used by the West, not for the benefit of Greek society, but for the West's own advantage.

In order to conduct the war of independence against the Ottomans, Greek élites borrowed large amounts of money from the West. In the 1820s, Greece received two loans of £800,000 and £2m., respectively. A primitive Greek state apparatus experienced its first bankruptcy in 1824–25, when it could not service the loans received from France and England. In 1832–33 another loan of 60m. (in gold francs) was contracted and entirely consumed for the expenses of the regency and the maintenance of the army. That loan led to another Greek bankruptcy in 1843. Clearly, imperial geopolitical necessities trumped economics and the origin of the Greek debt is geopolitical rather than economic. In the meantime, Western powers took care to turn Greece into a Christian Kingdom, implanting a Bavarian monarchy in Athens in 1833. The 'catching-up with the West' discourse began dominating the country's political spectrum from the very beginning. The élites were split between 'populist' and 'modernizing' factions, the former representing local farming interests and the latter merchant strata tied to the West. This conflict took a peculiar and partisan turn later in the century, personified in the antagonistic premierships of Charilaos Trikoupis (modernizer) and Theodore Diliyiannis (populist).

Between 1827 and 1877–78, Greece was excluded from western financial markets. During these five decades and beyond, governments resorted (rather unsuccessfully) to internal borrowing while encouraging investment projects from wealthy diaspora Greeks, whose comprador capital, together with that of Jewish and Armenian merchant classes, was prominent in the Ottoman

Empire. With low levels of industrial development, and unable to pursue economies of scale due to its small size, Greece was marked by a backward peripheral economy and a deeply dependent polity throughout the 19th century; in 1893 Greece declared bankruptcy once again making the words pronounced in the parliament by the late premier, Trikoupis, 'unfortunately, we went bankrupt', a phrase never to be forgotten by any Greek to the present day.

Yet, despite its dilapidated finances and its unsophisticated banking and industrial sectors, Greece was always viewed by Western powers through the prism of their imperial geopolitical interests. As the Austro-Hungarian and Ottoman empires retreated, new spaces opened up for Russia and West European imperialism, now renewed by emerging actors such as Germany and Italy. Christian Balkan micro-states offered the West splendid opportunities, providing proxies in ongoing wars against the Ottoman Turks. By the end of the First World War, the Ottomans were pushed out of Europe, and the borders of the Balkans/Eastern Europe and the Near/Middle East were redefined. This was colonialism at its best: the borders of the Balkans and the Near/Middle East were re-drawn on the map and, in secret gatherings, turned into Treaties by the general staff and the diplomats of the winning, yet declining, European empires. However, whereas Arabic factions, by and large, compromised to Western colonialism, Turkey's response was different.

Conquering land and incorporating populations—not all of whom were Greek—Greece saw substantive industrial activity in the first two decades of the 20th century under the liberal-nationalist leadership of Eleftherios Venizelos. Under British sponsorship, Venizelos led a losing proxy war against Kemalist-nationalist forces in Asia Minor. The aftermath was a total catastrophe for both Greece and modern Turkey. Although Greece saw the inflow of some 1.4m. Christian refugees, it achieved ethnic homogeneity for the first time in its history while Turkey, having lost its most enterprising merchant classes, relied heavily on a state-led authoritarian form of economic development, and failed to achieve ethnic or religious homogeneity. Cyprus, a majority ethnic Greek island, remained under British colonial control and the Dodecanese complex of islands remained under Italian colonial control.

Without a robust economic-industrial base, and with its ruling political élites closely tied to imperial interests due to their comprador character, the country could not capitalize on its geostrategic advantages and pursue an independent and sustainable economic course. This translated directly into a balance-of-payment problem, which, coupled with constant internal borrowing needed to fund a clientelistic and corrupt state machine, repeatedly produced unsustainable debts. In the wake of the 1929 global financial crisis, Greece suffered a fourth bankruptcy in 1932. Afterwards, the dictator Ioannis Metaxas, pursued an import substitution industrialization policy, substantially improving the country's balance of payments. Having sided with the victors during the Second World War and overcoming a bloody Civil War, which the Communists lost, Greece reaped economic and geopolitical rewards: the

Dodecanese were given to Greece and the Marshall Plan initiated the transfer of large amounts of money into the devastated Greek economy (Stathakis, 1995). Meanwhile, as the imperial torch was passed onto the new global hegemon, the USA, the Cold War produced dividends: Greece's geopolitical importance guaranteed a massive inflow of US capital and loans while marginalizing Greece's domestic communist forces during 'the Golden Age of capitalism' (1950–1970).

Yet, once more Greece remained peripheral and deeply dependent. Characteristically, in the 1960s, when the Governor of the Bank of Greece, Xenophon Zolotas, went to the US ambassador in Athens to ask for a loan, the ambassador replied by pointing to a geopolitical conflict. Effectively, the ambassador said that if Greece wanted a loan, then it had to accept Dean Acheson's plan for Cyprus—a plan secretly negotiated among North Atlantic Treaty Organization (NATO) powers proposing partition of the island between Greece and Turkey, dispensing with Archbishop Makarios, who was at that time Cyprus' elected leader and a founder of the non-aligned movement (Draenos, 2012). Thus, the geo-political issue and the debt problem were dealt with through a straightforward swap. Such was the importance of Cyprus for NATO and the West that the USA, via the Central Intelligence Agency, instigated a military dictatorship in Greece in order to facilitate a Cyprus solution based on Acheson's partition plan (Fouskas and Tackie, 2009). In fact, bourgeois democracy was only restored in 1974, when Cyprus was partitioned followed Turkey's two consecutive advances on the island.

From the 1950s through the mid-1970s, Greece did not manage to catch up with the Western core. Yet throughout this period—and in contrast to the demand-led Keynesian policies of the West—Greece, under the influence of its pro-monetarist central banker, Xenophon Zolotas, pursued policies that would later be termed neoliberal. Its economic development was supply-led and pro-monetarist, largely because of Cold War politics. Greek ruling élites, in co-ordination with the US Embassy in Athens, had to keep the masses as much as possible outside the corridors of democratic decision-making. Although the pro-Soviet Communist Left had been defeated during the Civil War (1944–49), it still enjoyed widespread popular support, which meant the conservative Government feared any attempt to open up politics in civil society. Both political participation and demand-led economic policy remained stalled until 1974.

However, after 1974 successive Greek cabinets under right-wing Constantine Karamanlis (1974–81) and socialist Andreas G. Papandreou (1981–89, 1993–96) shifted Greek policy-making to a demand cycle, replenishing the state machine with their party-political personnel, nationalizing major private enterprises and, especially in the 1980s, funding Greece's welfare state through unscrupulous borrowing (both external and internal) rather than through taxation. Even as it entered the European Economic Community (EEC) in 1981, Greece continued to pursue demand-led policies at a time when most of the West was already shifting to embrace neoliberal globalization/financialization.

In France, for example, the French socialists under François Mitterrand succumbed to the monetarist discipline of the European Monetary System (EMS) and abandoned their programme of nationalization, welfare spending and high wages. Greece's Papandreou, along with Scandinavian socialists, continued inflating the economy despite Greece's deteriorating competitiveness within the EEC notwithstanding two consecutive devaluations of the drachma.

Time and again, geopolitical considerations figure prominently: Greece was admitted to the EEC five years ahead of Portugal and Spain as part of a strategy to stabilize NATO's southern flank, at a time when US fixed capital investment in Greece was drying up. In the 1980s German and French capital increasingly dominated the Greek economy and pushed the country to adopt a neoliberal agenda so that it could use Greece as a launching pad from which to spread financial services across the 'transition' economies of the Balkans and the near East (Fouskas and Dimoulas, 2013).

Over the following two decades, and especially after the country's entry to the eurozone in 2001, Greece's competitive position deteriorated sharply. Traditionally profit-making industries such as textiles disappeared. Financial and banking services dominated Greece's economy, spreading out to the Balkans and the Near East. Credit became cheap and easily obtainable as the country could borrow on low interest rates. Public assets were privatized one after another. The country's dependence on external and domestic borrowing increased to such a degree that, given the opening up of public assets to foreign capital acquisition and the loss of monetary sovereignty, one wonders whether the term 'dependence' adequately describes the country's global economic relation with the core.

When the global financial crisis trickled down to the eurozone via the banking sector, the first to suffer were the most financialised economies of the core, such as Germany. The first banks that declared bankruptcy were German banks, followed by Irish ones (Wolfson and Epstein, 2013). Yet, Greece suffered most, because it was and is the weakest link of the neo-imperial financial chain of capital accumulation: Greece not only had a high current account deficit, it also had a massive budget deficit, as opposed to Ireland and Spain. Thus, by 2010 it became a hotbed for speculation when its debts matured. However, Greece was a member of the eurozone and currency devaluation was not an option. A debtor-led default and exit was refused by its entire political spectrum, including Synaspismos Rizospastikis Aristeras (Coalition of the Radical Left—Syriza), which capitulated to the creditors in the summer of 2015, having previously spent seven months in Government negotiating in vein a better bail-out agreement than the previous Centre-Right cabinets.

Twenty years of neoliberal financialization (1996–2016), followed by acute deflationist austerity measures—referred to rather euphemistically as 'internal devaluation'—and bail-out agreements, have solved none of Greece's historical economic problems: industrial backwardness; institutional malaise; high debt to GDP ratios, and a qualitatively peripheral position in the European and global political economy. Supply-side deflationist policies imposed by the troika (the International Monetary Fund—IMF, the European Union—EU and the European Central Bank—ECB) brought about no growth, let alone sustainable development, making the social situation unsustainable: the country lost 27% of its GDP; austerity measures lowered the minimum wage to poverty levels, yet direct taxation and the poll tax increased; unemployment oscillates between 22% and 27%; and pension funds are collapsing. In one of our forthcoming contributions to the debate on Greece and the global financial crisis (Fouskas and Dimoulas, 2018) we point out that a key social contradiction in Greece at present that cuts across the fundamental cleavage between capital and labour (and insofar as the number of pensioners, the unemployed and long-term unemployed is larger than the economically active population) is between those inside the workforce and those outside it.

II

What is the policy solution to the current deadlock in Greece and Europe, especially after the United Kingdom's so-called Brexit vote on 23 June 2016? From a Greek perspective, two questions are paramount: shall Greece default and exit the eurozone re-establishing the sovereignty of its monetary institutions and reissue a new drachma? Is exit from the eurozone good enough, or should exit *also* from the EU be put on the agenda as Stavros Mauroudeas argues in his contribution? Obviously, these questions make sense to the extent that the current economic programme pursued by Greece under the auspices of the troika is unsustainable. From a European, rather than an EU, perspective the key questions are more than obvious and, in fact, the first one has already been posed by the IMF: shall the EU cancel the largest part of the Greek debt so that the negative impacts of austerity could be absorbed in a relatively short period of time, getting the country outside the troika programme? Or, should the EU abandon its deflationist, supply-side ordoliberal rigidity (see below), cancel the debt of the periphery and move on towards a fiscal and political union democratizing its institutions and policy-making apparatus?

By 'democratization' we do not mean power for the people and by the people. This is not realistic because this is a matter of *socialist* democracy at a complicated supranational level. European societies have not posed this historical question yet because they cannot pose it. Instead, by 'democratization' we mean the opening up of the caucuses of European power structures to political and social struggle, that is opening up to negotiation and bargaining so that the disadvantaged position of labour compared to that of financial, banking and industrial capital is improved. This requires courage and realism on the part of the ordoliberal élites currently ruling the EU (see below). In addition, we should not forget the avenue taken by other economic and monetary unions, the most conspicuous historical example being that in the wake of the American civil war, when the triumphant North cancelled the debt of the South making the state of the federal union in the USA possible.

The aforementioned issues are only partially economic or political. Importantly, they are also social and geopolitical, especially for a country such as Greece, which is surrounded by volatile security zones (ethnic and religious/sectarian conflicts in the Balkans and the Near/Middle East, the refugee crisis, continuous neo-imperialist interventions) and critical geostrategic chokepoints (the Suez Canal, the Dardanelles). Moreover, Greece, by virtue of the 1960 Treaties, is directly involved in the Cyprus issue. Greece is a passage. Given the situation in Syria, the role of Russia and the crisis in Ukraine, destabilization of the Greek passage would undermine European peace head on. From this perspective, it is not in the geopolitical interest of Germany, let alone the USA, to clash with Greece over the debt issue, even though Germany and the USA do not share the same views on how to deal with the Greek debt crisis (Varoufakis, 2017; Fouskas, 2017). By the same token, Greece's negotiating team in 2015 paid lip service to the country by sidelining crucial geopolitical and geostrategic aspects of an eventual official Greek default and exit from the eurozone and, eventually, the EU. After all, the crises facing Europe and the world today are deeply and primarily geopolitical, in the sense that power-shifts in Eurasia and around the world are poignantly and intimately connected to the global financial crisis and the rise of China and Russia in international economy and security (Fouskas & Gökay, 2012).

This collection of inter-disciplinary essays should be read against this analytical and historical background. Their focus is the crisis period that began in earnest in 2010 extending to the present day, although some of them, such as the contributions by Alexander Kazamias and Tolis Malakos, are either far wider in scope or start their analyses, quite reasonably, from 1974. All the authors articulate their own perspective stemming from a variety of disciplines, such as political science, political economy, industrial relations or cultural studies. This is because we wanted to offer an inter-disciplinary and holistic approach to the Greek debt crisis, one that goes beyond economics, but without excluding economics.

However, as we said above, readers will find in this book views that do not share the same short of analysis of the Greek, European and global crises. As editors, we have done so deliberately. The perspectives here differ in terms of the way in which the crisis is analysed and the causes that lie behind it, because our aim has been and remains to open up a constructive dialogue between all those perspectives and analyses that oppose neoliberal and ordoliberal economics. Put simply, our effort has been to give to the reader not just an inter-disciplinary and informative understanding of the Greek crisis but also, quite importantly, a heterodox-pluralist approach, whose unity is defined by the 'other', the 'enemy': the *neoliberal globalization* led by the Wall Street and the City of London and the *ordoliberal* project of Germany that has guided the EU-eurozone process for several decades now.[1] Note that these two phenomena, although relatively distinct, are intrinsically connected, especially through banking and finance. As a matter of fact, the eurozone crisis was triggered by the global financial crisis of 2007–08 due to the high volume of junk paper (credit default swaps, collateralised debt obligations and other vehicles) bought by German and French banks in the first place. Ordoliberal rigidity and 'protection' proved unable to control the structural movement of globalized finance. The first banks that collapsed in the eurozone were French and German banks, not Greek or Portuguese banks, and when the German and French executives were asked by their central bankers to find hundreds of billions of euros to compensate for the losses in the banking sectors, those same executives found a way out by disciplining the embattled periphery of Greece, Spain, Ireland and Portugal. In this context, the contributions by Leila Simona Talani and Matthias Kaelberer are quite instructive, as they set out the argument about the structural asymmetries of the EU/eurozone and the way in which those asymmetries come to penalize the weak, the subaltern and the peripheral.

This book is not the venue to start a debate or discussion about the similarities and differences between German/Austrian ordoliberalism and Anglo-American led neoliberal globalization. Also, we do not wish to rehearse a 'varieties of capitalism' argument. Yet all contributions here, whether pro- or anti-European, make clear their opposition to free market economics and the catastrophic effects of their uncontrollable crises upon the majority of the population, especially the socially and economically weakest sectors of society. In particular, the text by Kees van der Pijl, taking Greece as its foremost example, demonstrates the connection between authoritarianism and the neoliberal/ordoliberal recipes produced by the troika of the ECB, the IMF and the EU in order to arrest the debt crisis. The European project may be heading towards a (permanent) state of exception capitalizing upon acts of terrorism in various European capitals in order to impose an even stricter discipline upon labour, the deprived, the less privileged and the poor. This trend also becomes clear and further exemplified in the case of Greece, as shown by Elias Ioakimoglou in his wide-ranging neo-Gramscian/Poulantzian contribution.

Clearly, the most interesting debate on the causes of the eurozone crisis—to the extent that there is one, as provocatively argued here by Turan Subasat—is that between post-Keynesians and Marxists. Effectively, the arguments rehearsed here by Talani and Kaelberer are post-Keynesian and neo-Gramscian. Also post-Keynesian, for example, are arguments by Costas Lapavitsas or Martin Wolf in their various contributions on the eurozone and Greek crises (although Lapavitsas has tried to ground them in Marxism), and Wolf in the asymmetrical structure of the EU.[2] However, there is an equally powerful argument advanced in this collection by Stavros Mavroudeas, who criticises post-Keynesians for interpreting the crisis as a mere disequilibrium in the sphere of capital circulation, that is, as a balance-of-payments crisis. This, Mavroudeas argues, is a cyclical argument dear to social democratic interpretations of the crisis, politically producing pro-capitalist 'solutions' in the field of policy, such as a default and exit strategy for Greece. Resembling in many respects a combination of Robert Brenner's and Ben Fine's theses, the root cause of the crisis in Greece and beyond, Mavroudeas says, is the falling rate of profit in the real economic sector, which, as in other parts of the West, can be traced back to the 1970s. The suggestion is clear: the crisis of over-accumulation that had been ushered in across western capitalist formations in the 1970s is still unresolved, and such is the case with Greece. From this perspective, the famous 'crisis of financialization', which is dear to heterodox economists, is but an epiphenomenon of the capitalist crisis of over-accumulation. Thus, defaulting on its debt payments and exiting from the eurozone alone will not cure Greece's problem. What Greece needs is also an exit from the EU by way of putting forth a socialist project alternative to the capitalist relations of production. Further, Subasat, in his comparative study, claims that the introduction of the euro in 1999, although it impacted the current account imbalances through trade, was not the only source of malaise; nor were the deficits accumulated by trade itself the result of trade among eurozone countries. In fact, much of the deficit in the periphery countries was caused by trade with the rest of the world. To all intents and purposes, this is an original argument rarely advanced in the vast literature on the eurozone crisis.

Elias Ioakimoglou's bracing account on the issue of 'internal devaluation' stands out because it examines matters from the point of view of *labour*. He shows how internal devaluation, fruitlessly aimed at boosting competitiveness via austerity under conditions of monetary union, produces a crisis of political hegemony that is a crisis in the ability of the ruling social classes to represent the general interest vis-à-vis the subaltern classes. Drawing on traditional Marxian theories of capital accumulation, unemployment and political power on the one hand, and modern social reproduction theories on the other, his chapter defines an analytical framework considering social reproduction crisis as the intermediate link between internal devaluation and hegemonic crisis. Using this framework Ioakimoglou finds that internal devaluation, imposing a dramatic fall in wages and pensions, dismantling social services and leading to massive long-term unemployment and widespread poverty, triggers a variety of processes deconstructing the existing regime of social reproduction. Thus, it generates two opposing tendencies: a strong tendency to hegemonic crisis and a counter-tendency to passivity of subaltern classes emanating from the disorganizing effects of massive unemployment and material deprivation on militancy and politicization. Which tendency will eventually prevail, Ioakimoglou argues, remains to be seen.

At the time of writing, Syriza is in office in coalition with a small right-wing party that provides Syriza with the necessary majority in parliament in order to rule. Syriza and its leadership argue that back in the summer of 2015 they did the right thing, namely, accepting harsh austerity without debt cancellation, and that this was a pro-European, progressive political strategy. After all, what does the recent experience of all those Eurosceptic neo-Nazi movements across Europe show? It shows, according to Syriza, that the Greek Left is not

Eurosceptic and introvert and, as such, cannot be thrown into the same cauldron with the extreme right. The Greek Left is a progressive and modernizing force and wants to reform Europe from within by way of enhancing European democracy and solidarity. However, Markantonatou's and van der Pijl's contributions to this book seem to suggest otherwise, despite the fact that their accounts are, in many respects, pro-European.

Van der Pijl, assessing Varoufakis' work, argues that Europe, as it stands, resembles an authoritarian coalition guided by predatory neoliberalism, whereas Markantonatou, reaching out to Wolfgang Streeck via Karl Polanyi and Max Weber, comes to the conclusion that the Greek case is a failed attempt by the European managers of the crisis that, intentionally or not, leave democracy defenceless. This is correct. The authoritarian, nationalist and racist movements that have sprung up across Europe over the last 20 years or so are the result of neoliberal/ordoliberal economic policies that have dismantled the welfare state and put downward pressure on wages and income in order to offset the falling rate of profit in every economic sector, whether 'real' (e.g. manufacturing) or 'fictitious' (e.g. financial services).

Political and party systems under capitalism always appear under a facade of democracy and liberal-pluralistic choices, yet they are deeply authoritarian. The bourgeoisie may concede to the subaltern classes and their political representatives some control of its bourgeois state machine, but it will never concede even an inch from the control it exercises over state power and key departments of the state (the military, the central bank, the finance and interior ministries, etc.). Syriza, argues Alexander Kazamias in his Poulantzian/neo-Gramscian political analysis, backed by the mass movement of the 2010–2014 period, managed to gain some important positions within the Greek state apparatus, reshuffling the party system and appearing as a hegemonic force capable of achieving socialist change. His wide-ranging chapter offers a splendid account of Greece's changing political spectrum; it explains the rise of Syriza, the demise of Panellínio Socialistiko Kinima (Panhellenic Socialist Movement—PASOK) and the endurance of the party founded by Constantine Karamanlis in 1974, New Democracy. Reading Kazamias' contribution we come to conclude that, in many respects, Greece can be viewed as a classical case of a party system that melts in face of a sweeping economic crisis, although it reluctantly comes back to rebalance its fundamentals without achieving any consolidation, at least for the time being. In this context, the Greek party system defies typologies, which are dear to political scientists. That said, and given the crisis of each and every single one of the polities of European states, we wonder whether the Greek case is setting the tone for the rest of Europe.

Crisis, in Chinese, means opportunity. In such times all sort of agencies try to take advantage of the fluid circumstances and the opportunities created by the structural and inter-subjective nature of the situation in order to advance towards positions of power. Harsh conflict is inevitable and if history provides a yardstick it is that, in periods of conflict and crisis, the winner, usually, is the one who manages to strike the right political and social alliances at the right time. We have assembled here a number of inter-disciplinary essays and arguments which, despite their differences, share the strategic aim of a critique of both neoliberalism and authoritarianism. In fact, as many contributors suggest here, including the opening essay by Kees van der Pijl, neoliberalism and authoritarianism share more similarities than differences. With this book, we hope to see this at the practical political level, rather than just a 'theoretical' exercise, in both Greece and Europe and, indeed, the world. If this collection of heterodox and scholarly essays has managed to add to the collective political subconscious such a progressive understanding of present circumstances, then it would be certainly vindicated.

III

Readers of the *Journal of Balkan and Near Eastern Studies* (JBNES, see www.tandfonline.com/cjsb), published by Routledge six times a year since 1998, must be familiar with some of the essays published in this book. The contributions by Matthias Kaelberer, Maria Markantonatou, Tolis Malakos and Leila Simona Talani first appeared in JBNES over the last five years, although the authors have reworked their argument and adapted it to the requirements of the book. We thank Routledge and the journal's team for allowing us to reproduce some of this material. We also wish to thank all the contributors to this volume for their excellent essays and co-operation throughout the editorial process. Our special thanks are reserved for Cathy Hartley, Europa Commissioning Editor at Routledge, who persevered with us after we had missed so many deadlines for delivering the final manuscript.

Notes

1 Although not an entirely coherent school of economic and political thought, ordoliberalism is, broadly speaking, the German-Austrian brand of Anglo-American (Thatcherite-Reaganite) neoliberalism. Its main tenets are: a strong state to enhance market competition; price stability; depoliticization of the policy process and complete independence of the central Bank mechanism; construction and institutionalization of policy rules based on a strict anti-inflation bias; and, for some of them, anti-trust legislation. On this basis, ordoliberalism, as relatively opposed to neoliberalism, sees the extension of free market principles in the social economy as an institutional act led by a strong state or, in the case of the EU, a seam of federated states (Bonefeld, 2017). A first original analysis of ordoliberalism comes from Michel Foucault (2010) in his pioneering 1978–79 lectures at the Collège de France on the 'birth of biopolitics'. In the English-speaking world, the 1979 article in *Socialist Register* by Andrew Gamble (Gamble, 1979), later turned into a book, remains an important contribution.

2 Lapavitsas' work is heavily influenced by the following sources: Rudolf Hilfreding's work on *Finance Capital*; the Japanese Uno School of Marxism; and the *underconsumptionist* argument put forth by authors of the *Monthly Review* group in the USA, first and foremost by Paul Baran and Paul Sweezy.

References

Bonefeld, W. (2017), 'Stateless money and state power: Europe as ordoliberal ordnungsgefüge', [*mimeo*]. York: University of York.

Draenos, S. (2012), *Andreas Papandreou: The Making of a Greek Democrat and Political Maverick*, London: I.B. Tauris.

Foucault, M. (2010), *The Birth of Biopolitics. Lectures at the Collège de France, 1978–1979*, New York: Palgrave.

Fouskas, V.K. (2017), 'A whistleblowers' tale' (Review of Yianis Varoufakis, Adults in the Room), *The Fabian Review*, summer.

Fouskas, V.K. and Dimoulas, C. (2012), 'The Greek workshop of debt and the failure of the European project', *Journal of Balkan and Near Eastern Studies*, 14(1) March 2010.

Fouskas, V.K. and Dimoulas, C. (2013), *Greece, Financialization and the EU. The Political Economy of Debt and Destruction*, New York: Palgrave.

Fouskas, V.K. and Dimoulas, C. (2018), 'Imperial Bondage: Austerity in Greece, 2008–2018', in Sturm, R., Griebel, T. and Winkelmann, T. (eds) *Austerity: A Journey to an Unknown Territory. Discourses, Economics and Politics* (Sonderband 9 der Zeitschrift für Politik) Baden-Baden: Nomos.

Fouskas, V.K. and Gökay, B. (2012), *The Fall of the US Empire. Global Fault-lines and the Shifting Imperial Order*, London: Pluto press.

Fouskas, V.K. and Tackie, A.O. (2009), *Cyprus. The Post-Imperial Constitution*, London: Pluto press.

Gamble, A. (1979), 'The free economy and the strong state: the rise of the social market economy', *Socialist Register*, v.16, London: Merlin press.

Stathakis, G. (1995), 'US economic policies in post-Civil War Greece, 1949–1953: stabilisation and monetary reform', *The Journal of European Economic History*, 24 (2).

Varoufakis, Y. (2017), *Adults in the Room*, London: Bodley Head.

Wolfson, M.H. and Epstein, G.A. (2013), *The Political Economy of Financial Crises*, Oxford: OUP.

1 Eurozone Authoritarianism and the Neoliberal Project in Greece and Southern Europe

Kees van der Pijl

The Syriza Government of Greece right from its inauguration in early 2015 engaged in skirmishes with the eurozone finance authorities about its election promise to end austerity. At the time movie director Costa-Gavras in *Le Monde Diplomatique* was quoted as saying that the dark cloud hanging over the left Government's head was probably not a military intervention like the one that in 1967 ushered in an ugly colonel's regime lasting seven years. Instead, the maker of *Z* and other gems of political cinema warned that in the circumstances one should rather expect merciless economic and psychological warfare, pursued to the bitter end. The Greeks would be forced to bite the dust if only to rule out that any other government ever would even consider departing from the eurozone's austerity dictate.

The first to experience the full brunt of this was the incoming Minister of Finance, Yanis Varoufakis, who was treated to a humiliating welcome by his eurozone colleagues who enjoined the author of *The Global Minotaur* to stop 'lecturing them' on the underlying issues. The media did not fail to label Varoufakis' arguments 'other-worldly' and indeed, to a consensus committed to untenable economic dogma, they were. But this was not a matter of theoretical dispute spilling over into personal abuse. After the referendum of 5 July 2015, which gave the Syriza Government a mandate double the vote that propelled it into office, Varoufakis was sacrificed to the populist fury whipped up in the bloc's creditor states against the spendthrift 'PIGS' (Portugal, Italy, Greece and Spain)—a ploy effectively exculpating speculative finance from responsibility for the austerity and turning it instead into a reality check for the weak.

With southern Europe framed as an object of disdain, Prime Minister Alexis Tsipras bowed to the demand to achieve the impossible goal of repaying the debts the country had incurred after it had surrendered its monetary sovereignty to the eurozone. It is not inappropriate to see the eurozone's treatment of Greece under the Syriza Government as an aspect of incipient fascism, the phase in which, still under bourgeois legality, sarcasm about the plight of others and scapegoating of the weak take the place of rational argument (cf. 'Fascismo' in *Dizionario Gramsciano*). If today, refugees and migrants are increasingly victimized in this way, the disciplining of Greece was a necessary phase in the hardening of the mood.

In this chapter I will investigate the longer-term process of class formation of which the authoritarian neoliberalism applied to Greece was one outcome. As I will argue below, it was a recipe meant to discipline not just the southern eurozone but European society as a whole. France in this respect occupies a central position. Here we can see the complex interconnections between neoliberal austerity and an authoritarian response to the crisis, in which proto-fascism becomes a legitimate political response to the growing hardships faced by the large mass of the population.

Class Compromise and Social Cohesion

All societies rely for their durability on a central class compromise that provides the grid on which further compromises are grafted and through which crises and dislocations are absorbed and overcome. This compromise originates in what David Harvey calls the 'human resource complex' in which production is embedded (Harvey 2006: 399). Over time, societies become 'national' and acquire what may conveniently be called a distinct 'national character' because of *cumulative* class compromises. These shape the collective reception of their own past and mould expectations, whilst inspiring the confidence needed to deal with future emergencies.

Before production was recognised as the bedrock of class compromise, liberal philosophers speculated on its role in various directions. David Hume in the mid-18th century argued that all societies rest on compromise, the English being the sole exception because of their individual liberty and religious diversity (Hume 1875, I: 248, 252). His younger contemporary, Edmund Burke, considered British exceptionalism from the opposite angle. Unlike societies liable to revolutionary convulsions like France, the Anglophone legacy of liberty and diversity instead fostered a political style that turns 'all change into a subject of compromise, which naturally begets moderation; they produce temperaments, preventing the sore evil of harsh, crude, unqualified reformations, and [render] all the headlong exertions of arbitrary power … for ever impracticable' (Burke 1790, III: 277).

Liberal ideologues would continue to ignore the anchorage in production of this largely mythological, but as a powerful myth, *central* characteristic of Anglophone society—the idea of a quasi-natural, pragmatic adjustment to changing circumstances. This may be traced to the fact that even when the United Kingdom was the workshop of the world, the imperial worldview of the commercializing aristocracy that took hold across the Lockean heartland was not discarded. Of course the society of agriculture and early manufacture in which it crystallized did not endure, and when it metamorphosed into mass industrial society, for which the principles of gentlemanly compromise and moderation proved ill-suited as a formula of social cohesion, epochal tensions threatened to dislodge it altogether.

Thus, in the run-up to World War One it was widely felt that European society was no longer able to contain the pressures for change and socio-cultural innovation emanating notably from the socialist labour movement and that a 'conflict between the two social orders—of privilege and the masses' was heading for a violent dénouement (Schmitt and Vedeler 1984: 20). Yet the epoch of mounting tensions and even the cataclysmic struggle that followed are best understood as deepening compromise in production, enlarged by social security arrangements and other, more intangible forces supporting national cohesion. Hence when the crunch came, the majority of socialists across Europe rallied to the defence of the fatherland, as long as the enemy could be depicted in terms 'beyond compromise'. Only in Russia the war led to the collapse of an autocracy ruling a pre-bourgeois society that was fundamentally unable to accommodate its working class. In Germany, north Italy and Hungary, revolutionary outbreaks remained sporadic in the face of social cohesion underpinned by past compromises and bonds welded in the factories and the trenches.

Indeed, in the main belligerent countries the war had demonstrated the viability of an economy organized entirely around large-scale production. This is the bedrock of class compromise, to the point where Lenin thought that the change from bureaucracy to democracy would suffice to shift the ground from state-monopoly capitalism to socialism (Lenin 1917, XXV: 337, 341). Certainly the depth of national economic integration around large-scale industrial complexes made any attempt to resurrect 19th-century-style liberal internationalism premised on the gold standard and speculative financial flows an illusion, as the 1929 stock market crisis and the Depression would reveal. Instead the locus of class compromise shifted in a radically different direction with the establishment of a corporate liberal capitalism pioneered by F.D. Roosevelt's New Deal in the USA.

This compromise was centrally anchored in the ascendant mass production industries of the Fordist complex, with automobile and other durable consumer goods production subordinating the coal and steel bloc of the previous era. In the end, another round of world war was necessary, not only to defeat the contender states led by Nazi Germany (which remained in the grip of a bankrupt heavy industry bloc that proved 'too big to fail'), but also to actually release the full potential of a demand-led mass production economy. Just as, in both cases, the war effort mobilized the mass psychological forces required to weld a new class compromise. For even fascism is a form of compromise—an agreement to draw together around a stock of common convictions and experiences in the face of forces considered entirely alien to that agreement. In the case of Germany, Versailles provided the common ground that would not otherwise have existed to permit the ascent of a criminal regime.

Given that the 1929 Wall Street Crash had been caused by the excesses of internationally active money-dealing capital (*Geldhandelskapital*), in the USA the bank crisis and the Depression were followed, after two years of economic collapse that ruined the heavy-industry-centred capitalist bloc, by the 1933 Glass-Steagall Act, a centre-piece of the New Deal. Glass-Steagall subjected money-dealing capital, its institutional presence in the economy as investment banks and brokerage firms, and the class fraction it catered to (the *rentiers*), to repression. Thus, money capital proper (the deposit banking business, insurance, and the finance departments of large corporations) would be able to perform its systemic function as the pivot of the cycle of industrial capital, undisturbed by the risks involved in speculative international operations of a fundamentally commercial form of capital, that is, capital in commodity form, trade; in contemporary terms, trade in services and more particularly, trade in financial services.

As a form of commercial capital, money-dealing capital does not add value but chases rewards from price differentials through the profit distribution process. These differences (value-adding production, P; money capital invested with an eye to keeping real accumulation going, M; and commercial, money-dealing capital, let us say, C^M as a specific form of C) are *intrinsically connected to different forms of class compromise determining whether and to which degree a capitalist society allows forms of political democracy to take hold.* Whereas class compromise in production works to enfranchise organized labour, the relocation of production to zones outside that compromise obviously undermines democracy; what remains is at best an *Ersatz* compromise between money capital and middle classes able to profit from its operations. However, once money-dealing capital encroaches on the operations of investment capital beyond a certain point, the basis for any social compromise becomes narrow indeed, and this is what is happening today.

Anglophone liberals from the early 18th century had theorized how politics should mobilize a following for the alternation of 'party' positions aligned with fractions of capital (landed property plus the money interest versus manufacture and trade). Whilst they ascribed the faculty of reason exclusively to the property-owning classes, they also believed that 'even if all men cannot reason, all men can feel', and that therefore it should be possible to sway the broader public with emotive themes such as patriotism (van der Pijl 2014: 8–10). The founders of modern political science at the turn of the 20th century, Mosca, Pareto, Michels, and others, were still confident that mass society, then pressing forward to obtain the right to vote, could be held in check by élites manipulating powerful emotive symbols and 'superstitions'.

This certainly inspired the aestheticization of politics by fascism, but the New Deal was a different matter. The 'rationality' of the North American class structure, famously highlighted by Gramsci, and unburdened by the social weight of what he calls the 'pensioners of economic history' as in Europe (or Japan), enabled the organized working class to press its interests directly, 'rationally'. Certainly the Fordist format of the relations of production worked to commodify any demand of organized labour into an economic one, thus deepening its insertion into the capitalist economy, its 'real subsumption' to capital. Collective bargaining from the start was only allowed to deal with wages in relation to productivity. Even so, political democracy critically depends on the organized working class, not on the bourgeoisie, which historically has been ambivalent on the issue and at best an ally of the workers clamouring for it (Rueschemeyer et al. 1992: 270–71 & *passim*).

In that light the restatement by Joseph Schumpeter of the original elitist understanding of democracy, which restricts the voting public to a passive role is best seen as an element in the panoply of ruling class power that was being assembled to deal with possible further democratic demands after the war (Schumpeter 1942). From the induced recession of 1937 through which the Roosevelt Administration sought to tame the workers after the New Deal had unleashed dangerous forces for change, to Joseph McCarthy's anti-communist witch hunt after the war, runs a political business cycle that allows capital accumulation to be adjusted to the requirements of class power whenever full employment threatens to break out of the production-consumption format of Fordism (Kalecki 1972). The vote, and what could be voted on, was always secondary to this fundamental equation; otherwise the presence of organized labour at the heart of the class compromise with capital nevertheless underpinned 'the best democracy money can buy'.

Let me now bring in Varoufakis' analysis of the global political economy in which class compromise was embedded.

The 'Global Plan' and its Limits

The New Deal compromise, extrapolated from the USA to Western Europe under the Marshall Plan, was premised on what Varoufakis labels 'the Global Plan' to use US surpluses to resurrect its wartime foes as bastions against the new contender, the Union of Soviet Socialist Republics (USSR) and its client state socialisms. The US project was a second-best to what was the truly visionary scheme to establish a functioning 'surplus recycling mechanism', the Keynes Plan placed before the Bretton Woods conference in New Hampshire in 1944. Here the British economist, an iconoclast and eccentric but otherwise dedicated to the long-term survival of capitalism, proposed an International Currency Union with the bancor as a universal currency. The plan envisaged giving each country an overdraft facility at 50% of its trade volume in bancors, at zero interest. More could be borrowed, at a fixed rate. A surplus country would be penalized if its surplus exceeded a given level, thus forcing it to revalue, and this would in turn finance the loans to deficit countries.

This proposal was referred to in a British Broadcasting Company interview in January 2011 by the then-director of the International Monetary Fund (IMF), Dominique Strauss-Kahn. Strauss-Kahn boldly declared that 'Keynes, sixty years ago, already foresaw what was needed; but it was too early. Now is the time to do it. And I think we are ready to do it!' A few weeks after the interview he was seen being driven off handcuffed in a New York Police Department car, suspected of sexual impropriety, and dismissed from the IMF before a magistrate had even indicted him (Varoufakis 2013: 254–55). Whilst Varoufakis does not address whether this was a deliberate honey trap or a lucky break for Strauss-Kahn's detractors, there is no doubt that today even less than in 1944, the USA is not inclined to allow anyone to meddle with the prerogatives it derives from the ability to print the world's reserve currency.

The Global Plan as the alternative to the original Keynes Plan aimed at securing a European market for West German industry while incorporating it into the Atlantic line-up against the Soviet bloc, and providing markets for Japan's output too. The latter was achieved by recruiting its industrial base for the Korean War and subsequently, the Vietnam War, and by actually opening the North American home market to Japanese products. In hindsight, we may see in this generosity also a paradoxical reward for the ability of both German and Japanese capital to press down wages and impose maximum discipline on their work forces, which short-lived labour militancy right after the war was not able to reverse. Even at the time of the establishment of the original European Economic Community, the differential between French wage costs bolstered by workers' gains in the Popular Front and West German wages and conditions still remained a major bone of contention.

The Atlantic class compromise, within the aforementioned limitations, was no less real. It worked, in Europe even more than in North America, to create the one period in the history of capitalism in which the wage share in society enjoyed modest rises, even briefly jumping in the inflationary early 1970s (when wage indexation still held)—before entering the long-term decline that is continuing today (Bengtsson and Ryner 2015). Yet the real net beneficiaries of corporate liberal capitalism were the middle classes, whose relative enrichment 'was the principal structural transformation of the distribution of wealth in the developed countries in the twentieth century', even if the gains for this 40% of the population remained confined to one-third of wealth in Europe and one-quarter in the USA; the rest remaining in the hands of the top 10%. Otherwise, the benefits of class compromise in production consisted of the consolidation of one-quarter to one-third of all wealth as public property (Piketty 2014: 137, 184, 260–61).

In the meantime, what Keynes had foreseen happened in the course of the 1960s. There was no sustainable surplus recycling mechanism in place once the US, which wanted to remain in control, became a deficit country on account of the huge expenditures for the Vietnam War. These by 1965 began pushing down corporate profits and living standards alike, and as a result the gold cover of the US dollar agreed at Bretton Woods became untenable. By early 1971 US liabilities stood at more than US $70,000m., backed up by $12,000m. in gold. And that was after Washington, DC, had already been compelled to throw 20% of its gold stock into the breach when the UK devalued in 1967 (by 14%, well beyond the 1% limit of the Bretton Woods rules). Varoufakis recounts how French President Georges Pompidou in August 1971 sent a French destroyer to New Jersey, USA, to redeem US dollars for gold from Fort Knox; a few days later Prime Minister Edward Heath made a polite request for the same on behalf of the UK. Nixon was livid and on 15 August announced the end of gold convertibility.

This was step one in a dramatic turn around of the postwar surplus recycling mechanism, the setting up of the Global Minotaur structure Varoufakis sees as having remained until the crisis of 2008. Named after the Cretan monster to which Athens had to supply annual human sacrifices until Theseus ended the tribute, the US Minotaur henceforth was fed with the surpluses of the rest of the capitalist world, industrial as well as financial.

Architects of the Minotaur's Labyrinth

The abrogation of the New Deal/post-war class compromise in production and the concomitant restrictions of political democracy transpired during the 1970s. It culminated in the 'revolutions' of Margaret Thatcher and Ronald Reagan and came about through a process of class formation in which strategic élites abandoned the corporate liberal principles of Fordism and Keynesianism (the 'Warfare/Welfare state') and converged on ideological themes discredited or marginalized in the post-1945 Golden Age. From disparate angles at first, and over time reworking positions initially adopted into a more comprehensive stance, the period illustrates how such epochal reconfigurations of capitalist class power acquire their internal consistency and outward cogency. Without these exploratory processes a class bloc's position cannot achieve the cohesion through which it ultimately imposes itself on society at large as a concept of control, and neither would it be recognized as a viable project on the part of the larger sections of the population with which a compromise is sought.

It all starts with uncertainty and minority positions challenging the orthodoxy of the period coming to a close. Thus in the Nixon Administration only Secretary of Labor George Shultz initially subscribed to the provocative thesis of MIT economist Charles Kindleberger that *as long as the rest of the world recognized the necessity of US leadership*, foreign creditors would continue to cover any deficits, knowing that they were in fact investing in the provision of certain public goods serving the system as a whole. The majority stuck to the classical position, represented in academia by Robert Triffin, that the USA too should balance the books first. (Bassosi 2006: 34–40). The Kindleberger position then resonated with a task force led by Paul Volcker, whose curriculum vitae included previous positions in the Federal Reserve of New York, Chase Manhattan Bank, and a first stint at the US Treasury in the mid-1960s. Volcker, appointed by Nixon to the post of Under Secretary of the Treasury for International Affairs with a brief to report to the National Security Council under Henry Kissinger, in May 1971 submitted the plan to suspend gold convertibility.

Volcker's boss at Chase Manhattan, David Rockefeller, in an attempt to assuage disquiet among US allies over Nixon's unilateralism, from 1972 put his right-hand man, Columbia scholar Zbigniew Brzezinski, to work on what became the Trilateral Commission (TC), an offshoot of the Bilderberg Conferences but including a Japanese contingent, to provide a strategic forum in which a consensus on the new international order could be worked out (and of which Volcker would later become the North American Chairman).

From the TC emanated the first explicit proposal to roll back the democratic format of the compromise with organized labour in production, the oft-cited *Crisis of Democracy* report of 1975 written by Michel Crozier, Samuel Huntington, and Joji Watanuki. The report stated that 'In recent years, the operations of the democratic process...have generated a breakdown of traditional means of social control, a delegitimation of political and other forms of authority, and *an overload of demands on government*, exceeding its capacity to respond'. To underline that the demand load coming from the working class was the key problem, Huntington in his chapter argued against making democracy synonymous with equality (Crozier et al. 1975: 9, 62). These were the years of the aftershocks of the May 1968 movement, the oil crisis, the USA's defeat in Vietnam, the Portuguese revolution and the collapse of the Central Intelligence Agency (CIA)-imposed dictatorship in Greece (Fouskas 2001, Fouskas 2005), years in which the open-ended quest for ways out of the crisis, the first simultaneous recession after World War Two, threatened to prolong, even *expand*, the role of organized labour and the political Left in new class compromises.

Already in 1969, the idea of bracketing economic expertise from democratic interference, and assign it the status of scientific certainty led the Swedish central bank, a hotbed of the emerging neoliberalism, to ask the Nobel prize committee to be granted a licence to award an annual prize under the Nobel brand. The Mont Pèlerin Society (MPS), the network in which Friedrich Hayek, Milton Friedman and their peers from 1947 had groomed an alternative to Keynesianism restoring the *rentier* (recommended for euthanasia by Keynes) to respectability, would become the main supplier of its laureates. Its commitment to ending the class compromise with organized labour dated from the founding MPS meeting, which identified the 'power of the trade unions' as the key obstacle to be removed in order to return to sound capitalist practice.

From 1978 Edwin Feulner, Jr., the President of the Heritage Foundation, was Treasurer of the MPS. Heritage had been launched five years earlier by Paul Weyrich and was funded by a group of socially revanchist multimillionaires such as the beer magnate, Joseph Coors, Mellon heir Richard Scaife, and others, before gaining the support of, again, Chase Manhattan, Mobil Oil, and other mainstream corporate giants. Feulner was prominent among those attacking the Third World advocates of a New International Economic Order on account of their strategy to use the post-1971 dollar inflation for a grand redistribution of global power and influence under the guise of 'self-determination' (Feulner 1976: 66). From 1979 Volcker, appointed by President James Carter as head of the Federal Reserve, used a series of interest rate hikes to disorganize that very project. A year prior to his appointment, in a Warwick University talk, he tellingly dismissed the idea that the market was 'an impartial arbiter', because 'retaining freedom of action for national policy' comes first. He added that 'a controlled disintegration of the world economy' should be the target in the 1980s. In other words, as with the Global Plan, the project of the Global Minotaur feeding on the world's surpluses would tolerate no entities capable of sustaining an alternative order (cited in Varoufakis 2013: 100).

At his confirmation hearing in August 1979, Volcker warned that inflation was eating into profits as well, indicating the need to use anti-inflation measures to right the balance of strength with labour. This of course had been the concern of many other networks formed in response to the democratic surge of the late 1960s and early 1970s, among them another Bilderberg offshoot, the Pinay Circle or *Cercle Violet*, named after the former French Prime Minister and his lawyer, respectively (Teacher 1993). Constituted in 1969, its members included the Far Right Bavarian fief-holder, Franz-Josef Strauss; and from Italy, the consummate politician, Giulio Andreotti, '*il Divo*'; as well as the cement king close to the Vatican, Carlo Pesenti, and many others. The Pinay Circle interfaced with various other networks operating in the shadow world of intelligence services and neo-fascist operatives active in Latin America and Europe; a section of its Italian membership was included in the infamous Masonic Lodge, *Propaganda Due*, whose Grand Master, Licio Gelli, (a former fascist intelligence officer, liaison officer with US intelligence, and guest of honour at Ronald Reagan's inauguration in 1981) played a key role in the North Atlantic Treaty Organization (NATO) 'strategy of tension'. This strategy among others aimed at derailing the inclusion of the Italian Communist Party into the Government and culminated in the assassination of Christian Democratic party leader Aldo Moro in 1978. Gelli's philosophy was that 'dictatorship and democracy always march side by side, because democracy is being undermined by dictatorship and dictatorship is being undermined by democracy'. A stable equilibrium between the two had not yet been reached and was in fact difficult to imagine (cited in Willan 1991: 211).

Having jolted the balance away from the democratic configuration of the previous decades by his monetary interventions, Volcker in December 1979 participated in a two-day conference of the Pinay Circle in Washington DC, which was also attended by Feulner, European Commissioners K.-H. Narjes (also a TC member) and F.M. Pandolfi (former Italian finance minister and a member of *Propaganda Due*) and a series of intelligence officers including William Colby, the architect of the Gladio covert network in Europe and former director of the CIA. This array of participants made the event a worthy conclusion of a protracted process of strategic élite realignment through which a fundamental reordering of Atlantic class society from capital-labour compromise in production to a different configuration of forces, came about. As Volcker would put it himself in 1985, the new hegemonic formula was perhaps 'not implemented as smoothly as it could have been … [but] there is … more emphasis on market orientation … , more concern and effort to reduce the proportion of government in [gross national product] GNP, more emphasis on private initiative', and all this was not confined to the USA either but even extended to France and the developing world (cited in Gill 1990: 114).

The Volcker Shock built on the rolling back of democracy through the bracketing of neoliberal economics, the assault on the working classes in the developed world (where necessary enlarged with military coups and covert operations creating terror scares), the New Cold War announced by the NATO decision to aim intermediate-range missiles at Warsaw Pact command centres, the Contra counteroffensive in the areas where socialist or socialist-inspired forces had still been advancing the 1970s, and so on. Yet the mobilization of the aforementioned networks and the adoption of their neoliberal/neoconservative ideas by successive US presidencies (in the Carter Administration, more than 20 TC members held senior office from the President down, whilst the Far Right, including also the mid-1970s Committee on the Present Danger, had an even firmer grip on the Reagan Administration, cf. Brownstein and Easton 1983: 533–34 *& passim*) still was accompanied by a class compromise outside the strategic élites involved in them.

Since production was now evacuating the zones of class compromise with organized labour (whether inside countries to non-unionized regions or sectors, or abroad), whilst public property was being axed by privatization drives, the one substantive social force available to a neoliberal class compromise was the asset-owning middle class, which as we saw had been the beneficiary of the previous period in terms of private property. So, as Duménil and Lévy highlight, besides 'a strict alliance with top management … achieved by paying out astounding remunerations, as "wages" and stock options', the [new] compromise took the form of giving asset-owning upper middle classes a chance to profit from capital incomes and asset price rises, 'either directly or through investment funds' (Duménil and Lévy 2004: 30).

Thus, with the abrogation of the class compromise with organized labour in production, the balance among fractions also shifted to money capital *qua money*, and without the restrictions imposed by domestically anchored class compromise in production. Even so, the priority awarded to restoring global class discipline lent Volcker-style neoliberalism a *systemic* quality, because his prime objective and that of the majority of the forces he spoke for, was the restoration of profits from real capital accumulation, 'M–P–M', albeit under conditions far more favourable to capital. Combating inflation was mandatory for the Minotaur structure: first, because the credit-financed industrialization and modernization projects of the Soviet bloc countries, Yugoslavia, and the Third World coalition clamouring for a New International Economic Order, had to be scuttled; second, because wages in the USA had to be brought down to attract foreign investment into the US economy; and third, because a strong dollar would bolster demand for US corporate and treasury securities, and vice versa.

The Many-Headed Hydra of Money Capital

Just as the Global Plan had been a conscious creation rather than a spontaneous economic miracle, the Global Minotaur was based on strategic calculations that owed little to the market magic propagated by neoliberal economists. The Minotaur structure however lacked the element of generosity towards West Germany and Japan and their respective regional economic spaces that the Cold War and the fresh memory of the Depression and World War Two, as well as fear of Soviet state socialism, had imparted on its predecessor. It was truly an insatiable monster and that was also what it was set up to be, just as it attacked, on the recommendations of a microeconomics no longer subject to political dispute, the actual working classes. That the abrogation of the class compromise with labour was most ferociously executed in the USA, follows from the above-mentioned need to attract foreign investment. As Varoufakis documents, when unit labour costs in Japan, West Germany and even Thatcher's UK were still rising at average annual rates between 11% and 15% in the period 1985–90, the US labour cost growth rate was already down to 1.6% per annum, and when in the next decade, wage rises froze everywhere, the US growth rate was still lowest and the USA the cheapest developed economy to produce in (Varoufakis 2013: 104–5).

Now money capital is a many-headed Hydra, and removing the controls imposed on it will let its different faces appear all at the same time. On the one hand, it represents the totality of capital, the imaginary ('fictitious') control panel from which investment funds are being distributed over the different branches of production. On the other, it is the specific form of capital handled by money capitalists, i.e. banks and finance departments of other companies competing among each other, to be used either as credit to productive, profitable activities, M; or as money-dealing capital, C^M, which as we saw is a form of commercial capital that appropriates its share of total profit via the price system, by exploiting price differentials. The relaxation of the Keynesian controls on money capital, culminating in the Volcker shock of 1979 and the neoliberal policies of the 1980s, inevitably allowed money-dealing capital, too, to make a come-back from the euthanasia Keynes had recommended for it in the Depression.

In the words of R.T. Naylor, 'Tight credit encouraged, even forced, legitimate money into patterns of behaviour historically associated with the cash hoards of drug peddlers, tax evaders, contraband traders, and others who have something to hide – namely, the search for short-term havens in highly liquid assets, instead of seeking opportunities for long-term productive investment' (Naylor 1987: 13). The *rentiers* (recipients of rent, interest and dividend and the beneficiaries of capital gains on assets) now regained strength as wages declined. *Rentier* income had never been entirely repressed, but 'the big acceleration in its rise began around 1979 or 1980. During the period of the Volcker monetary policy of high real interest rates and the Reagan policy of large budget deficits, the rentier share leaped.' (Epstein and Power 2002). The USA led in absolute terms (38% of GNP in the 1980s, slightly declining in the 1990s). The class compromise with asset-owning middle classes, although heavily skewed towards home ownership, also relied on *rentier* incomes; just as changes in the bond market allowing government bonds to be traded over the counter and tax measures replacing the take on top incomes with paying out interest on government bonds, all worked to consolidate it.

However, since the components of bank capital separated by Glass-Steagall had by the mid-1980s effectively blended again (the act would eventually be abolished by the Clinton Administration in 1999), these benefits to the (upper) middle classes inadvertently became exposed to the instability and risk that come with the ascendancy, on account of its superior profitability, of money-dealing capital. Peter Gowan captures the shift when he writes that 'trading activity here does not mean long-term investment…in this or that security, but buying and selling financial and real assets *to exploit – not least by generating – price differences and price shifts*' ('speculative arbitrage', Gowan 2009: 8–9, emphasis added). Thus after a relatively brief period the neoliberalism projected by the bloc of forces of which Volcker was the spokesman, that is, the *systemic* correction of the compromise with organized labour, fell prey to the inevitable corollary of unleashing money capital, money-dealing capital—*predatory* neoliberalism. The Big Bang in the City of London and the replacement of Volcker at the head of the Federal Reserve by J.P. Morgan banker and Ayn Rand aficionado Alan Greenspan mark the transition from the systemic to the predatory variety of neoliberalism in terms of managing the Anglophone financial sector.

From 'national' class compromise with organized labour in production, via compromises with the asset-owning domestic middle classes in a context of relocating production, to the predatory rule of money-dealing capital, capitalist society in the West thus slowly assumed the oligarchic profile more and more evident today. Simultaneously, as it removes itself from the need to strike compromises dictated by the requirements of long-term investment, *capital also loses its interest in democracy.* Of course, the vestiges of post-war class compromise are never entirely obliterated, and public sector unions especially may hold on to certain privileges, just as 1970s–1980s middle class formation has entrenched through inherited home ownership and the like. However, the drift is towards oligarchy, and importantly, along with it, authoritarian rule and foreign adventurism, because as Charles Kupchan and Peter Trubowitz write, with the loss of domestic class compromise, 'growing disparities in wealth have reawakened class tensions; and political pragmatism has been losing ground to ideological extremism' (Kupchan and Trubowitz 2007: 9).

In this light we must now analyse the situation that arose when the one contender to capitalist imperialism, the Soviet bloc, collapsed in 1991, and the West, removing the remaining restrictions on money-dealing capital, adopted a more aggressive international posture under the auspices of the one surviving superpower. This will allow us to understand the formation of the eurozone and the epochal significance of the Greek rebellion.

Predatory Raiding and War

The collapse of Soviet state socialism and the People's Republic of China's transition to state capitalism opened up new hunting grounds for money-dealing capital, both by raiding foreign economies and by engaging in commercial operations notably in the military industrial sphere threatened by the winding down of the Cold War arms race. Operation Desert Storm meanwhile deepened the connections with the orthodox Sunni Muslim monarchies in the Middle East that dated from the first oil crisis and Western-sponsored *jihad* in Afghanistan (Scott 2015). Here we see the beginning of how the ascent of money-dealing capital dovetails with the shift from the New Cold War (in which the emphasis was on bringing down the USSR and regimes relying on it) to 'full spectrum dominance' by the West.

In June 1991 US presidential candidate Bill Clinton was subjected to what the *New York Times* later called a job interview on Wall Street with Goldman Sachs banker Robert Rubin and others, and once elected, he did not fail to include key bankers into his cabinet. Rubin became Secretary of the Treasury and Richard Holbrooke, whose investment bank assignments included stints at Lehman Brothers and Crédit Suisse-First Boston, became Assistant Secretary of State (van der Pijl 2006: 261–62, 273). The Administration's neoliberal globalization project very soon was enlarged by a more militant defence posture, carrying some of the same signatures. Wall Street bankers and investment funds had become commercially involved in the post-Cold War mega-mergers in the aerospace sector (Lockheed and Martin Marietta, Boeing-Rockwell-McDonnell Douglas, Raytheon and Hughes…), and their interest was typically in fees and price differentials, buying cheap and selling dear. Thus, the fast-rising Carlyle group in 1992 bought the aerospace interests of bankrupt Ling-Temco-Vought (LTV) just before Lockheed Martin got their hands on it, only to sell them again to Northrop Grumman for more than three times what it had paid originally, and many other examples can be given (Briody 2003: 46–50).

NATO expansion, which would require new members to standardize equipment, was another area the aerospace industry and Wall Street shared an interest in. The 'US Committee to Expand NATO' was chaired by the director of strategic planning of Lockheed Martin, whilst Holbrooke was entrusted with the sensitive Yugoslavia portfolio that saw two NATO bombing campaigns against Bosnian Serb and Serbian targets in 1994 and 1999, respectively. As Holbrooke put it in a 1995 article in *Foreign Affairs*, 'the West must expand to central Europe as fast as possible in fact as well as in spirit, and the United States is ready to lead the way' (Holbrooke 1995: 42). Today we might repeat those words for *eastern* Europe as far as Ukraine (Sakwa 2015).

More fundamentally, NATO expansion, in breach of the reassurances given to Gorbachev at the time of German reunification, as well as the bombing, notably, of Belgrade and the bridges over the Danube, were first of all the consequence of the Anglo-American lead in replacing the previous, cataclysmic mass war model by a more targeted military strategy that accompanied the substitution of class compromise in production and mass conscription by the rule of money. The changes specifically targeted the persistence of the Fordist-Keynesian pattern of capitalism on the European continent. If left to deal with the collapsing state socialisms in Central and Eastern Europe, 'Old

Europe', although revamped along neoliberal lines at Maastricht, might be tempted to allow the legacies of planned economies to persist in a new, German-dominated Europe that no longer required an interventionist USA. In addition, establishing bridgeheads among Islamic communities in Yugoslavia fitted into a design to gain access to energy resources in Central Asia left unprotected after the dissolution of the USSR.

Parallel to supporting the NATO foray into the former Warsaw Pact and the establishment (sponsored by the USA, the UK and Turkey) of the GUAM regional security bloc in 1998 (comprising Georgia, Ukraine, Azerbaijan and Moldova), money-dealing capital also went about raiding the globe on its own. The Mexican crisis of 1994 marks the beginning of a series of short-term investment booms and busts, and the fact that hot money now had a firm grip on state institutions in the financial sphere was brought out when the hedge fund Long-Term Credit Management (LCTM) crashed in 1998. Set up by the financier credited with inventing 'proprietary trading' (speculative arbitrage with a bank's own or borrowed money) and two 'Nobel' economics laureates, LTCM was saved by Greenspan's Federal Reserve with US $3,600m. of public money. In combination with the handling of the Asian Crisis (a predatory raid on economies that had not yet joined the neoliberal move out of direct involvement of money capital in production) this bail-out 'allowed the financial turmoil to transmute into yet another stock market/housing bubble' (Rude 2008: 211).

That particular bubble would then lead the capitalist economy into the abyss in 2008. In the process it would also deal a terminal blow to the remaining democratic foundations of liberal capitalist society, clearing the way for authoritarianism and populism (Deppe 2013). For apart from its involvement in the new wars of the post-1991 period, which already worked to foster the forces of collective hatred and indifference to suffering, money-dealing capital also gambled away the finance-led compromise with the asset-owning middle classes. The techniques of inter-bank lending based on packaging mortgage and other debt of different quality into the notorious collateral debt obligations (CDOs), insured by the, by now, equally ill-reputed credit default swaps (CDSs), proliferated especially after 2000. This entailed subjecting the maturation process (attached to real accumulation) of the underlying contracts (paying out a pension, paying back the mortgage, etc.) to the unregulated, short-term market movement of funds through which money-dealing capital, meanwhile the leading fraction of capital, generates its income.

The voracious nature of the latter process is expressed through 'financial deepening', a relentless process of securitization of assets. It was the demand for asset-backed securities (CDOs) by investors that made the derivatives market balloon to US $630,000,000m. outstanding in 2006, 14 times the value of global GDP; insuring the CDOs into which they had been packed by CDSs rather than by proper insurance then triggered the collapse of 2008 (Sassen 2015: 535–39).

The idea of capital evacuating the zones of class compromise was now taken to its logical conclusion by money-dealing capital (with its preference for 'short-term havens in highly liquid assets', that is, physically and/or legally offshore). On the eve of the crash the parallel universe of off-balance-sheet, shadow banking entities like hedge funds, so often located in offshore jurisdictions and operating beyond regulatory oversight, had grown to a trading volume twice the size of transactions in the regulated banking system (Chesnais 2011: 71–72). Money-dealing capital operates with complete disregard for the sort of considerations that flow from democratic government, such as employment conditions, social security and general welfare. Yet whilst it fosters oligarchic enrichment and then seals it off by authoritarian control (just think of the response to the Occupy Wall Street movement in the USA, or to the *Indignados* in Spain), this does not remove it from the sphere of politics as such. For bankers all along had been literate about '"hot money" flows as … a mechanism by which the financial markets discipline profligate government' (Burn 2006: 89). This takes us to the eurozone.

The Eurozone as a Playground for Hot Money

Varoufakis calls Germany's role in the eurozone the simulacrum of the Global Minotaur in the global political economy, but a simulacrum in the postmodern sense, so it is the same except that everything is different. If we focus on the period after 1991, when money-dealing capital was abandoning all constraints that Western societies inherited from past compromises, first with organized labour in production and then in finance with asset-owning middle classes, we see Germany fast catching up in the key domains in the transition to predatory neoliberalism.

First, the attack on labour. The incorporation of the defunct German Democratic Republic by the Federal Republic weakened labour's bargaining power now that the workforces of East Germany and the rest of the former Soviet bloc and Ukraine became available to German capital. In the 1990s the annual rise of unit labour costs fell to levels pioneered by the USA, to which the Gerhard Schröder Government added the Hartz I–IV reforms of labour law, leaving a core of protected labour untouched but disciplined it nevertheless by making the descent into precarious jobs and the reserve army of labour far more painful (Holman 2015). Once the euro had been introduced and German industry was protected against competitive currency depreciation, its gains from the fall in wages were made permanent. The beggar-thy-neighbour policies towards the other EU countries then slowly undermined the trade and payments balances of the southern eurozone member states, which were refinanced through short-term capital movements until the 2008 crash threw the entire structure into disarray (Varoufakis 2013: 202; Lapavitsas et al. 2010).

The second component of the simulacrum was the new German assertiveness in international affairs. Indeed, its first use of the external freedom regained by the restoration of full sovereignty was the extension of diplomatic recognition to the Slovenian and Croatian secessions without demanding prior minorities protection, forcing the other EU states to fall in line. Of course this prompted the aforementioned US response in Bosnia and, eventually, the joint NATO campaign against Serbia over Kosovo, in which the first signs of a confrontation with Russia and China became evident. Even so, the fact that Germany joined the dissidents in the UN Security Council over the Anglo-American invasion of Iraq in 2003, and largely maintained their distance from the NATO air war in Libya, is important. It shows that although German preferences were consistently overruled by the USA, through NATO or otherwise, the current stalemate in Ukraine, in which Germany and France have helped negotiate a ceasefire in the civil war whereas Anglophone NATO powers keep bolstering the regime (brought to power by the coup of February 2014), fits into a longer lineage of dissent.

With France on the other hand, the post-war division of labour, in which Paris had used its status as one of the occupying powers to contain the inevitable political and economic resurgence of Germany through structures of permanent European consultation, was reversed in the 1990s. This was one reason for France to rejoin NATO's military organization in the Kosovo campaign. At that point Paris used its advantage in the two key areas that Varoufakis identifies as domains of French superiority in Europe, i.e. its policy-making civil service and its highly sophisticated banking sector, for a last hurrah. Indeed, the pattern of European structures being erected around German aspirations was to play itself out for one last time when Bonn surrendered the Deutschemark for a common currency.

However, while the original European integration process built on the then prevailing format of corporate liberal class compromise in production, and the 1985 decision by European Commission President Jacques Delors to complete the Single Market may be read as an uneasy adjustment to systemic neoliberalism, *the euro was a project of and for money-dealing capital.* The committee consisting mainly of central bankers that worked out the euro project in 1988–89 could not miss the pre-eminence of this form of capital even if it had wanted to—certainly after the European Exchange Rate Mechanism collapsed under the attacks of speculators in the early 1990s. Hence it recommended that the euro's role as a means of exchange would remain confined to the eurozone, making the euro an investment object first of all. To attract short-term money flows, its interest rate (the sole monetary policy instrument of the European Central Bank—ECB), was set just above the US rate (Chesnais 2011: 120, cf. 90). The anti-inflationary caps of Economic and Monetary Union also were not because of the supposed painful memories of 1920s inflation in Weimar Germany, etc., but because, as noted above, '"hot money" flows [are] … a mechanism by which the financial markets discipline profligate government'.

Thus, the German advantage obtained by wage repression in the 1990s was consolidated by the common currency, which prevented the deficit countries from adjusting their exchange rate to compete. After 2004, when the

Minotaur's voraciousness appeared insatiable, German trade surpluses boomed, unemployment fell from almost 4m. to 2m. and corporate profits increased by 37%, while its banks along with French and other financial operators were scouring the market for speculative gains on government paper, especially after 2006 when the spread in bond yields among surplus and deficit eurozone countries increased (Varoufakis 2013: 203; Anand et al. 2012: 7). In addition, the eurozone countries followed the neoliberal trend by radically slashing top income tax rates, covering the shortfall by selling bonds, i.e. paying the wealthy instead of taxing them. This obviously fed into the oligarchic trend while laying the groundwork for the post-2008 austerity policies, given that in several countries debt service would soon become the second or third largest item in the government budget after education and health.

Thus, the simulacrum was made complete. Just as the Global Minotaur lacked a surplus recycling mechanism, forcing deficits to be covered by borrowing, the Germans ruled out a proper surplus recycling mechanism for the eurozone. This set in stone the obligation of the deficit countries and France to continue providing German exports with demand. When the 2008 crash happened, the weakest link of the system, the eurozone, cracked first. That the eurozone had been set up as a playground for hot money was now brought out for everyone to see, for although there was much sniping at the financial practices prevalent in Wall Street, the City and their orbit of offshore centres, European banks were actually submerged much deeper in money-dealing practices. German banks, even the reputedly solid Landesbanken, on average had a leverage level of 52 in borrowed euros for every euro of their own funds, French banks held 33,000m. euros in CDOs, and in all, European banks were exposed to the indebted eurozone countries to the tune of 849,000m. euros and to other indebted non-dollar regions at the rate of a further 500,000m. euros (Varoufakis 2013: 200–203).

Redefining the Crash

The crash of 2008 has mortally wounded the Minotaur, for as Varoufakis details, US demand for the world's net exports, foreign direct investment and financial assets held by foreigners, have all gone into meltdown. Foreign funding of its government deficit is the only remaining lifeline for the USA. Paradoxically, confidence in the USA remains because the dollar share of global reserves stood at 62% in 2009 and has even climbed in response to Europe's post-2010 sovereign debt crisis (Varoufakis 2013: 226–31).

The world would have slid into a major depression straightaway had not the governments learned the lesson of the 1930s and stepped in to bail out the banks—forgetting Keynes' strictures against speculative finance though. For the crash interrupted but ultimately did not stem the ascent of speculative money-dealing capital, although it had been at the origin of the debacle. In uncanny resemblance of Nazi Germany when the bankrupt part of capital politically prevailed over its economically more viable competitors, the trading desks of the large banks have largely escaped formal default, but this time, not in one country but in the Western capitalist system as a whole. So unlike the 1940s, there is no new configuration of forces such as New Deal Fordism (or the Soviet planned economy for that matter) waiting in the wings to take over once the predatory neoliberalism of the defunct Minotaur truly collapses.

In five years the socialization of bank debts raised sovereign debt relative to GDP by 51.7 percentage points in Japan, 41.6 points in the UK, 33.1 in the eurozone, and 27.3 in the USA. The UK and the eurozone passed the 100% debt to GNP mark in 2011 (the USA remained just under 100, Japan's debt stood at 200% but is owed mostly to domestic creditors). Crucially however, the bail-outs included restocking the trading desks of the banks with public funds so that the very instruments that had caused the crash could again be brought into operation, making governments the prisoners of the high priests of hot money who should have been expropriated by the very principles of market economy. Thus saving the insurance company AIG in September 2008 by a US $85,000m. rescue package in exchange for a 80% Federal share, included paying out outstanding credit default swaps at face value, with Goldman Sachs receiving between $12,900m. and $20,000m. according to different sources; Merrill Lynch and its new owner, Bank of America, together received $12,000m., Société Générale (France) and Deutsche Bank $12,000m., and Barclays $8,500m., to name only the largest beneficiaries (Nesvetailova 2010: 35). What else was this but restarting the fatal cycle of speculative arbitrage, the proliferation of CDOs and CDSs that had run aground so completely?

In the eurozone, which does not enjoy the 'Kindleberger privilege' of the USA, ensuring that the rest of the world will continue to fund its deficits, there was the additional problem of the differentials between the member countries and their constitutional inability to defend themselves by devaluation. This in itself fuelled speculation as banks and hedge funds began to issue CDSs targeting the weakest member states such as Greece and Ireland, and as this market grew, it siphoned off capital (supplied to them by the bail-outs) for renewed speculative movement of funds. Sovereign debt was now packaged into CDOs or CDO-like debt instruments; Varoufakis in this light considers the May 2010 Special Purpose Vehicle (SPV), Europe's version of the American Geithner-Summes plan, a straightforward case of publicly funded speculation. Subsequently renamed the European Financial Stability Facility (EFSF), this was not remotely an assistance programme for countries in difficulty, but like its US prototype, premised on the mode of operation of money-dealing capital.

Thus, an EFSF loan would be raised on the European money market under a guarantee of the other countries in proportion to GDP (Greece had been removed from this market in May 2010). The bond would be packaged with one part guaranteed by Germany, a smaller one by France, the smallest by Portugal, etc. and sold to Asian investors and Europe's own quasi-bankrupt banks. These semi-creditworthy assets would then begin to circulate by the billions, 'insured' by CDSs (e.g. a CDS that will pay out when Portugal defaults, and then a price rise of these CDSs will push up the interest rate Portugal has to pay for new loans to the point where it has to apply to the EFSF again), and so on. In combination with a 'euro carry trade' in which banks, but also governments of the low-debt, low-interest rate eurozone countries, pursue speculative hedging operations targeting southern Europe, this has created a new money-dealing bonanza that not only absolves the CDO form as such (by reviving it) but allows the banks, insurance companies, hedge funds, etc. to continue to create new forms of private money as if the crash of 2008 never happened.

At the same time austerity policies, in order to service the debt, are not only blocking a return to social protection for the foreseeable future, but also work to shrink the economy and makes deleveraging ever-more difficult. Once interest rates start to climb again, the amount of borrowing due to cheap credit will prove too much for the downsized economies and they will once again be exposed to the vagaries of speculative arbitrage. Already in 2010 the total amount of outstanding over-the-counter derivatives surpassed the pre-crisis level, reaching US $700,000m. and once again Europe is at the heart of the impending storm, as European banks according to the latest figures top the list of holders of derivatives ($370,000m.), followed by the USA ($220,000m.), Asia, $40,000m., and the rest of the world in all, $140,000m. (Mirowski 2013: 350–51; Hutchinson 2013; *Le Monde* 6 May 2014).

Thus, the shock-like abandonment of class compromise and the corollary restriction of democracy reached its logical conclusion under the auspices of the form of capital most removed from the social contract, money-dealing capital. That the bail-outs also worked to transmit the moment of crisis from a crisis of speculative finance to a crisis of sovereign debt has completely altered the public perception of the origin of our current predicament. By this metamorphosis, in the words of Chrystos Lynteris, 'an officially sanctioned and governmentally organised Economic Crisis, a structural counter-event … that … manages to substitute [the initial crisis] as the true field of decision, as the real crisis', states are being empowered as enforcers of their own downsizing, state aid to bankers is sold as 'saving Greece' (Lynteris 2011: 210). This then feeds into the rise of nationalist populism and neo-fascism, directed against countries in southern Europe now blamed for having been forced, under eurozone rules, to cover their deficits by borrowing. Absurdities such as 'not one more cent to Greece' are now commonplace also among mainstream politicians.

However, the capture of state policy by money-dealing capital and the concomitant drift to oligarchic authoritarianism, fed by the upward redistribution implied in austerity policies, has graver implications as well. It also coincides with a new irrationalism and adventurism in foreign policy. The depicting of foreign leaders as so many incarnations of evil for not submitting to Western guidance (first Slobodan Milosevic, then Saddam Hussein and Muammar al-Gaddafi, and today, Vladimir Putin), is a way of projecting repressed hatred of one's own Government and the inability to ward off the injustices of painful austerity policies. It satisfies a desire for opposition and enmity in a situation in which domestic dissent has effectively been stifled, which is one reason why such large parts of the Left have joined in 'dictator-bashing'. The phenomenon was already noted when German troops in World War One committed large-scale atrocities against Belgian life and property, as if to compensate for the fact that in the Second Empire itself any real opposition or substantive redistribution was blocked (Alff 1976: 49)· Of course an added consequence of this projection of evil on the foreign leader is the mistaken expectation that if only 'he' were out of the way, the society in question would happily and orderly join the West in its selfless campaign for global civilization.

Thus, the overt and increasingly racist disdain for the southern eurozone countries blends with Putin-bashing and other forms of bellicose consensus. Because they are still entrenched in a corporate liberal class configuration with capital/labour compromise surviving, welfare state elements likewise, and an unbeaten labour movement, Greece and the other southern eurozone societies are now bearing the brunt of 'reform'. What they are facing today is the full impact of the nihilistic thrust of predatory neoliberalism, the combination of relentless austerity with growing authoritarianism. This takes us to France, which as I indicated above, is the real target of the northern eurozone credit and export economies' predatory neoliberalism. There too the complex interconnections between austerity and authoritarianism, neo-fascism and violence are most clearly in evidence—as is the resistance to them.

The French Drift to Authoritarianism

Redefining the bank crisis caused by reckless speculation as a crisis of state finances and sovereign debt, with the attendant rhetoric of clearing the desk, honouring 'our' debts and not passing them on to future generations, etc., lends credibility to attacking the remaining structures of social protection. In the eurozone, the main effort is directed at enforcing predatory neoliberalism, *uncompromising capitalism*. It is here that the Greek stand acquires its true significance. For when Prime Minister Tsipras made his initial tour to several southern eurozone capitals and the newspapers gloated that his ideas had fallen on deaf ears, this was because he encountered government leaders who had already signed up to the worst consequences of the disastrous austerity policy, and who did not miss the chance to demonstrate to their patrons in Brussels and Frankfurt they were committed to staying the course.

The most dramatic alternative to the Syriza stand, and under 'socialist' auspices at that, is France. In contrast to the ultimatums delivered to Athens, Paris for one has been given two years to implement the necessary reforms. This will once again take the form of a 'shock therapy' in the sense of Naomi Klein and cover the entire scale from covert operations to an economic 'war of manoeuvre' against the population at large (Klein 2007). However, whereas in the meantime we know a lot about the earlier transition from corporate liberal to neoliberal capitalism, including its darker hues, to decipher the current situation the genius of a Costa-Gavras would be necessary to disentangle how economic dogma and violence, constitutional twists and authoritarian impulses, have all blended in a web of deceit that is leading French society into the abyss.

The French Socialist Party has effectively been marginalized as a political force, falling behind the neo-fascist National Front of Marine Le Pen and Nicolas Sarkozy's right-wing bloc. August 2014 already brought the desertion of the Minister of the Economy, Industrial Renewal and Digital Affairs, Arnaud Montebourg, and his replacement by Rothschild banker Emmanuel Macron. Montebourg had protested the fact that a vote for the Socialists in France had effectively come to mean one for Schäuble's right-wing in the Christian Democratic Union of Germany, but his successor wasted no time before writing a neoliberal omnibus bill named after him (the *loi Macron*, the official title of which is of course, 'for growth, etc.') that covers an entire revamping of the social contract that France had lived with for half a century or more. The bill has been applauded by Chancellor Angela Merkel and EU President Jean-Claude Juncker alike, but only as the beginning (Bulard 2015: 1, 4–5).

This bulky piece of legislation abrogates not just the skeleton class compromise with organized labour or the compromise with the asset-owning middle classes, *it abrogates the social contract itself.* Key among the bill's provisions is the rolling back of social protection. The labour code (adopted in 1806 under Napoleon) can now be side-lined as employers will be entitled to sign private contracts as civil parties with individual workers, disregarding provisions of the labour code. The new labour law, signed by Minister of Labour Myriam El Khomri, in the spring of 2016 provoked a nation-wide youth revolt under the slogan *Nuit Debout,* a conflation of staying up/standing firm in the night. Compared to that, the provisions of the *loi Macron* on lowering the tax on shares distributed to top management only underline the boost to inequality that the bill aims to provide. Not since liberation in 1945 has a French Government dared to engage in such a radical removal of social protection, along with the further erosion of employment benefits, Sundays and holidays worked, and actual wage reductions.

In January of 2015, when chances that the unabashedly anti-social thrust of the *loi Macron* might still mobilize French society and even sections of the Socialist Party against it were still alive, the dramatic events in Paris changed the political mood. The murderous assault on the anti-Islamic 'satirical' magazine, *Charlie Hebdo*, followed by a hostage-taking in a Jewish supermarket, also with deadly outcome, prompted a massive demonstration against violence that resonated across Europe and beyond. Political leaders not necessarily known for their championing of press or other freedoms had themselves photographed, arms locked, at what looked like the first row of a demonstration. In fact as pictures taken from a higher angle revealed, the leaders had just been assembled in a side-street, away from any demonstration and with police on all sides shielding them from unwanted attention.

Unlike the subsequent terror attacks in November 2015at the Bataclan rock music hall and the Stade de France in Paris, the supposed perpetrators of the *Charlie Hebdo* attack were both executed by police, as was the hostage-taker in the Jewish supermarket. It was claimed that a police officer familiar with the attackers committed suicide while working on a report on the matter. Although much remains unknown, it would seem that the *Charlie Hebdo* episode had more in common with a similar, two-pronged terror incident (a 'random' attack followed by a specific anti-Jewish one) in March 2012, during the presidential campaign eventually lost by Sarkozy (Guyenot 2015), than with the November 2015 attacks, which bore the hallmarks of an authentic assault on the part of 'third-generation' *jihadists* (Kepel 2015).

What matters is that the response of the French media, which are almost without exception the personal property of individual billionaires and multi-millionaires, converged on a call for a strong state that would push through the neoliberal *loi Macron*. Television station BFM (property of media mogul Alain Weill) called for 'the moment of national unity evoked by what has happened [to] be extended in the vote over this legislative project [i.e., the *loi Macron*], because the signs were there, a sort of consensus on the need to liberalise the economy'. A commentator of the weekly *Le Point* (owned by François Pinault, third richest man in France) actually claimed that the demonstrations were not even in need of interpretation; this and nothing else was what they were held for. 'On 11 January 2015 the French addressed the world and their leaders with a message of dignity and courage, of which the spirit is clear: to get away from denial, the lifting of taboos, and pass from words to deeds. *These principles…will only be credible if they are to be applied also to economic and social reforms.*'

The editor of *Le Point* in the issue of the previous week had already indicated that the shock of the attacks could work out favourably for the Government of Prime Minister Manuel Valls.

> The government of Manuel Valls has come into a strong position to push aside the wailing of the dissidents [*frondeurs*], the lamentations of the trade unions and of all those resisting comprehensive reforms. France needs these to overcome its archaic structures and create manoeuvring room for its economy, for example in the domain of the organisation of the labour market or the 35-hours' working week. To reinforce the liberal wind that was the inspiration for the *loi Macron* and go even much further … we can only hope for France that Mr. Valls *will not allow this unique economic 'opportunity', offered by the tragedy of the terrorist attacks, to pass him by.*
>
> (Rimbert 2015: 2, emphases added)

Anyone familiar with the 'strategy of tension' that in the 1970s helped keep Italy from 'falling' to communist government participation, will recognize the brazen attempt to give a steer to terror events, which of course is not the same as claiming that they were staged with that purpose. Yet that the state of exception was being used to push through a neoliberalism for which no social consensus existed otherwise, is beyond doubt (Fouskas and Gökay 2015). In the case of France the rule that under article 49(3) of the Constitution of the Fifth Republic, a bill can be enacted by decree unless Parliament votes a non-confidence motion—a rule reflecting the emergency conditions of the original constitutional reforms by Charles de Gaulle in 1958 and 1962—offers the opportunity to bypass even parliament; never mind that François Hollande prior to his presidency had labelled this provision 'brutal' and a 'denial of democracy' (Bulard 2015). Eventually the *loi Macron* was pushed through under this provision, and the El Khomri labour law too was slated for being enacted in this way (*Le Nouvel Observateur*, 17 February 2015; *Le Monde*, 10 May 2016).

The French case illustrates the ascendancy of predatory neoliberalism in Europe, combining the oligarchic pursuit of commercial-financial profit with mounting authoritarianism exploiting terror incidents paralysing public debate. The post-2008 political culture has abandoned any pretence of winning populations for projects other than straightforward manipulation, as the radical erosion of class compromise reduces the field of politics to back door operations or worse. The threat of international terrorism itself works to erode democracy and accelerates its demise through 'law enforcement, intelligence gathering, and covert operations – activities that entail bureaucratic coordination, but not national mobilization' (Kupchan and Trubowitz 2007: 29). Simultaneously the heightened sense of society being under attack is expressed in the steady rise of the National Front, from 4.8% in the elections of 2008, to 15.1% in 2011, to one-quarter of the vote in the first round in March 2015.

If social cohesion rests on cumulative compromise anchored in production, the successive impacts of the abrogation of the compromise with organised labour and the surrender of public and middle-class assets to securitization run amok, have obviously undermined it. As neoliberalism has come under the spell of the predatory variety championed by money-dealing capital, the very idea of a domestic class compromise is being replaced by a tentative compromise achieved horizontally, among the oligarchies of the different countries. Austerity policies propagated across the West may be interpreted as the expression of such a transnational consensus of the oligarchies that have drained worker, public and middle-class assets and income and turned it into private hoards managed for them from offshore centres. The EU, and the eurozone in particular, has become a key vehicle of this consensus, since no democratic control exists at this level.

Indeed, whenever an electorate is given a chance to vote on a topic remotely connected to 'Europe', it votes No. The rejection of the so-called European Constitution by referendums in France and the Netherlands in 2005, both traditionally pro-European countries, was a case in point. In the Netherlands, the referendum on the ratification of the EU Association Treaty in April 2016 again resulted in a two-thirds' majority for rejection even though the earlier lesson of the Constitution (which was simply repackaged as the Lisbon Treaty in 2007) discouraged many to even vote.

In Greece it was obvious from the start that Syriza was not leading a revolution but at best a rebellion. Putting it down, and doing so in a way that stamped out the very idea of an alternative route, even within capitalism, was the key aim of the troika composed of the IMF, the EU and the ECB. An *Economist Intelligence Unit* meeting in Athens in March 2015 concluded that the treatment allotted to Greece had nothing to do with repairing anything in the country's economy. It was merely to send a message to:

> the countries of southern as well as of northern Europe, in order to figure out up to which point it was possible to impoverish a population and to destroy its middle class. The effect of exemplarity being sought aimed at convincing union organizations in other countries and political parties that it is better to accept a relatively orderly dismantling of social legislation (as is happening in France for instance with the *loi Macron* but as is also happening in Italy) rather than finding oneself in the situation of Greece or of Spain.
>
> (Sapir 2015)

In addition Sapir suggests that the 'demonstration' being played out here is also to lock in austerity in current economic policy to avoid that the surplus countries, in the absence of a federal budget at the EU level, become permanent sources of subsidy for the weaker economies of the eurozone. This highlights that the ultimate imposition of discipline is not a matter of northern against southern Europe, but of the dominant fraction of contemporary capital on all of them.

Instead of proceeding on the assumption that a class compromise can still be founded on the carcass of a defunct economic system, which through its successive configurations has seen all social vitality flow from it, Europe's peoples therefore face the task of rewriting *a social contract beyond capitalism*. With the ongoing carnage under the banner of the War on Terror and the adventurism on the Russian borders on the part of the USA and NATO combining with the spread of ever-more intrusive authoritarianism, we should not be led to thinking that this is something of only academic interest. It is an urgent task that we cannot afford not to take up.

References

Alff, W. (1976), *Materialien zum Kontinuitätsproblem der deutschen Geschichte.* Frankfurt: Suhrkamp.

Anand, M.R., Gupta, G.L., and Dash, R. (2012), *The Eurozone Crisis. Its dimensions and implications.* Working Paper, Economics Division, Department of Economic Affairs. New Delhi: Ministry of Finance.

Bassosi, D. (2006), *Il governo del dollaro. Interdipendenza economica e potere statunitense negli anni di Richard Nixon (1969–1973)*. Firenze: Edizioni Polistampa.

Bengtsson, E., and Ryner, M. (2015), 'The (International) Political Economy of Falling Wage Shares: Situating Working-Class Agency', *New Political Economy* 20(3) 406–430.

Briody, D. (2003), *The Iron Triangle. Inside the Secret World of the Carlyle Group* [foreword C. Byron]. Hoboken, NJ: John Wiley.

Brownstein, R., and Easton, N. (1983 [1982]), *Reagan's Ruling Class. Portraits of the President's Top One Hundred Officials*, 2nd ed. New York: Pantheon.

Bulard, M. (2015), 'Pour amadouer Bruxelles. Loi Macron, le choix du "toujours moins"'. *Le Monde Diplomatique*, April.

Burke, E. (1790), *Reflections on the Revolution in France*, in *Works*, 12 vols. Gutenberg.org. [orig., *The Works of the Right Honourable Edmund Burke*. London: John Nimmo, 1887].

Burn, G. (2006), *The Re-emergence of Global Finance*. Basingstoke: Palgrave Macmillan.

Chesnais, F. (2011), *Les dettes illégitimes. Quand les banques font main basse sur les politiques publiques*. Paris: Raisons d'agir.

Crozier, M., Huntington, S.P., and Watanuki, J. (1975), *The Crisis of Democracy. Report on the Governability of Democracies to the Trilateral Commission*. New York: New York University Press.

Deppe, F. (2013), *Autoritärer Kapitalismus. Demokratie auf dem Prüfstand*. Hamburg: VSA.

Dizionario Gramsciano 1926–1937 (2009), Guido Liguori and Pasquale Voza, eds. Roma: Carocci.

Duménil, G., and Lévy, D. (2004), 'Neo-Liberal Dynamics – Towards a New Phase?' in K. van der Pijl, L. Assassi, and D. Wigan, eds. *Global Regulation. Managing Crises After the Imperial Turn*. Basingstoke: Palgrave Macmillan.

Epstein, G. and Power, D. (2002), 'The Return of Finance and Finance's Returns: Recent Trends in Rentier Incomes in OECD Countries, 1960–2000', *Research Brief, Political Economy Research Institute* (University of Massachusetts Amherst) no. 2, November.

Feulner, E.J., Jr. (1976), *Congress and the New International Economic Order*. Washington, DC: The Heritage Foundation.

Fouskas, V.K. (2001), 'Reflections on the Cyprus Issue and the Turkish Invasion of 1974'. *Mediterranean Quarterly* (Winter) 99–127.

Fouskas, V.K. (2005), 'Uncomfortable Questions: Cyprus, October 1973–August 1974'. *Contemporary European History*. 14(1) 45–63.

Fouskas, V.K. and Gökay, B. (2015), 'Cannibalisation and the State of Exception'. *Open Democracy*. 30 November. www.opendemocracy.net/can-europe-make- it/vassilis-k-fouskas-bulent-gokay/cannibalisation-and-state-of-exception (last accessed 23 April 2016).

Gill, S. (1990), *American Hegemony and the Trilateral Commission*. Cambridge: Cambridge University Press.

Gowan, P. (2009), 'Crisis in the Heartland. Consequences of the New Wall Street System'. *New Left Review*, 2nd series (55) 5–29.

Guyenot, L. (2015), 'Prequel to Charlie Hebdo: The March 2012 Mohammed Merah Affair (a Mossad-DCRI Co-Production?)' in K. Barrett, ed. *We Are Not Charlie Hebdo. Free Thinkers Question the French 9/11*. Lone Rock, WI: Sifting & Winnowing Books.

Harvey, D. (2006 [1982]). *The Limits to Capital*, rev. ed. London: Verso.

Holbrooke, R. (1995), 'America, A European Power', *Foreign Affairs*, 74(2) 38–51.

Holman, O. (2015), 'Flexibilisation of labour in the European Union' in K. van der Pijl, ed. *Handbook of the International Political Economy of Production*. Cheltenham: Edward Elgar.

Hume, D. (1875 [1742, 1752]). *Essays. Moral, Political, and Literary*, 2 vols. [eds T.H. Green, T.H. Grose]. London: Longmans, Green & Co.

Hutchinson, M. (2013), 'Finance sector fading'. *Asia Times Online*. www.atimes.com/atimes/Global_Economy/GECON-01-101213.html, (last accessed 10 May 2016).

Kalecki, M. (1972 [1943]). 'Political Aspects of Full Employment', in E.K. Hunt and J.G. Schwartz, eds., *A Critique of Economic Theory*. Harmondsworth: Penguin.

Kepel, G. (2015), *Terreur dans l'Hexagone. Genèse du djihad français* [with Antoine Jardin]. Paris: Gallimard.

Klein, N. (2007), *The Shock Doctrine. The Rise of Disaster Capitalism*. Harmondsworth: Penguin.

Kupchan, C.A. and Trubowitz, P.L. (2007), 'Dead Center. The Demise of Liberal Internationalism in the United States'. *International Security*, 32(2) 7–44.

Lapavitsas, C., Kaltenbrunner, A., Labrinidis, G., Lindo, D., Mitchell, J., Panceira, J.P., Pires, E., Powell, J., Stenfors, A., and Teles, N. (2010), 'Eurozone crisis: beggar thyself and thy neighbour'. *Journal of Balkan and Near Eastern Studies*, 12(4) 321–373.

Lenin, V.I. (1917), The Impending Catastrophe and How to Combat it, in *Collected Works*, vol. 25. Moscow: Progress.

Lynteris, C. (2011), 'The Greek Economic Crisis as Evental Substitution' in A. Vradis and D. Dalakoglou, eds. *Revolt and Crisis in Greece. Between a Present Yet to Pass and a Future Still to Come*. Oakland, CA: AK Press, and London: Occupied London.

Mirowski, P. (2013), *Never Let A Serious Crisis Go to Waste. How Neoliberalism Survived the Financial Meltdown*. London: Verso.

Naylor, R.T. (1987), *Hot Money and the Politics of Debt*. London: Unwin Hyman.

Nesvetailova, A. (2010), *Financial Alchemy in Crisis. The Great Liquidity Illusion*. London: Pluto Press.

Piketty, T. (2014), *Capital in the Twenty-First Century* [trans. A. Goldhammer]. Cambridge, MA: Harvard University Press.

Rimbert, P. (2015), 'Loi Macron, obscur objet du désir'. *Le Monde Diplomatique*, March.

Rude, C. (2008), 'The Role of Financial Discipline in Imperial Strategy' in L. Panitch and M. Konings, eds. *American Empire and the Political Economy of Global Finance*. Basingstoke: Palgrave Macmillan.

Rueschemeyer, D., Stephens, E.H., and Stephens, J.D. (1992), *Capitalist Development and Democracy*. Chicago, IL: University of Chicago Press.

Sakwa, R. (2015), *Frontline Ukraine. Crisis in the Borderlands*. London: IB Tauris.

Sapir, J. (2015), 'Where is Greece going?' *RussEurope* (17 March). http://russeurope.hypotheses.org/3640 (last accessed 10 May 2016).

Sassen, S. (2015), 'Conclusion : Emergent predatory logics', in K. van der Pijl, ed. *Handbook of the International Political Economy of Production*. Cheltenham: Edward Elgar.

Schmitt, B.E. and Vedeler, H.C. (1984), *The World in the Crucible, 1914–1919*. New York: Harper & Row.

Schumpeter, J.A. (1942), *Capitalism, Socialism, and Democracy*. New York: Harper.

Scott, P.D. (2015), *The American Deep State. Wall Street, Big Oil, and the Attack on U.S. Democracy.* Lanham, MD: Rowman & Littlefield.

Teacher, D. (1993), 'The Pinay Circle Complex 1969–1989', *Lobster. Journal of Parapolitics* 26, 9–16

van der Pijl, K. (2006), *Global Rivalries from the Cold War to Iraq*. London: Pluto and New DelhiSage Vistaar.

van der Pijl, K. (2014), *The Discipline of Western Supremacy.* Vol. III of *Modes of Foreign Relations and Political Economy.* London: Pluto.

Varoufakis, Y. (2013 [2011]), *The Global Minotaur. America, Europe and the Future of the Global Economy* [rev. ed]. London: Zed Books.

Willan, P. (1991), *Puppet Masters. The Political Use of Terrorism in Italy.* London: Constable.

2 Sovereign Debt or Balance-of-Payments Crisis?

Exploring the Structural Logic of Adjustment in the Eurozone

Matthias Kaelberer

Political observers and European policy makers conventionally describe the economic crisis that engulfed many of the peripheral countries of the eurozone after 2009 as a sovereign debt crisis. The popular account of the crisis has been that of irresponsible fiscal policies in those countries—most importantly Greece, Ireland, Portugal and Spain. Consequently, policy prescriptions to address the crisis have focused on reducing government debt, primarily through austerity measures. In contrast to this prevailing perspective, I argue in this article that the eurozone crisis represents a balance-of-payments crisis rather than a sovereign debt crisis—only this time the crisis is taking place *within* a common currency. The common factor among the countries most severely affected by the euro crisis was not government debt. Actually, Greece was the only country with a sizable but stable government deficit and debt problem before the economic downturn started in 2007. Spain and Ireland even had budget surpluses before the crisis. Instead, the common denominator for Greece, Portugal, Spain, and Ireland was their deficit in the external payments position. Their national economies all had lost competitiveness in the eurozone.

This interpretation of the euro crisis as a balance-of-payments crisis has significant consequences for the adjustment measures governments can take. Despite the expectation of many observers at the time of the creation of the euro that the common currency would distribute the burden of adjustment more evenly across its member countries, the opposite is actually true. Compared to the Economic and Monetary Union (EMU)'s predecessor regime, the European Monetary System (EMS), deficit countries are saddled with even higher adjustment costs in the common currency than before. In particular, they no longer have the tool of a nominal exchange rate change to address balance-of-payments disequilibria. This situation allows surplus countries—most importantly Germany—to exercise leverage over the narrative of the crisis and the key bargaining issues at stake in solving the crisis (for example, on the conditionality of bail-outs or on the rules that govern joint financing facilities).

This article seeks to provide an alternative interpretation of the euro crisis to the dominant sovereign debt narrative. I argue that the basis of the euro crisis is a balance-of-payments disequilibrium. The frame of reference—sovereign debt crisis or balance-of-payments crisis—makes a significant difference not only for determining the causes of the euro crisis but also for the adequacy of policy measures to address it. The first section of this paper develops the argument and provides evidence that the euro crisis is fundamentally a balance-of-payments crisis rather than a sovereign debt crisis. The sovereign debt crisis is a symptom, not the cause of the eurozone crisis. Section two explicates the structural logic of adjustment in the eurozone. My central argument here is that, contrary to the initial expectations, a common currency actually worsens the asymmetries between core and periphery compared to the situation prior to the formation of monetary union. The third section will finally hint at some of the policy implications of a balance-of-payments crisis within a single currency. The austerity measures advocated by many policy-makers of the core countries reflect their misdiagnosis of the eurozone crisis as a sovereign debt crisis. Indeed, the sovereign debt crisis narrative has missed the fact that the euro crisis reflects deeper imbalances in the real economy and it has failed to catch the interrelated nature of the macroeconomic imbalances within the eurozone. Instead, interpreting the euro crisis as a balance-of-payments crisis allows the perspective to open up to a more complex array of appropriate policy measures.

Sovereign Debt Crisis or Balance of Payments Crisis?

The global financial crisis produced asymmetrical consequences for different parts of the eurozone. While many of the northern European countries experienced a much milder downturn, countries such as Greece, Ireland, Spain and Portugal—a group of countries I will refer to as the eurozone peripheral countries—were much more severely impacted. They saw a significant drop in economic activity, a rise in unemployment and a growing government deficit. Greece essentially served as the trigger mechanism when financial markets realized during the autumn of 2009 that the Greek government deficit and debt were significantly worse than commonly assumed at the time. This discovery initially led to a significant rise in interest rates on Greek government bonds. It also created spillover effects into bond markets for other peripheral countries, leading to a rise in interest rates for numerous other peripheral eurozone countries.

This development reversed trends that had prevailed in the early years of the eurozone. The introduction of the euro initially helped to lower borrowing costs for the peripheral countries in the eurozone. Since the European Central Bank (ECB) now sets a single interest rate for the whole eurozone, the former high-inflation countries benefitted from a significant reduction in their real and nominal interest rates. Nominal interest rates approached Germany's low levels, and with still higher inflation, real interest rates came down significantly—and were actually negative for some of these countries at times. Ironically, it was Germany and its low inflation neighbours who faced the

Table 2.1 EMU Bond Yields

	2003	*2005*	*2007*	*2008*	*2009*	*2010*	*2011*	*2012*	*2013*	*2014*	*2015*
Germany	4.07	3.35	4.22	3.98	3.22	2.74	2.61	1.50	1.57	1.16	0.50
Ireland	4.13	3.33	4.31	4.53	5.23	5.74	9.60	6.17	3.79	2.37	1.18
Greece	4.27	3.59	4.50	4.80	5.17	9.09	15.75	22.50	10.05	6.93	9.67
Spain	4.12	3.39	4.31	4.37	3.98	4.25	5.44	5.85	4.56	2.72	1.73
France	4.13	3.41	4.30	4.23	3.65	3.12	3.32	2.54	2.20	1.67	0.84
Italy	4.25	3.56	4.49	4.68	4.31	4.04	5.42	5.49	4.32	2.89	1.71
Portugal	4.18	3.44	4.42	4.52	4.21	5.40	10.24	10.55	6.29	3.75	2.42

Source: Eurostat.

highest real interest rates during the early years of the eurozone, given their lower inflation rates and the now common nominal ECB interest rate. Thus, borrowing was cheaper for the peripheral countries than before the creation of the monetary union. Relatively slow economic growth in the Northern core facilitated capital flows into the higher growth countries of the European periphery.

The relatively easy access to capital enabled greater consumption and investment in the non-tradable sector and the domestically oriented sectors of the economy, such as the real estate market and construction sector in Spain and Ireland. Economic growth in the peripheral countries was driven by strong domestic demand and provided for a time the appearance of economic strength (Blankenburg et al. 2013). Thus, even though not all countries necessarily fed consumption directly, investments in the non-tradable sector had the same effect as consumption from a balance of payments perspective. Flows into the non-tradable sector of the economy do not allow for generating enough funds to repay their external debt, and therefore function in a similar fashion as capital flows to finance consumption (Belke and Dreger 2013). Capital inflows by and large did not reach the export-oriented sectors of the economy and therefore failed to improve the long-term competitiveness of these economies through innovation and efficiency gains. Instead, capital inflows facilitated domestic consumption and construction, fed a housing bubble and produced inflation. Ironically, greater capital mobility in the Single European Market did not produce greater efficiency in the real economy, but rather produced market failure (Tombazos 2011). Left to its own devices, free capital mobility merely misallocated resources in the early years of the eurozone.

The initial expectations attached to the introduction of the euro also included the belief that monetary union would lead to convergence in inflation rates. Indeed, through fixing nominal exchange rates in the euro the formerly high-inflation countries were supposed to gain anti-inflationary credibility and be able to import low inflation from the core countries of the eurozone at no costs. The ECB was meant to serve as the guarantor of low inflation and lend even greater credibility to the disinflation efforts of the peripheral countries in the eurozone.

Table 2.2 clearly demonstrates the persistent inflation differentials among eurozone member countries even after the introduction of the euro. It represents an ironic twist that one goal of monetary union—greater capital mobility—helped undermine another goal, that of inflation convergence. The introduction of the euro facilitated deeper financial integration and greater capital flows. Within a common currency, investors no longer had to fear nominal exchange rate changes. With the ECB in control of monetary policy, peripheral countries seemingly gained credibility, leading to a reduced risk assessment for foreign investment in these countries. Thus, peripheral countries initially benefitted from lower interest rates permitted by financial markets. Indeed, the increased capital mobility was believed to be very beneficial.

Table 2.2 Consumer Price Index: HICP (1996 = 100)

	2013	*2009*	*2005*	*2000*
Germany	128.7	120.2	111.3	103.6
Ireland	142.9	142.1	129.3	108.2
Greece	167.4	152.7	135.8	113.2
Spain	152.8	140.4	125.0	107.7
France	131.3	122.4	113.5	103.3
Italy	142.9	130.7	120.0	106.9
Portugal	147.1	136.6	125.9	107.3

Source: Eurostat.

First of all, according to neoliberal theory and practice, free capital mobility would create greater efficiency as it would allow capital to find the most productive forms of investments unconstrained by barriers. Funds would flow from Germany and other northern countries to the peripheral countries in the European Union (EU), where they would presumably stimulate investments, raise productivity and therefore produce convergence among the members of the eurozone.

Thus, deeper financial integration in Europe—expressed through larger capital flows—increased the payments imbalances within the eurozone, compared with the pre-euro era. Paradoxically, the durably fixed exchange rates of the eurozone actually heightened the risk of a balance-of-payments crisis compared to its predecessor regime, the pegged exchange rate regime of the EMS. With rising capital mobility, imbalances in capital flows could become larger and trigger balance-of-payments crises, even though they could no longer produce exchange rate crises. The link that normally exists between balance-of-payments crises and exchange rate crises is broken when countries belong to a common currency. It was the global financial crisis that brought the underlying, but largely ignored imbalances to the attention of financial markets. The global financial crisis changed risk perceptions among investors. With the Greek fiscal situation serving as the trigger mechanism, investors charged premiums on government bonds that they viewed as risky. This change in perception led to a rise in nominal and real interest rates for the countries of the eurozone's periphery.

The overall fiscal picture of the eurozone since the creation of the euro nicely illustrates this alternative interpretation of the euro crisis. Ironically, it was not Greece or any of the other peripheral countries that triggered the first fiscal rule violations in the eurozone. Rather, Germany and France were the first countries to violate the criteria of the Stability and Growth Pact in the early 2000s when higher real interest rates in these countries facilitated rather slow economic growth, and with it higher deficits in excess of the prescribed limits.[1]

Table 2.3 Real GDP Growth (% change compared with previous year)

	2002	*2003*	*2004*	*2005*	*2006*	*2007*	*2008*	*2009*	*2010*	*2011*	*Average 2002–11*
Germany	0.0	–0.4	1.2	0.7	3.7	3.3	1.1	–5.1	4.2	3.0	1.2
Ireland	5.9	4.2	4.5	5.3	5.3	5.2	–3.0	–7.0	–0.4	0.7	2.1
Greece	3.4	5.9	4.4	2.3	5.5	3.0	–0.2	–3.3	–3.5	–6.9	1.1
Spain	2.7	3.1	3.3	3.6	4.1	3.5	0.9	–3.7	–0.1	0.7	1.8
France	0.9	0.9	2.5	1.8	2.5	2.3	–0.1	–3.2	1.7	1.7	1.1
Italy	0.5	–0.1	1.7	0.9	2.2	1.7	–1.2	–5.5	1.8	0.4	0.3
Portugal	0.8	–0.9	1.6	0.8	1.5	2.4	0.0	–2.9	1.4	–1.7	0.3

Source: Eurostat.

Not surprisingly, Germany and France were not punished for their profligacy. Not only did Germany and France lack fiscal discipline, Ireland and Spain—countries that were severely impacted by the eurozone crisis later on—were among the fiscal role models during the early 2000s. Both countries actually featured government budget surpluses until 2007 when the financial crisis began. Spanish and Irish budget surpluses exemplify that a sovereign debt crisis is not the underlying cause for the eurozone crisis.

The one country in the eurozone that arguably has a sovereign debt problem is Greece. Capital inflows here financed mainly a bloated state apparatus and helped maintain a clientilistic political structure. In addition, the Greek Government masked the true extent of its deficit and debt level until Prime Minister George Papandreou started to reveal the real numbers in the autumn of 2009. However, it was not that Greece (or for that matter any of the other eurozone countries) surpassed some objective threshold of government debt. Japan, for example, had all along—and continues to have—a higher government debt level than Greece. Rather, the revelations about the real Greek debt situation produced uncertainty and nervousness in financial markets. What became unsustainable was not the government debt *per se*, but rather the interest rates demanded for the debt by financial markets. Thus, the Greek crisis served as a trigger event that spilled over into other peripheral eurozone countries.

Germany was able to use currency unification to pursue a beggar-thy-neighbour policy in reverse. By forcing its partner countries to keep their nominal exchange rate stable, Germany could engineer the depreciation of its real exchange rate by exercising wage restraint coupled with stagnation of domestic demand. In particular, the labour market reforms of the Gerhard Schröder Government with emphasis on greater flexibility in the low-skill service sector as well as the consensual industrial relations system produced slow wage growth (Simonazzi et al. 2013, Hall 2012). Within a currency union, the partner countries cannot react with a corresponding devaluation of their nominal exchange rate. Thus, Germany would gain competitiveness not through depreciation of the nominal exchange rate as in conventional beggar-thy-neighbour-policies, but rather through depreciation of the real exchange rate. The tremendous rise in Germany's current account surpluses since the introduction of the euro supports this interpretation (see Table 2.6).

Table 2.6 reveals just how beneficial the durable fixing of nominal exchange rates has been for Germany's external balance. Since the introduction of the euro, Germany's current account surplus ballooned to unprecedented heights—levels that would not have been sustainable in a pegged or flexible exchange rate regime. Most likely, a depreciation or devaluation of other currencies would have taken some bite out of Germany's current account surpluses. As Table 2.7 below shows, the German current account surpluses of 6%–7% of GDP after 2005 were extraordinary. These current account surpluses are the main source of German economic growth. Productivity growth in Germany has remained weak since the introduction of the euro. As Costas

Table 2.4 General Government deficit/surplus as % of GDP

	2001	*2003*	*2005*	*2006*	*2007*	*2008*	*2009*	*2010*	*2011*	*2012*	*2013*	*2014*
Germany	–3.1	–4.2	–3.3	–1.6	0.2	–0.1	–3.1	–4.1	–0.8	0.2	–0.1	0.3
Ireland	0.9	0.4	1.7	2.9	0.1	–7.4	–13.9	–30.8	–13.4	–7.6	–5.7	–3.9
Greece	–4.5	–5.6	–5.2	–5.7	–6.5	–9.8	–15.6	–10.7	–9.4	–10.6	–12.4	–3.6
Spain	–0.5	–0.3	1.3	2.4	1.9	–4.5	–11.2	–9.7	–9.4	–10.6	–6.9	–5.9
France	–1.5	–4.1	–2.9	–2.3	–2.7	–3.3	–7.5	–7.1	–5.3	–4.8	–4.1	–3.9
Italy	–3.1	–3.6	–4.4	–3.4	–1.6	–2.7	–5.5	–4.5	–3.8	–3.0	–2.9	–3.0
Portugal	–4.8	–3.7	–6.5	–4.6	–3.1	–3.6	–10.2	–9.8	–4.4	–6.4	–4.8	–7.2

Source: Eurostat.

Table 2.5 Government Gross Debt as % of GDP

	1995	*2000*	*2005*	*2006*	*2007*	*2008*	*2009*	*2010*	*2011*	*2012*	*2013*	*2014*
Germany	55.6	60.2	68.5	68.0	65.2	66.8	74.5	82.4	80.4	81.9	77.4	74.9
Ireland	80.1	35.1	27.3	24.6	25.1	44.5	64.8	92.1	106.4	117.6	120.0	107.5
Greece	97.0	103.4	100.0	106.1	107.4	112.9	129.7	148.3	170.3	156.9	177.0	178.6
Spain	63.3	59.4	43.2	39.7	36.3	40.2	53.9	61.5	69.3	84.2	93.7	99.3
France	55.5	57.3	66.4	63.7	64.2	68.2	79.2	82.4	85.8	90.2	92.3	95.6
Italy	120.9	108.6	105.7	106.3	103.3	106.1	116.4	119.3	120.8	127.0	128.8	132.3
Portugal	59.2	50.7	67.7	69.4	68.4	71.7	83.7	94.0	108.3	123.6	129.0	130.2

Source: Eurostat.

Table 2.6 Current account balance with the rest of the world ('000m. euros)

	2001	*2003*	*2005*	*2006*	*2007*	*2008*	*2009*	*2010*	*2011*	*2012*	*2013*	*2014*
Germany	0.0	40.5	112.6	144.7	180.9	153.6	140.6	150.7	147.7	187.3	182.0	219.7
Ireland	–0.2	0.0	–5.7	–6.3	–10.1	–10.2	–4.7	0.8	1.1	2.7	7.6	11.5
Greece	–10.6	–11.3	–14.7	–23.8	–32.6	–34.8	–25.8	–23.0	–21.1	–4.6	1.1	1.6
Spain	–26.8	–27.5	–66.9	–88.3	–105.3	–104.7	–50.5	–47.4	–37.5	–3.0	15.1	8.5
France	26.3	11.5	–8.3	–10.3	–18.9	–33.7	–25.1	–30.2	–38.9	–32.2	–30.3	–21.1
Italy	3.4	–10.4	–12.6	–22.3	–19.9	–45.2	–30.1	–54.7	–50.3	–8.2	15.0	31.2
Portugal	–13.9	–9.2	–15.9	–17.2	–17.1	–21.7	–18.4	–17.2	–11.0	–3.5	2.4	1.0

Source: Eurostat.

Lapavitsas et al. point out: 'Germany has been marked by low growth, flat investment, stagnant consumption, rising savings and falling household debt. This is not a dynamic capitalist economy on any score. The only source of dynamism has been exports' (Lapavitsas et al. 2010: 335).

Even the pegged exchange rate regime of the EMS, which allowed Germany to periodically undervalue the deutschemark, did not produce comparable surpluses. In addition to the occasional realignment of exchange rates in the EMS, the financing facilities that existed under the EMS represented a mechanism that would reign in extreme imbalances balance of payments in member states. Before the various bail-outs, the bond purchasing programme of the ECB and the establishment of the European Stability Mechanism (ESM), no comparable arrangement existed within the EMU. Thus, Germany was able to use the nominal exchange rate fix as a means to produce economic growth through a competitive devaluation of its real exchange rate with peripheral members of the eurozone.

The Structural Logic of Adjustment in the Eurozone

Many observers at the time of the formation of monetary union in Europe believed that the EMU would solve the inherent asymmetry problem in European monetary relations. Under the previously existing regime of the EMS, Germany served as the de facto standard-setter for the system (Kaelberer 2001). All other participants were forced to adjust their macroeconomic policies to avoid disequilibrium with Germany. As the principal strong currency country and low inflation leader Germany determined the interest rate floor for the system as a whole. Germany was free to set its interest rate according to its domestic priorities. All others needed to adjust their macroeconomic policies accordingly.

Obviously, under the EMS the macroeconomic options to create equilibrium included a nominal exchange rate change—a possibility that no longer exists within a monetary union. Initially, observers expected that this situation would lead to some kind of 'average' economic standard among all members of the EMU. After all, the ECB would now set interest rates for the eurozone as a whole, while the German *Bundesbank* only had to take German economic conditions into account during the EMS years. Because Germany could no longer determine the macroeconomic standard single-handedly it would presumably lose some of its power. In a sense, the members of the eurozone believed that they traded in sovereignty (i.e. their right to print money) in favour of regaining de facto authority (i.e. their participation in joint ECB decision-making). Indeed, one of the most important French goals in creating monetary union was a desire to tie down Germany and gain back some of the monetary authority it had lost to Germany under the EMS. The euro crisis, however, reveals that this is hardly the case. To the contrary, the absence of the nominal exchange rate instrument actually has aggravated asymmetries within the European monetary order.

Table 2.7 rent Account Balance as % of GDP

	1975	*1980*	*1985*	*1990*	*1995*	*2000*	*2005*	*2008*	*2010*	*2012*	*2014*
Germany	1.13	–1.72	2.44	2.80	–1.17	–1.83	4.99	6.19	6.12	7.03	7.42
Ireland	–	–	–	–0.70	2.58	–0.32	–3.48	–5.61	1.14	4.42	1.65
Greece	–	–	–	–	–2.69	–7.80	–7.60	–14.95	–10.22	–3.49	–1.63
Spain	–	–	–	–	–0.32	–3.97	–7.36	–9.62	–4.49	–1.11	1.08
France	–	–	–	–	0.70	1.44	–0.47	–1.77	–1.36	–2.21	–1.06
Italy	–	–	–	–1.47	2.04	–0.53	–1.65	–2.88	–3.53	–0.55	1.91
Portugal	–	–	–	–	–	–10.36	–10.70	–12.64	–10.57	–1.53	0.11

Source: Organisation for Economic Co-operation and Development.

The striking feature of the EMU is the continued if not enhanced power of Germany (and other strong currency countries). Germany's power in the monetary realm ultimately is outsized. It has a far greater ability to shape the outcomes in this area than one should expect on the basis of such conventional indicators as a country's economic size or military power. Monetary relations have an inherent power dynamic that is driven by a country's balance-of-payments position, regardless of whether we are dealing with a flexible exchange rate regime, a pegged exchange rate system or a currency union.

Why did observers initially overlook these structural similarities between a common currency and other exchange rate regimes? I argue in this section that the original architecture of the eurozone relied on an inconsistent trio of assumptions. Policy-makers maintained that (1) there could not be a bail-out of eurozone member countries,[2] that (2) no country was allowed to exit from the euro, and that (3) no country was allowed to default within the eurozone—the no bail-out/no exit/no default trilemma. These foundational premises of the eurozone are incompatible. Essentially this inconsistent trio rested on the implicit assumption that balance of payments disequilibria could not develop among the member states of a common currency. In particular, the lack of any pressure on a country's nominal exchange rate and the effective cut in interest rates for weak currency countries after entering the euro further facilitated that feeling initially. With entry into the EMU, weak currency countries apparently had achieved low interest rates without major economic efforts and without ever again having to fear speculation against their national currency. Since all euro member states had accepted the Maastricht Treaty criteria it was felt that no further convergence was necessary (Boltho and Carlin 2013). The inconsistent trio represented a harmonious narrative about life within the eurozone.

The euro crisis reversed that situation. Underneath the absence of currency crises and the low interest rates that prevailed in the early years of the euro's existence, balance-of-payments disequilibria continued to exist. The countries that used to be strong currency countries before the adoption of the euro, carried their strong currency status over into the eurozone. This means that the popular storyline in the days of the Maastricht Treaty negotiations that Germany would give up power and status by joining the EMU was incorrect. This narrative rested on the assumption that balance-of-payments disequilibria could no longer exist in a common currency and facilitated a misunderstanding of macroeconomic adjustment in the eurozone.

Indeed, balance-of-payments disequilibria can still arise within a common currency and macroeconomic adjustment is still necessary in a currency union, even though the common currency now prevents some of the conventional means of adjustment.[3] Most importantly, of course, the currency union precludes the adjustment of nominal exchange rates. Under a truly floating exchange rate regime, adjustment could—in theory—always happen through a nominal exchange rate change. Even in a pegged exchange rate regime, such as the EMS, occasional adjustment of central parities allowed for addressing a disequilibrium through a nominal exchange rate change. In a monetary union, however, nominal exchange rates are irrevocably fixed. Thus, adjustment would have to happen through a change in the real exchange rate, rather than the nominal exchange rate. Politically, of course, adjustment through a real exchange rate change is much more difficult to achieve.

However, the absence of the nominal exchange rate instrument is not the only complication for macroeconomic adjustment within a common currency. Fiscal policy also does not provide a lot of room for macroeconomic adjustment. First of all, the Maastricht Treaty restricts the fiscal policy flexibility of individual EU member states. However, more importantly, there does not exist a sizeable central budget in the EU at this point. Fiscal policy for the most part still rests with the member states. The size of the individual member states' budgets dwarfs the EU's own budget. Individual member states still have control over the largest chunks in typical government budgets, such as national security and social welfare spending. Thus, the central budget of the EU cannot properly serve as a shock absorber that counterbalances differential economic shocks affecting the eurozone countries (for example, through the flow of unemployment and other counter-cyclical funds across the Union).

In addition, labour migration is not a very flexible adjustment mechanism in Europe either. In theory, the Single European Market allows for the free flow of labour across the 28 EU member countries. In terms of macroeconomic adjustment, this should lead to a flow of labour from low growth/high unemployment areas (e.g. Greece, Ireland, Portugal and Spain) to higher growth/lower unemployment areas (e.g. Germany and most of Northern Europe). Indeed, the financial crisis has facilitated some modest movement of workers from the periphery into the rest of Europe.[4] However, European labour migration flows are nowhere near the scale of flows within the single market of the USA, for example. Cultural and linguistic constraints in particular limit an efficient adjustment through labour migration.

Thus, adjustment would have to come through a change in the real exchange rate, i.e. changes in wages and prices. While there are many causes for Greece's fiscal debt, it is in part an expression of Greece's inability to compete economically with Germany and the other strong currency countries. The low interest rates resulting from integration into the euro had merely served to finance consumption, but not to improve Greece's competitiveness. Indeed, from a critical perspective, Milios and Sotiropoulos (2010: 225) view Greek membership in the EMU as 'the strategy *par excellence* for capital' precisely because it forces the national economy to gain competitiveness by keeping labour costs down. As they argue, 'The EMU puts into effect an extreme variant of the strategy of exposure to international competition which only through continual "adjustment" of labour can continue to exist' (Milios & Sotiropoulos 2010: 226). The euro, in their view, represents the ideal capitalist mechanism to continuously exert pressure on labour to reduce costs and increase competitiveness.[5]

Of course, during the first 10 years of the euro's existence Greece and other peripheral countries pursued high economic growth policies fuelled by low interest rates. The resulting inflation was partially hidden by the fact that the euro averaged national inflation rates and the ECB ran interest rate policy for the eurozone as a whole. However, this effectively led to even lower real interest rates in Greece and an explosion of public borrowing, setting in motion a vicious cycle of ever higher inflation and ever lower real interest rates. As a result, Greece's real exchange rate appreciated, reducing the competitiveness of the Greek economy. Germany, on the other hand, used the discipline imposed by the euro to drive down wage costs. Thus, Germany's real exchange rate depreciated, improving its competitive position.

Germany's co-ordinated market economy puts the country into a favourable position to achieve a depreciation of the real exchange rate and to gain competitiveness within the common currency.[6] The relatively consensual nature of German labour relations and industrial institutions helps to keep down labour costs and makes sure that Germany's highly skilled labour force remains competitive in European and global markets. Countries with less consensual labour relations, such as Greece, have a tougher time engineering a depreciation of the real exchange rate. They often have to rely on a depreciation of the nominal exchange rate to restore some degree of competitiveness. Thus, adjustment within a common currency and without the nominal exchange rate tool becomes politically much more costly for them.

Balance-of-Payments Imbalances and Macroeconomic Policy-Making in a Single Currency

Identifying the eurozone crisis as a balance-of-payments crisis instead of a sovereign debt crisis allows this paper also to evaluate the appropriateness of policy measures dealing with the crisis. Key to understanding the policy implications is the realization that a balance-of-payments crisis is based on inter-related macroeconomic imbalances and not on one country's profligacy, as would be the case in a sovereign debt crisis. A balance-of-payments crisis is an inter-related phenomenon because someone's surplus is someone else's deficit. Instead of resulting from individualistic action, a balance-of-payments crisis is structural. One country's debt represents another country's excess savings; overconsumption somewhere in the system has to be underconsumption somewhere else. The systemic impact of imbalances is that capital moves from countries with a trade surplus to countries with a deficit. In the years following the adoption of the euro, this led to speculative capital flows that contributed to the build-up of real estate bubbles and domestic inflation in the peripheral countries.

Maintaining a fixed exchange rate through the common currency allowed Germany to pursue a reversed version of beggar-thy-neighbour-policy. By forcing its partners to keep their nominal exchange rates stable, Germany could engineer a depreciation of its real exchange rate through wage moderation. De facto, Germany pursued a neo-mercantilist strategy to improve its competitive position within a framework of fixed nominal exchange rates (Armingeon and Baccaro 2012). This model of gaining competitiveness can work for one country (or a few countries), but, by definition, it cannot work for all countries. Thus, the interdependent nature of balance-of-payments crises makes it logically impossible to generalize the German recipe as a formula of macroeconomic adjustment for all members of the currency union. Consequently, the alternative narratives of balance-of-payments crisis or sovereign debt crisis have real political consequences. While a sovereign debt crisis interpretation identifies one culprit, a balance-of-payments crisis perspective assigns responsibility for the disequilibrium to both sides. In a balance-of-payments crisis narrative, then, policy measures are two-sided, whereas the sovereign debt crisis reading of the situation requires adjustment only from the 'profligate' country.

The policy setting for macroeconomic adjustment within a common currency is unique. As elaborated earlier, members of a currency union lack access to the nominal exchange rate instrument to address balance of payments imbalances. While governments that control their own currency rarely pursue a nominal exchange rate change in isolation from other policy measures (for example, monetary and fiscal policy), the absence of the nominal exchange rate instrument in the eurozone restricts the options available for governments that experience a balance-of-payments disequilibrium. This necessitates a search for alternative ways to restore external balance.

Of course, many observers have suggested the break-up of the eurozone and the return to national currencies. Such an option would make the nominal exchange rate instrument available again to those countries that restore their own national currencies. Indeed, the general expectation is that such a move would immediately lead to a sizeable depreciation of the peripheral currencies. However, both the political and the economic costs of a eurozone break-up would be dramatic and the reintroduction of national currencies appears unlikely at the moment. A frequently discussed variation of this scenario—the split of the eurozone into a 'Northern euro' and a 'Southern euro'—remains very remote as well.

At first sight, a reintroduction of national currencies might seem attractive for the peripheral countries, because they would regain the power to devalue their nominal exchange rates. An orderly depreciation would indeed help countries to restore some degree of short-term competitiveness. However, depreciation would not help resolve some of the underlying issues, such as the weak economic base and the fraught political structures of the peripheral countries, as well as Germany's easier ability to achieve a depreciation of its real exchange rate. Moreover, in all likelihood a break-up of the eurozone would not result in an orderly depreciation but rather in a massive currency crisis with devastating effects for both core and peripheral countries. A large devaluation would trigger a run on banks, bankruptcies of financial institutions and desperate measures of governments to safeguard the financial system.

Among those measures could be restrictions on the use of money by citizens or law enforcement measures to protect financial institutions, with problematic consequences for the quality of democracy in those devaluing countries.[7] Moreover, devaluation of the peripheral currencies would lead to an increase in foreign-denominated debt, with the most likely consequence a default by governments in the peripheral countries and bankruptcies of numerous financial institutions in both peripheral and core countries.

In the end, this would bring many peripheral countries back to where they started. They would need the co-operation of core countries to sort through a government default, and bargain for the restructuring of debt and for aid that will be attached to conditions that are likely less lenient than they are within the current Troika process inside the eurozone. Once the peripheral countries are outside the eurozone, core countries would be less inclined to offer concessions to peripheral countries (Lapavitsas et al. 2010).[8] Core countries so far have exhibited a preference for keeping the eurozone together. In addition, core countries would have to fear that a collapse of the eurozone would also lead to the unravelling of other areas of European integration, in particular its core project, the single market. Most likely, countries would introduce barriers to trade in the context of such monetary turmoil. In leaving the eurozone, peripheral countries would abandon the bargaining leverage that comes with the preferences core countries have for continued European integration and monetary co-operation.

Thus, the reintroduction of national currencies appears to be a fairly remote possibility. The costs would be staggering for peripheral countries and the incentives for core countries are, at this point, to do as much as necessary to preserve the eurozone. Given that distribution of costs and preferences, it is important to talk about policies that help to address the *internal* disequilibrium within the eurozone. Under the sovereign debt crisis narrative, that adjustment solely needs to come from a depreciation of the real exchange rate of the deficit countries within the eurozone. The austerity measures imposed in recent euro crisis negotiations are consistent with this reading. They reflect the power of surplus countries to interpret the crisis as a sovereign debt crisis and to seek adjustment by the 'profligate' countries in the eurozone. Overall, German policy-makers have viewed economic activity as a morality play, in which debt and guilt are nearly synonymous.[9] German proposals for dealing with the crisis have focused on the responsibility of debtor countries for safeguarding the euro and for adjustment (Dyson 2010). They have emphasized such things as fiscal austerity, the conditionality of loans, surveillance of fiscal policies, possible sanctions against deficit countries, the abolition of wage indexation systems, and harmonizing pension systems and corporate tax systems. Thus, according to the sovereign debt crisis interpretation, adjustment is one-sided action by the deficit countries.

The balance-of-payments crisis narrative, however, views the euro crisis as an interdependent phenomenon. While some actions on the part of deficit countries, including austerity measures, are necessary, the balance-of-payments crisis narrative opens the perspective to additional, more complex and ultimately reciprocal measures. One of those areas is that of broader structural adjustment and modernization in the peripheral countries. Part of the political attractiveness of joining the euro for the peripheral countries was the desire to modernize and to become part of the community of advanced industrial societies in Europe. While responsibility in the case of structural adjustment would still rest primarily with the peripheral countries, some mutual commitments are conceivable. For example, EU members could strengthen structural funds that tie the flow of financial assistance to modernization efforts, such as upgrading the industrial structure of the peripheral economies, reforming the institutional structure of government or investing in skill-building education (Mazier and Petit 2013). In particular, modernization of Greek political structures would help the country move away from a clientilistic system that has hampered its economic development. While the modernization process itself is painful, the goal coincides with the desire of the peripheral countries to achieve greater equality with the eurozone's core. Increasing EU structural funds to achieve this goal would be an area where the interests of core and peripheral countries could converge.

Upgrading structural funds could also be a first step towards a more unified fiscal policy within the EU. Ultimately, Germany cannot simultaneously have perennial trade surpluses in the eurozone without some form of economic redistribution (Bibow 2013). As long as the eurozone comprises economically heterogeneous countries, some form of fiscal transfer union is necessary (Armingeon and Baccaro 2012). Joint fiscal policy should achieve some redistribution and create through investment a productive base in peripheral countries.[10] The problem for the peripheral countries is not that labour costs *per se* are too high. Their productive structure does not let them compete with Germany (or for that matter with the People's Republic of China and some of the former Soviet bloc countries) (Simonazzi et al. 2012). A depreciation of the real exchange rate through productivity gains is a politically more acceptable and constructive strategy than achieving the same result through wage cuts and austerity. Investment into the productive structure of the peripheral countries through joint fiscal policy would make up for the lost opportunity after the introduction of the euro fuelled a low-interest-rate-driven consumption boom rather than investment growth.

In addition to fiscal integration, increased coordination of policy-making in the financial and monetary field would be quite consistent with the balance-of-payments crisis narrative as well. Overall, there is an astonishing disjuncture between the financial market integration that the EU pursued through the Single European Act and the Maastricht Treaty and the lack of financial market governance. The private banking sector played a deplorable role in the euro crisis. Banking and finance facilitated the easy credit that fed the consumption and real estate boom during the early 2000s and as a result exposed themselves to the bursting of the real estate bubble in the USA and several European countries (most prominently, Ireland and Spain). The financial crisis then brought with it an additional risk factor—the stack of precarious government bonds. The bail-out packages for Greece and other peripheral countries were clearly designed to shift adjustment costs away from French and German banks (and save these banks in the process), putting even more emphasis on the austerity measures required of crisis-ridden countries. Strengthening banking supervision and financial regulation at the European level with a strong mandate for the ECB would thus represent a step toward a more symmetrical solution to financial crises.[11]

Additional symmetrical measures would have to come in the area of monetary policy as well. The issuing of joint eurobonds would reflect and underscore the interdependent nature of the eurozone balance-of-payments crisis. The German Government, of course, has so far ruled out eurobonds. However, political conditions inside and outside Germany can change, turning eurobonds into an area of potentially overlapping interest between core and peripheral countries in the eurozone. Depending on what precise rules the eurozone members would be able to agree on for the issue of eurobonds, adjustment obligations could still be distributed quite asymmetrically. As a matter of fact, such asymmetry would have to be expected given the differences in bargaining power and German reluctance on that issue. However, even with remaining asymmetry, eurobonds would be a powerful symbol for greater unity and solidarity.[12]

Another step in the direction of closer integration would be the development of the ECB into a true lender of last resort. While the Maastricht Treaty did not provide for this function, the eurozone has de facto moved beyond the treaty's restrictions to cope with the no exit/no bail-out/no default trilemma established at Maastricht. When ECB President Mario Draghi announced in the summer of 2012 that the central bank would do 'whatever it takes' to preserve the euro, he essentially committed the ECB to a quasi-lender of last resort obligation in coping with financial panic. Even though the ECB's government bond purchases did not solve underlying structural issues, the relative calm that returned after Draghi's announcement underscores how much a full lender of last resort could contribute to financial stability and with that to lower borrowing costs for peripheral countries.

In the end, the creation of a more symmetrical adjustment structure in the eurozone would come down to building a politically more integrated Europe as well as a greater integration of European societies. If European-level labour unions and employer associations were strengthened, one could envision the move of wage bargaining to the supra-national level. Such co-ordination of wage bargaining would help keep wages in line with productivity growth and trigger appreciation of the real exchange rate in the core countries through wage increases and moderate reflation.

Ironically, the idea of a politically more integrated Europe coincides with Germany's general preferences as well. It represents an area where the interests of core and periphery countries could potentially converge. Reaching such a goal will not be easy. At this point, Germany clings to an interpretation of the euro crisis as a sovereign debt crisis and not as a balance-of-payments crisis. My analysis of the adjustment logic in a balance-of-payments crisis reveals the power of core countries to impose that narrative on any policy solutions to the crisis. The peripheral countries have little power on their own to change that dynamic. The exit option for them is costly. Thus, a change in Germany's reading of the crisis would have to come from within. Most importantly, Germany itself would have to feel the costs of continued balance-of-payments disequilibria. Fear of continued chaos in financial markets and in the societies of the peripheral countries that threatens the stability of the euro and the EU as a whole, coupled with enticing Germany into greater political union—a goal that is still very popular with German citizens—could go a long way towards achieving such a goal.

The EU has clearly moved away from the rigidity of the Maastricht Treaty and toward a stronger political union in response to the euro crisis. The old trilemma of no bail-out, no exit and no default has been resolved in favour of allowing bail-outs (Greece, Ireland, Portugal and Cyprus) and partial defaults (Greece and Cyprus). The ECB has taken over some de facto lender of last resort functions and is most likely to gain greater banking supervision functions as well. The creation of the ESM and the adoption of the Treaty on Stability, Coordination and Governance in the EMU have produced stronger political integration than existed before the crisis. Thus, there have been some developments on the policy side that are consistent with the balance-of-payments crisis narrative.

Nevertheless, the sovereign debt crisis reading of the euro crisis remains the dominant interpretation of the euro crisis. This situation will remain unchanged until surplus countries re-evaluate their interests. Such a change in surplus countries' interests will most likely take place when the perceived costs of macroeconomic as well as political instability force a course correction. The measures adopted so far in dealing with the euro crisis demonstrate the typical pattern of such changes. On occasion, Germany and the other core countries made critical concessions on financing the balance-of-payments problems of deficit countries (such as the bail-outs and the ESM). Financing facilities have historically been the policy area where Germany is most inclined to make concessions, because German policymakers perceive them as the least costly of all potential compromises.[13] It is noteworthy that these compromises were largely driven by Germany's broader interest in European integration and the stability of the EU, as well as the need to safeguard its own banking system. If deficit countries can link needs for reform in the monetary union with the self-interest of surplus countries this pattern of gradual change is most likely to continue at a moderate pace, even though a fully symmetric system is unlikely in the foreseeable future. Germany needs an economically stable EU and benefits substantially from the euro's existence. It therefore treats the defence of the euro as a fundamental national interest. Germany cannot risk a break-up of the euro and peripheral countries should use the leverage that results from the preference to bargain for German concessions on macroeconomic adjustment in the EMU.

Conclusion

This paper argues that the euro crisis at its core is not a sovereign debt crisis—as suggested by the dominant public narrative—but rather a balance-of-payments crisis. Several of the peripheral countries hit worst by the financial crisis were actually in fairly good fiscal shape prior to the crisis. Most ironically, Spain and Ireland had much lower debt and deficit levels than Germany. Whether we are dealing with a sovereign debt crisis or balance-of-payments crisis, however, is not simply a question of semantics. The sovereign debt crisis narrative seriously misdiagnoses the underlying causes of the euro crisis and, therefore, ends up specifying the wrong policy prescriptions to address the crisis.

The architects of the EMU largely assumed that balance-of-payments crises were no longer possible in a common currency. Thus, they built into the eurozone a trilemma where no country could be bailed out, could exit the euro, or could default. The euro crisis revealed that balance-of-payments crises are still possible and the built-in trilemma left the eurozone without effective tools to address the crisis. The continued possibility of balance-of-payments crises also demystified another narrative the Europeans had told themselves, namely that monetary union would create a more balanced monetary system in Europe. The EMU's predecessor regime had functioned asymmetrically. Germany set the macroeconomic standard for the rest of the system by determining the interest rate floor. The German *Bundesbank* was free to pursue macroeconomic policies according to German domestic needs, while the others needed to adjust their policies according to German priorities.

While the architects of the EMU believed that monetary union would create a more symmetrical system, the opposite actually happened. The impossibility of nominal exchange rate changes meant that a balance-of-payments crisis within a monetary union actually enhanced the power asymmetries compared to the EMS. Its domestic political economy enables Germany to devalue its real exchange rate through wage and price restraints in a beggar-thy-neighbour fashion. Because others are unable to counter with nominal exchange rate changes, Germany was able to build up unprecedented external surpluses. Germany and its surplus country allies have used their power position to adhere to a narrative of the euro crisis as a sovereign debt crisis and not as a balance-of-payments crisis. Such an interpretation allows core countries to unilaterally blame the 'profligate' countries and force adjustment on them. The balance-of-payments crisis narrative, however, interprets the disequilibrium as interdependent and reciprocal. From that perspective policy measures to address the crisis should be more complex and multifaceted than the singular attention to austerity measures in the current adjustment process.

Acknowledgements

This article represents a revised and updated version of a paper initially published in the *Journal of Balkan and Near Eastern Studies*. I would like to thank Vassilis K. Fouskas for his comments on the current as well as the previous version of the article and I would like to thank the anonymous reviewers of the *Journal of Balkan and Near Eastern Studies* for their comments and suggestions. Earlier versions of this paper were presented at the Annual Convention of the International Studies Association 2014 in Toronto, Canada, and the Brown Bag Lunch talk series of the Department of Political Science at the University of Memphis, Texas, USA. I would like to thank all the participants in these venues for their thoughtful questions and suggestions—especially Şeniz Avcioğlu, Jacqueline Best, Robert Blanton, Nicole Detraz, Katharine Rietig and Sharon Stanley. In the context of my research on this subject I had valuable conversations with European central bankers and policy-makers. I would like to thank them for their time and their willingness to share their thoughts on the subject. Clint Thompson, Jennifer Marshall, Brooke Shannon and Anna Talley provided outstanding research assistance on the paper.

Notes

1 German growth rates were particularly weak at an annual average of 1.1% between 1999 and 2005 (Simonazzi, et al. 2013: 653–75).

2 Technically, the Maastricht Treaty included a no-bail-out clause. However, governments eventually circumvented that by using the 'emergency' clauses of the treaty to provide the legal justification of the bailout.

3 For a broader discussion of the recycling of surpluses in the international economy, see Varoufakis 2011 and Pettis 2013.

4 The number of foreign migrants settling in Germany increased from 573,815 in 2008 to 965,908 in 2012. The number of Greek immigrants with at least one year of residence in Germany increased from 4,110 in 2008 to 14,300 in 2011, while for Spaniards the number more than doubled from 3,431 to 8,266 (Bundesamt für Migration und Flüchtlinge, Migrationsbericht 2012).

5 According to Fouskas and Dimoulas (2013) this perspective leaves out the domestic origins of the Greek debt problem. Indeed, there are domestic causes for Greece's balance-of-payments position, as I will argue momentarily. However, the structural logic espoused by Milios and Sotiropoulos, as well as the present article, uncovers a fundamental—if tautological—truth: someone's surplus has to be someone else's deficit. Germany's recipe for economic success cannot work in an interdependent economy.

6 On the contrast between co-ordinated and liberal market economies see Hall and Soskice (2001). For an application of the Varieties of Capitalism framework to the euro crisis see Hall (2012) and Vermeiren (2013). For a related discussion of domestic Greek politics and for what he calls 'disjointed corporatism' in the Greek case, see Featherstone (2011).

7 Critics are quick to point out the undemocratic nature of the Troika-driven restructuring process. However, a devaluation of a reintroduced national currency equally poses risks for democracy. In addition, there is no guarantee that a national currency would restore real authority alongside the renewed sovereignty.

8 Lapavitsas, et.al. (2010: 327–28 and 368–71), distinguish between a 'conservative exit' and a 'progressive exit' from the eurozone. That distinction illustrates precisely the problem. At this point, a shift in social power toward labour in both the peripheral and the core countries represents more wishful thinking than a realistic

alternative in European societies. Moreover, the benevolent co-operation required from core countries to restructure the peripheral countries' debt is anything but guaranteed after a eurozone break-up.

9 As Friedrich Nietzsche observed in the *Genealogy of Morality*, the German words for sin and for debt—*Schuld* and *Schulden*—share the same word origin and are related concepts. See: Nietzsche 1887 (2006). Thus, the close association between guilt and debt in German economic thinking is hardly surprising, even from a linguistic perspective.

10 As Varoufakis (2011) points out, during the years of large US surpluses after 1945, the USA recycled these funds into rebuilding war-torn Europe and Japan. Germany finds itself in a similar position these days vis-à-vis peripheral Europe.

11 For the significance of banking policies in the euro crisis, see Angeloni, et al. (2012).

12 For symbolic aspects of European monetary cooperation, see Kaelberer (2004).

13 For the broader history of these concessions, see Kaelberer (2001).

References

Angeloni, C., Merler, M. and Wolff, G.B. (2012), 'Policy lessons from the Eurozone crisis,' *The International Spectator*, 47(4): 17–34.

Armingeon, K. and Baccaro, L. (2012), 'Political economy of the sovereign debt crisis: the limits of internal devaluation,' *Industrial Law Journal*, 41(3): 254–275.

Belke, A. and Dreger, C. (2013), 'Current account imbalances in the euro area: does catching up explain the development?' *Review of International Economics*, 21(1): 6–17.

Bibow, J. (2013), 'The Euroland crisis and Germany's euro trilemma,' *International Review of Applied Economics*. 37: 360–385.

Boltho, A. and Carlin, W. (2013), 'EMU's problems: asymmetric shocks or asymmetric behavior?' *Comparative Economic Studies*, 55: 387–403.

Blankenburg, S., King, L., Konzelmann, S. and Wilkinson, F. (2013), 'Prospects for the Eurozone,' *Cambridge Journal of Economics*, 37: 463–477.

Bundesamtfür Migration und Flüchtlinge, *Migrationsbericht* 2012.

Dyson, K. (2010), 'Norman's malent: the Greek and Euro area crisis in historical perspective,' *New Political Economy*. 15(4): 597–608.

Featherstone, K. (2011), 'The Greek Sovereign Debt Crisis and EMU: A Failing State in a Skewed Regime' *Journal of Common Market Studies*, 49(2): 193–217.

Fouskas, V.K. and Dimolas, C. (2012), 'The Greek Workshop of Debt and the Failure of the European Project' *Journal of Balkan and Near Eastern* Studies, 14(1): 1–31.

Fouskas, V.K. and Dimolas, C. (2013), *Greece, Financialization and the EU: The Political Economy of Debt and Destruction*, New York: Palgrave Macmillan.

Hall, P. (2012), 'The economics and politics of the euro crisis,' *German Politics*, 21(4): 355–371.

Hall, P.A. and Soskice, D. (eds) (2001), *Varieties of Capitalism: The Institutional Foundations of Comparative Advantage*, Oxford: Oxford University Press.

Kaelberer, M. (2001), *Money and Power in Europe: The Political Economy of European Monetary Cooperation*, Albany, NY: State University of New York Press.

Kaelberer, M. (2004), 'The euro and European identity: symbols, power, and the politics of European monetary union,' *Review of International Studies*, 30: 161–178.

Lapavitsas, C., Kaltenbrunner, A., Lindo, D., Mitchell, J., Painceira, J.P., Pires, E., Powell, J., Stenfors, A. and Teles, N. (2010), 'Eurozone crisis: beggar thyself and thy neighbour,' *Journal of Balkan and Near Eastern Studies*, 12(4): 327–371.

Mazier, J. and Petit, P. (2013), 'In search of sustainable paths for the eurozone in the troubled post-2008 world,' *Cambridge Journal of Economics*, 37: 513–532.

Milios, J. and Sotiropoulos, D. (2010), 'Crisis of Greece of crisis of the euro? A view from the European "periphery",' *Journal of Balkan and Near Eastern Studies*, 12 (3): 223–240.

Nietzsche, F. (1887 [2006]), *On the Genealogy of Morality*, Cambridge: Cambridge University Press.

Pettis, M. (2013), *The Great Rebalancing: Trade, Conflict, and the Perilous Road Ahead for the World Economy*, Princeton, NJ: Princeton University Press.

Simonazzi, A., Ginzburg, A. and Nocella, G. (2013), 'Economic relations between Germany and southern Europe,' *Cambridge Journal of Economics*, 37: 653–675.

Tombazos, S. (2011), 'Centrifugal tendencies in the euro area,' *Journal of Contemporary European Studies*, 19(1): 33–46.

Varoufakis, J. (2011), *The Global Minotaur: America, Europe and the Future of the Global Economy*, London: Zed Books.

Vermeiren, M. (2013), 'Monetary power and EMU: macroeconomic adjustment and autonomy in the Eurozone,' *Review of International Studies*, 39: 193–217.

3 Greece and the Crisis of the Eurozone: A Structural Analysis

Leila Simona Talani

Introduction

This chapter addresses the position of Greece in the eurozone crisis. In particular, it focuses on the structural imbalances and internal contradictions of the Economic and Monetary Union (EMU). Within this context, the global financial crisis acted as an asymmetric shock, hitting different economic structures in different ways. This structural analysis explains why certain countries, such as Greece, were singled out by the markets as the weakest links of the system and were subjected to massive speculative attacks against their sovereign debts.

Thus, in this chapter, the sovereign debt crisis affecting Greece and the other members of the so called 'PIIGS' group (made up of Portugal, Ireland, Italy, Greece and Spain) is discussed within the context of the structural imbalances characterising the EMU from the start. (Similarly, Krugman 2012; De Grauwe 2013; Eichengreen 2014).

The main argument is that the global financial crisis hit Member States in differing ways, acting as an asymmetric shock due to the structural differences between the euro area states. This exacerbated the structural problem of competitiveness inherent in the way in which the European currency union was conceived. As such, the sovereign debt crisis can hardly be read as merely a fiscal crisis. On the contrary, it was the result of an existing problem of the sustainability of a structurally asymmetric monetary union made more serious by the economic shock represented by the global financial crisis. In a way, the global financial crisis acted as a catalyst for the prevailing imbalances embedded in the EMU, signalling to the financial markets which countries to speculate against (Chang and Leblond 2015). Speculation continued unhindered until the ECB eventually decided, or was allowed, to act as a de facto lender of last resort. Because of this, Greece was brought to the verge of the abyss and needed to adopt emergency measures.

This Chapter is concerned with the above issues, starting with addressing the unfolding of the eurozone crisis and its nature. It will then assess the extent to which Greece faced competitiveness threats exacerbated by the outbreak of the global crisis.

The unfolding of the crisis

There is no doubt that the global financial crisis represented a substantial blow to the global economy, leading to wide-ranging and long-lasting consequences. In the literature there is a tendency to distinguish five stages in the unfolding of the crisis (Orlowski 2008). If the first stage is clearly represented by the collapse of the US subprime mortgage market, this was followed by a credit crunch leading to a liquidity crisis. The subsequent phase was a commodity price bubble and finally the demise of investment banking in the USA (Orlowski 2008).

Although the bailing-out of financial institutions by national governments all over the globe avoided a global financial meltdown, by that time the global financial crisis had already provoked a global economic crisis (Talani 2010). Just two years after the collapse of Lehman Brothers, the global economy experienced its sharpest ever decline of gross domestic product (GDP), going from 5.2% to −0.8% (Sinn 2010). This was particularly serious in the eurozone, where the GDP fell by an unprecedented 9%, from 3.8% in 2007 to −5.2% in 2009, with Ireland being the first eurozone country to technically enter into recession in September 2008 (Sinn 2010). Finally, the euro area also experienced a sovereign debt crisis starting in Greece, in May 2010, moving to Ireland at the end of November, and eventually to the other members of the PIIGS group.

The first country to be attacked by speculation was Greece in May 2010, immediately after the credit rating agency Moody's downgraded the rating of its debt. This can be considered a signal to the markets to start speculating against a country. It certainly also did not help that a reaction from the European Union (EU) institutions took a long time to come and resulted merely in the establishment of an ad hoc, temporary and underfunded initiative: the European Financial Stability Facility (Chang and Leblond 2015). Instead of quashing the markets' thirst for speculation, the Facility might have even excited it (De Grauwe 2013).

By November 2010 financial markets were targeting Ireland. The country was still plagued by the crisis of its banking system and despite the fact that the EU had decided to approve a rescue package of €85,000m., which included €35,000m. to bail out the Irish banking system and €50,000m. to support the Government's day-to-day spending, financial markets did not seem satisfied. They kept on selling Irish bonds, as well as Greek, Portuguese, Spanish and Italian bonds, thus substantially increasing the yields paid on them.[1] The situation then worsened, threatening to bring the entire system to collapse, on 16 and 17 December 2010. The European Council, amid serious worries about broader stability in the eurozone decided to institutionalize the European Stability Mechanism, a rescue measure officially launched on 8 October 2012.[2]

The seriousness of the eurozone economic situation could not be underestimated. A report by the ECB in December 2010 identified in the interplay between sovereign debt difficulties and the weakness of the banking sectors of some countries a potentially disruptive threat for the sustainability of the whole eurozone The assessment of the ECB varied in its view of the sources of instability for the EMU to those outside the financial system or risks existing inside it.[3] The outside sources of concern came from macroeconomic imbalances between the different Member States, which were reflected in increasing unemployment levels and, related to that, a reduction of credit to private economic actors. This was accompanied by the re-emergence of global imbalances and some residual concerns about the fiscal stances of some eurozone Member States. Clearly, fiscal concerns were not the only source of trouble identified by the ECB at the height of the sovereign debt crisis and macroeconomic imbalances both within and without the euro area featured extensively among the most worrying problems.

Furthermore, the risks identified inside the financial system included the possibility of more volatility of financial markets in the case of a lacking macroeconomic recovery.[4] In this way, the ECB identified an adverse feedback loop between economic recession, the credit crunch and fiscal imbalances at the root of the persistently increasing spread between eurozone sovereign bond yields.[5] That the problem had shifted from the financial side to the real economy was further demonstrated by the fact that in the second and third quarters of 2010, the profitability of many large and complex banking groups (LCBGs) in the eurozone had continued recovering.[6] Concerns were expressed in relation to global financial imbalances that could create new threats to the fiscal and financial positions of some countries within the EMU if they emerged again.[7]

Although the analysis of the ECB was clear enough, the solutions identified by EU institutions did not seem to be able to stop the crisis, to the extent that in July 2011 the Greek, Irish and Portuguese spreads with the German *Bund* hit, respectively, 1600, 1200 and 1100 basis points. Equally, the Spanish and Italian sovereign debt spreads with the *Bund* reached 400 basis points, Belgium hit 200 basis points and France hit 90 basis points.[8] By 2012 Spain had to accept around €100,000m. as a sort of bail-out for its banking sector,[9] which was on the verge of bankruptcy.

The fiscal rationale of the eurozone crisis

The eurozone crisis has often been blamed on the fiscal profligacy of the PIIGS (De Grauwe 2013). Regarding this, it is difficult to deny that some of the countries affected by the wave of speculation against their sovereign debt in 2010 and 2011 had had, in the past, and still had at the time, compromised fiscal situations. However, it is worth noting that the fiscal stimulus and bail-out of the financial system came at a high price for the budgets of other countries as well, which had not been singled out by the financial markets. Just to give an example, in 2009 the first US Administration under President Barack Obama approved a stimulus package in the USA of $800,000m., raising the country's deficit to GDP ratio to 10%. Similarly, Japan recorded a 10% deficit to GDP the same year and in the United Kingdom the deficit to

GDP achieved the astounding level of 13%. On the other hand, the eurozone average deficit to GDP was only 6% in 2010, lower than its average level of more than 7% in the mid-1990s.[10] Obviously, the performance of deficit to GDP in different countries in the eurozone varied, but if we look at the countries that were eventually involved in the sovereign debt crisis, then some points need to be noted. First of all, not all countries that were under fire from financial markets had been experiencing bad performance in terms of their deficit to GDP during the crisis. For example, Greece in 2010, at the onset of the sovereign debt crisis, had a deficit to GDP which was only 4.3% above the 6% average of the eurozone. Equally, Portugal and Spain had a deficit to GDP ratio of just about 3.8% and 3.3% above that average, at 9.8% and 9.3%, respectively. Italy had even achieved a lower than average deficit to GDP during the global financial crisis, reporting a figure of 5.4% in 2009 and only 4.6% in 2010.[11]

Of course, looking at the performance of the debt to GDP ratio the picture for Greece changes. However, with reference to general government consolidated debt, it is clear that there were dramatic increases in Germany and the UK too over the period considered.

Equally, all the above fiscal indicators have to be assessed within the context of an unprecedented decline in GDP, which increased debt and deficit to GDP ratios. This is not only for mathematical reasons, but also for economic and political ones. Just to be clear, Ireland lost 12.2% of its real GDP, Greece 6.5%, Spain 7.2%, Italy 6.8% and Portugal 5.3% in the period between 2007 and 2009 (see figure 3.2 below).

So if the eurozone crisis cannot easily be conceptualized as a fiscal crisis, what was its true nature?

The global financial crisis and asymmetric shocks

There has been much lengthy speculation in the literature (Krugman 2012, De Grauwe 2013, Eichengreen 2014) on what the asymmetric shock that hit the

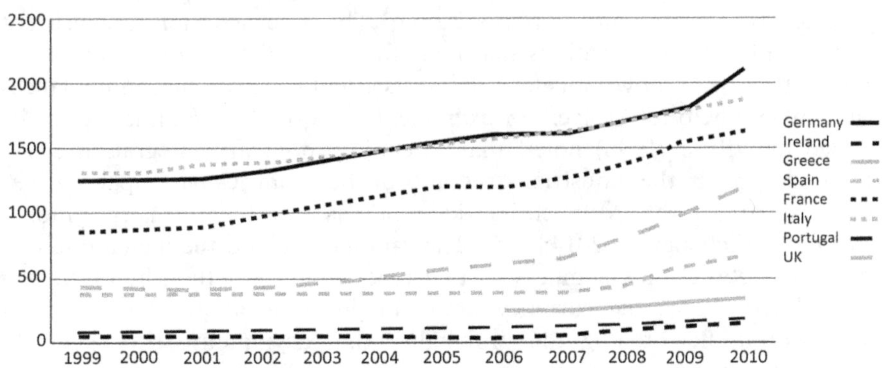

Figure 3.1 General government consolidated gross debt, 1999–2010
Source: European Commission, Annual Macro-economic Database (AMECO).

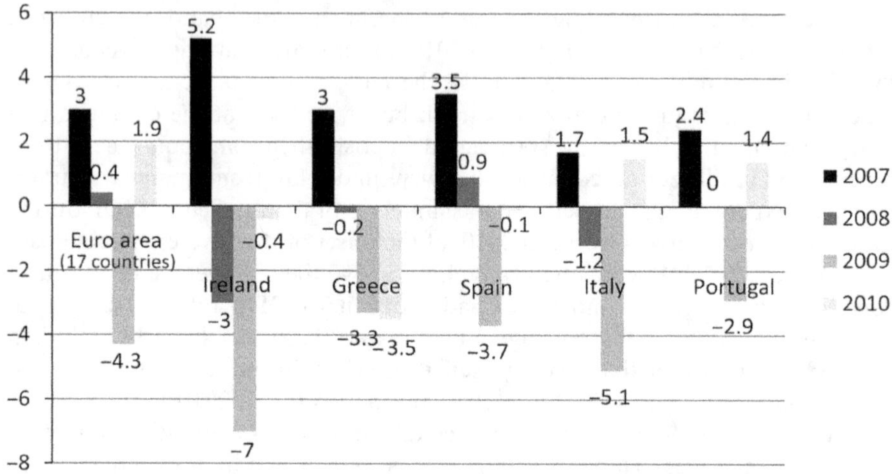

Figure 3.2 Real GDP loss 2007–2010
Source: European Commission, Eurostat, elaboration of the author.

eurozone on the eve of the sovereign debt crisis, signalling to the market that the time was ripe to increase the stakes on weaker countries credibility, actually was all about. It is difficult to deny that something unforeseeable and difficult to control had indeed happened prior to the eurozone crisis. As we highlighted above, that was, clearly, the global financial crisis of 2007–08, leading to the ensuing global economic crisis of 2009–10. It is therefore not inconceivable to hypothesize that the element that tilted the already precarious balance of the EMU to the side of the crisis might have been precisely represented by the financial turmoil.

In a way, we could consider the financial crisi and the following economic crisis as a sort of asymmetric shock.[12] This had different effects in different Euro-zone countries given the asymmetries existing before the creation of the eurozone which the EMU exacerbated, instead of reducing, as sometimes forecasted by the economists (Artis 2009.[13] This interpretation is consistent with a number of contributions that had stressed, at the eve of the establishment of the EMU, how monetary union itself could create more imbalances than it would help to resolve. For example, before the EMU came into place Frankel and Rose (1998) noted that extending monetary integration could lead to changes in the industrial structures of the countries participating in it. This is something that Mundell had identified as a problem to keep a monetary union (Eichengreen 2014: 4–5). The rationale behind the increase in discrepancies between the members of a currency union was that, by increasing inter-industry trade, the currency union might bring about more regional specialization, heightening the probability that asymmetric shocks would happen or that a single shock could have varying effects across regions.

An even more pertinent source of concern was, however, represented by the ever-relevant 'Walters critique' (1990). This was a theory that had already been brought into question to explain the crisis of the Exchange Rate Mechanism of the EMS in 1992 (Talani 2000). It posited that, despite the currency union, inflation rates would not converge across the members of the EMU. In particular, in the periphery of the EU, inflation rates 'would continue' to be higher than in the rest of the EMU. It is important to stress that inflation rates in the PIIGS countries had indeed always been higher than in the core countries and, according to Walters, they would remain so. This is a vital counterpoint to widespread interpretations of the increase in inflation rates of peripheral countries within the EMU as a consequence of their economies overheating due to lower interest rates. Eichengreen (2014), for example, noticed that indeed Walters (1990) was right because peripheral countries of the EMU experienced spending booms at home, reflected in soaring construction spending (Ireland, Spain), consumption spending (Portugal) and government spending (Greece) owing to the fact that borrowing became less expensive (Eichengreen 2014: 4–5). Similarly, De Grauwe (2013: 6–7) seems to believe that inflation in the PIIGS countries picked up after the establishment of the EMU when the low interest rates that had been enjoyed as a result of a single monetary policy produced an unsustainable expansion of the economy.

However, and this is a key point, inflation rates of peripheral countries had always been higher than the rest of the eurozone, and especially higher than that of Germany. However, harmonized inflation had not increased because of the availability of cheaper credit within the EMU. The Walters critique, in sum, was not activated by the establishment of the EMU but was already valid before the currency union came into existence.

Looking at the performance of the harmonized inflation rates of the PIIGS countries from 1991 it emerges that they all kept higher inflation rates than Germany or even of the EU 15 average until 2009. This dynamic was not a novelty introduced by the EMU, but was rather a confirmed reality that had already existed before the establishment of the EMU, when inflation rates were actually much higher (see figure 3.3 below).

But why is the performance of inflation rates in the PIIGS countries so important? To answer we need to go back to the notion of competitiveness.

The eurozone crisis as a crisis of competitiveness

There is by now a relative consensus in the literature that the eurozone crisis was a crisis of competitiveness and not a fiscal crisis (Krugman 2012; Eichengreen 2014; De Grauwe 2013; Bourgeot 2013; Gros 2011). A crisis of competitiveness manifests itself as a current account crisis (Bourgeot 2013). In this vein, it is undeniable that the trade account and the current account balance of the PIIGS countries experienced an opposite dynamic to that of Germany, from the start of the EMU through to the onset of the sovereign debt crisis.

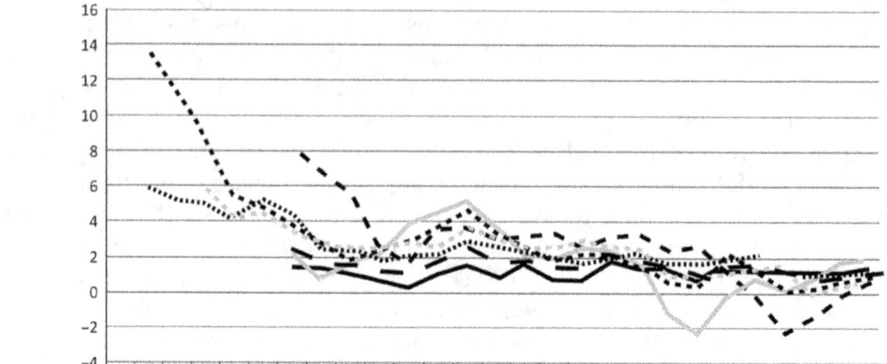

	1991	1992	1993	1994	1995	1996	1997	1998	1999	2000	2001	2002	2003	2004	2005	2006	2007	2008	2009	2010	2011	2012	2013	2014	2015	2016
Germany						1.381	1.33	1.035	0.495	0.167	1.036	1.407	0.66	1.481	0.621	0.675	1.854	1.325	1.34	0.625	1.18	1.314	1.174	1.1	1.076	1.324
Greece						8.148	6.687	5.54	2.415	1.614	3.479	3.572	2.995	3.172	3.259	2.439	3.095	3.12	2.263	2.612	1.078	-0.329	-2.4	-1.491	-0.169	0.55
Ireland						2.063	0.708	1.683	2.043	3.788	4.47	5.197	3.879	2.088	1.825	2.484	2.326	1.605	-1.291	-2.353	-0.219	0.748	0.137	0.726	1.696	1.911
Italy	5.831	5.183	4.998	4.275	5.104	4.28	2.446	2.428	1.894	2.04	2.055	2.911	2.553	2.134	1.911	1.633	1.82	2.231	1.583	1.659	2.021	2.019	1.253	0.717	0.746	1.065
Portugal	13.618	11.351	8.815	5.442	4.754	3.498	2.526	1.7	2.446	2.885	3.699	4.673	3.321	2.531	1.815	2.157	2.151	1.61	0.511	0.319	2.034	1.186	0.12	0.179	0.635	0.944
Spain			5.753	4.275	4.514	3.447	2.533	2.457	2.352	2.839	2.541	3.665	2.966	2.487	2.546	2.826	2.526	2.409	0.875	0.792	1.156	1.28	1.257	-0.104	0.363	0.663
Euro area (15 countries)						2.321	1.593	1.552	1.164	1.081	1.838	2.436	1.808	1.867	1.424	1.439	1.876	1.831	1.372	1.001	1.399	1.52	1.074	0.768	0.837	1.151

Figure 3.3 Harmonized inflation rates, % changes: PIIGS and Germany
Source: Organization for Economic Co-operation and Development (OECD) online database, as accessed on 18 January 2016.

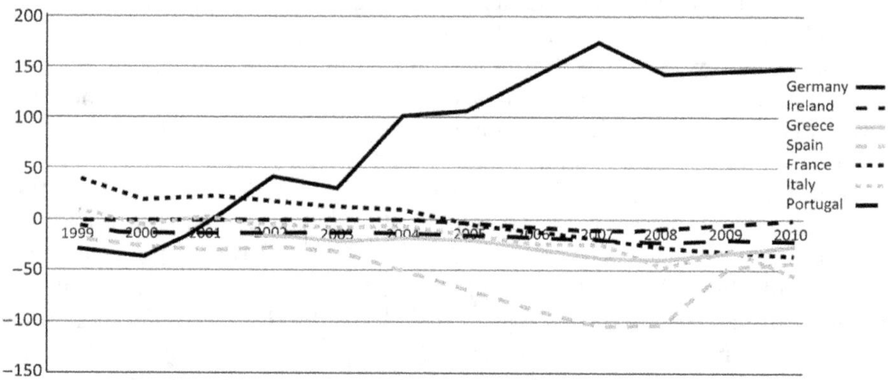

Figure 3.4 Balance on current account transactions with the rest of the world: PIIGS and Germany, 1999–2010
Source: European Commission, AMECO.

What remains to be discussed, however, is what exactly is meant by a 'crisis of competitiveness'. There are various ways to define it and they bring us to different conclusions and even varying policy proposals.

The most important measure of competitiveness, and the one that is often quoted in the literature is given by Unit Labour Cost (ULC). The nominal ULC is basically given by the ratio of total wages (which are nominal wages) to real GDP. It represents how much it generally costs in terms of labour to produce a unit of real GDP. Another way to calculate nominal ULC is to divide the average wage (total wages over number of employees) by the

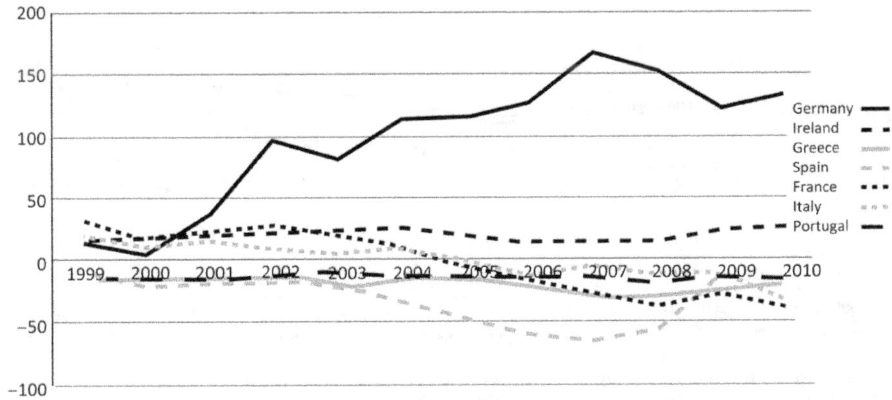

Figure 3.5 Net exports of goods and services at current prices: PIIGS and Germany, 1999–2010
Source: European Commission, AMECO.

productivity of one unit of labour (total real GDP divided by the total units of labour of a country).

Given the definition of ULC above it is clear that, even when a country's competitiveness has been affected by an increase in nominal wages, it is also a function of inflation rates. Furthermore, a loss of competitiveness can also be the consequence of a decrease in a country's productivity. Summing up, to correctly assess the factors contributing to a fall in competitiveness, the following indicators need to be considered: the harmonization of inflation rates, real costs of labour and productivity levels. In this way, a study by Bourgeot (2013) clearly shows that divergences in nominal ULC within the EMU were not a consequence of a wage drift, but of divergences in inflation rates and productivity levels. Indeed, if we look at real ULC we see that the wage share of GDP experienced a notable decline in peripheral countries between 1999 and 2007, with Spain decreasing by around 7%. This was almost as much as Germany's 8% decline after the implementation of Agenda 2010 by Gerhard Shröder in 2003.[14] It is also worth noting that the Italy, Ireland and Greece have always had, before, during and after the eurozone crisis, a wage share of GDP below the EU average, the eurozone average and the level of Germany. Even Ireland, which experienced a sharp increase in real wages between 2002 and 2008, always remained far below EU and eurozone averages and below the level in Germany.

Bourgeot (2013) also notices that over the past 40 years the share of wages has generally declined around the world. This is attributed to the falling power of trade unions and the impact of globalization, the same reasons why the share of profits has generally increased. So an explanation of increases in nominal ULC needs to be related to changes in inflation rates, which clearly were already diverging even before the establishment of the EMU. The effects of inflation on the competitiveness of the eurozone periphery countries are

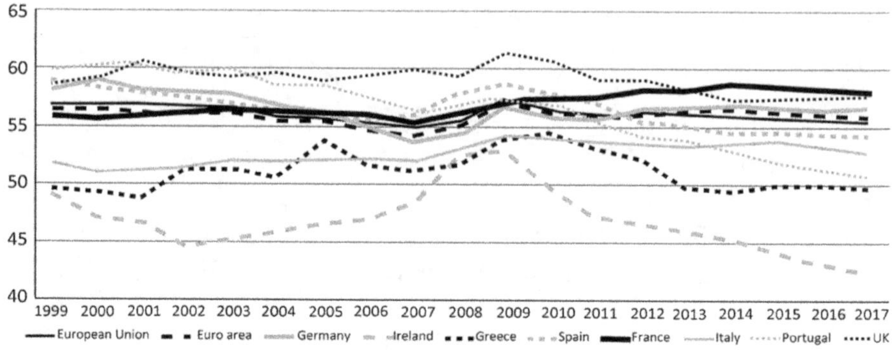

Figure 3.6 Adjusted wage share: total economy as a % of GDP, 1999–2017
Source: European Commission, AMECO.

undeniable, especially in light of the evolution of the national consumer price index (CPI).

The role played by inflation on the crisis of competitiveness emerges clearly in data on the performance of nominal ULC, real ULC, labour productivity and the CPI for each of the countries involved in the sovereign debt crisis, and for Germany. In particular, in Greece real ULC remained basically stable for all of the EMU period, productivity followed more or less the same trend and this means that the loss of competitiveness can be explained exclusively by the role played by inflation. The same dynamic is clearly recognizable in the case of Italy and even more so in the case of Spain, where the increase in nominal ULC and the performance of the CPI actually coincide. A key difference is the situation in Ireland and Portugal, where although the trend is similar there was a marked increase in labour productivity that kept the real ULC lower. Indeed, worsening productivity would exacerbate the loss of competitiveness by increasing real ULC, whereas an increase in productivity would decrease real ULC (Bourgeot 2013). In contrast, in Germany, nominal ULC does not seem to have been particularly influenced by the performance of the CPI, which, although increasing, was still far below the CPI of the periphery countries and therefore enabled Germany to make gains in relative competitiveness.

Bourgeot (2013) calculates that it is in the manufacturing sector, the most relevant in terms of competitiveness, where these trends have been particularly striking. Thus, we need to reassess the whole question of diverging competitiveness, resulting mainly from divergent inflation performances within the context of the currency union. As indeed Walters (1990) had rightly noted for the ERM of the EMS, in a fixed exchange rate system and, even more so, in a currency union, the competitiveness lost because of increasing rates of inflation leads, automatically, to divergences in real exchange rates. It must be noted, however, that in the EMU, exactly as in the ERM of the EMS, real exchange rates would not diverge randomly, but

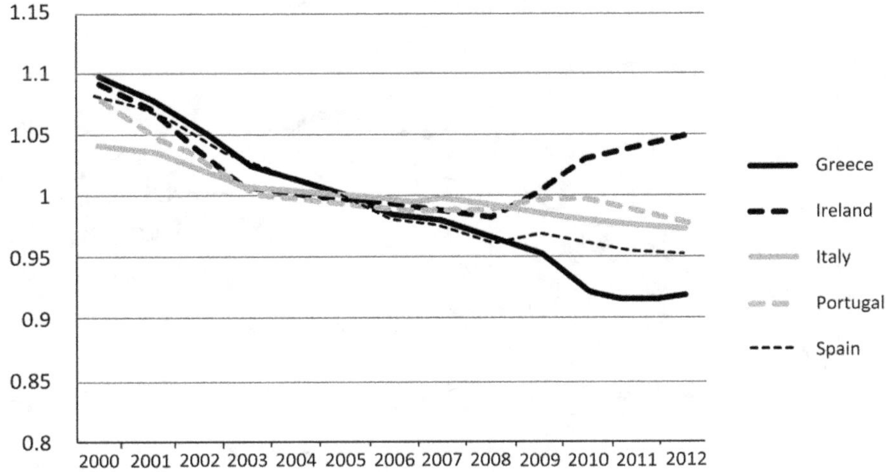

Figure 3.7 Italy: nominal ULC breakdown (2010 = 100)
Source: European Commission, AMECO.

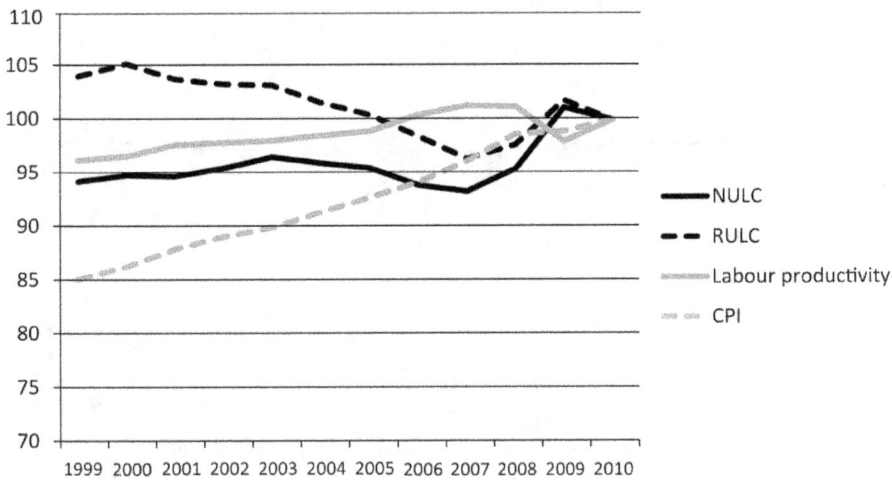

Figure 3.8 Germany: nominal ULC breakdown (2010 = 100)
Source: European Commission, AMECO.

would follow the so called 'n-1' country problem. To this, and to the special position of Germany in the EMU, we turn in the next section of this chapter.

Germany and the problem, for the others, of the 'n-1'country

In the literature on the relationship between the global financial crisis and the eurozone crisis two questions seem to be particularly puzzling[15]: The first question asks to what extent the financial markets increased the returns they required on sovereign debt and whether this was as a result of larger fiscal

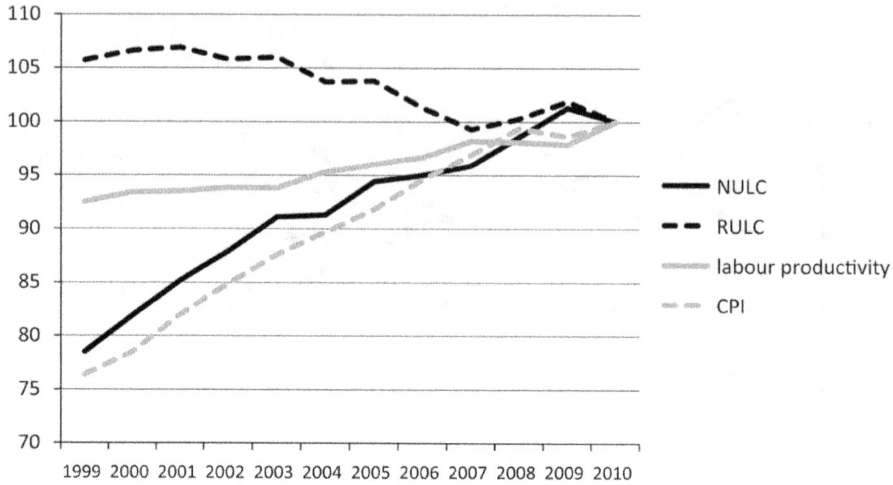

Figure 3.9 Portugal: nominal ULC breakdown (2010 = 100)
Source: European Commission, AMECO.

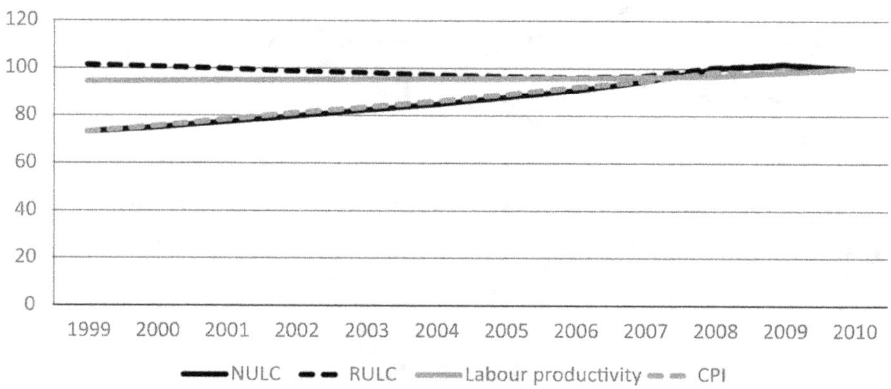

Figure 3.10 Spain: nominal ULC breakdown (2010 = 100)
Source: European Commission, AMECO.

deficits and debt or a change in their attitude towards the pricing of government credit risk. The second question is to what extent increased premiums on risk were the consequence of more risk aversion.

It is indeed evident, as a study conducted by the ECB shows, that following the collapse of Lehman Brothers in September 2008 financial markets attributed much more importance than before to fiscal imbalances. More precisely, after the global financial crisis markets asked coefficients for debt and deficit differentials that were 7–8 and 3–4 times higher, respectively, than before (Manganelli and Wolswijk 2009).

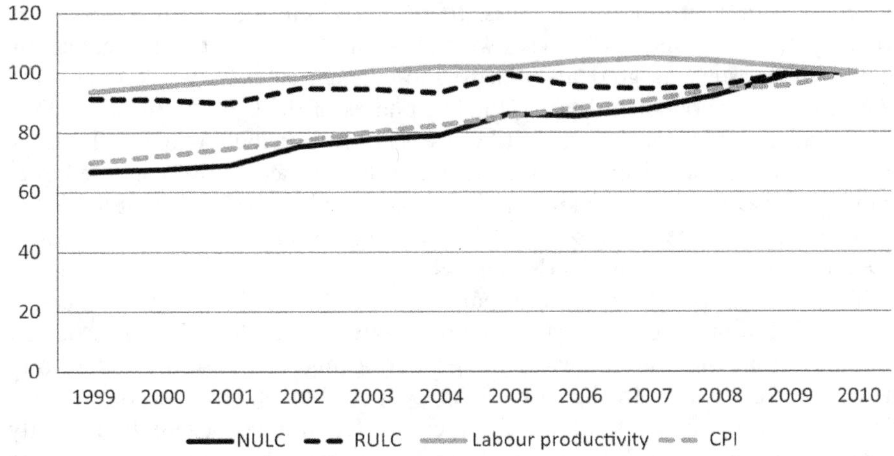

Figure 3.11 Greece: nominal ULC breakdown (2010 = 100)
Source: European Commission, AMECO.

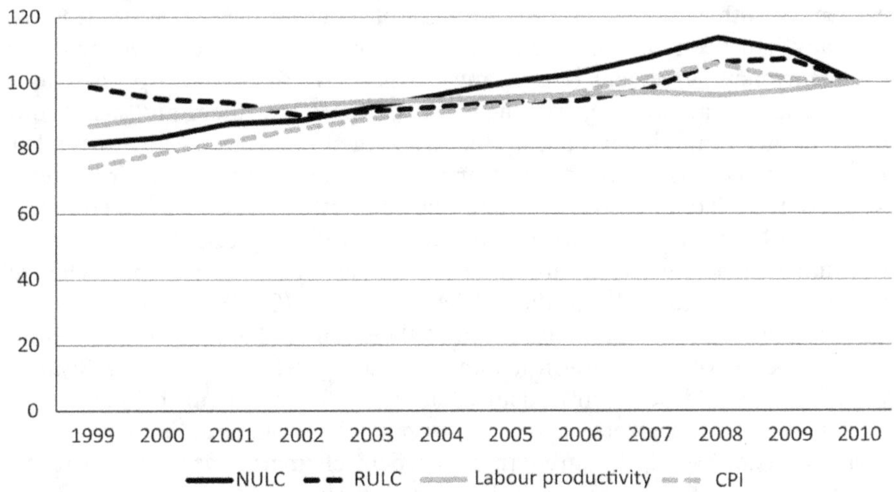

Figure 3.12 Ireland: nominal ULC breakdown (2010 = 100)
Source: European Commission, AMECO.

This clearly means that the markets changed their attitude towards countries with high fiscal imbalances after the crisis and they did so massively, thus demonstrating that there was a clear link between the GFC and the crisis of sovereign debt. Also, increased spreads not only showed a lack of credibility of a particular government under fire, but also signalled a desire of the markets to put their investment on more secure assets (similarly Krugman 2012). Risk aversion was indeed very sensible in a period in which the stock exchange had collapsed, the housing market was devastated and the banking sector had just experienced a severe liquidity crisis. In similar circumstances investors were looking for safe havens. These were first and foremost represented by commodities, such as gold and oil, to the extent that scholars recognise the commodity price bubble as one of the five phases of the GFC (Orlowski 2008). However, a safe haven investment status was also attributed to US Treasury Bonds and German Euro-denominated bonds. Consequently, increased premiums on fiscal imbalances and increased risk aversion both account for much of the increase in the spreads of all EU countries treasury bonds with respect to US and German benchmarks (Manganelli and Wolswijk 2009).

If it might be puzzling that the markets had attributed the status of investment safe haven to US government bonds, given that the GFC had started there and that the country was experiencing a huge increase in its debt and deficit to GDP ratios. In the case of the German bonds, however, the reasons are much more understandable. In fact, as DeGrauwe (1996) had rightly pointed out from before the start of the EMU, over the course of the whole evolution of the European monetary integration process Germany had enjoyed a very privileged position.[16]

Germany was, and had been always in the past, the one country of the 'n-1' problem. In other words, precisely because of its anti-inflationary credentials, Germany had been able to set the monetary policy of all the other members of the currency agreement (De Grauwe 1996: 27). To be more precise: in a fixed exchange rate system, like the ERM of the EMS, there are 'n-1' countries, the more inflationary prone ones and, therefore, the ones with weaker currencies, which will have to use their monetary policy to keep their bilateral exchange rates fixed. On the contrary, one country, the one with the strongest currency, Germany in this case, will not have to worry about the exchange rate, and will be free to set its monetary policy independently of exchange rate constraints. Indeed, in the ERM of the EMS all currencies would depreciate vis-à-vis the deutschmark and their central banks would therefore have to ask for very short-term lending facilities (VSTLFs) from the *Bundesbank*. These would be given in deutschemarks to enable them to intervene in foreign exchange markets, so as to support their bilateral exchange rate. Germany, because of the strength of its deutschemark, was always in the upper band of the system and the *Bundesbank* would, de facto, provide liquidity to the whole system. In this way, the *Bundesbank* defined the monetary policy for all other members.

Moreover, by needing to keep the nominal exchange rate at levels that were not necessarily consistent with the evolution of their inflation rates, the 'n-1' countries would be constantly losing competitiveness and worsening their structural problems. Seen from another angle, one country would improve its competitive stance as it would be able to keep the exchange rate at a lower level than the one that would be set if the system was flexible. The loss of competitiveness of the 'n-1'countries would eventually become unsustainable, reaching the point at which their exchange rate peg loses credibility and the markets can successfully speculate against their currencies.

As we have seen in the previous sections, divergent inflation rates, which already existed before the establishment of the EMU, did not disappear after the currency union entered into force. In particular, all countries were experiencing inflation rates higher than Germany, exactly has had been the case under the ERM of the EMS. This can only mean that all countries within the EMU were losing competitiveness vis-à-vis Germany. At the same time, by entering the currency union Germany itself could indefinitely enjoy a less appreciated currency, or at least as long as its inflation performance was better than the rest of the eurozone.

Thus, the more inflationary 'n-1' countries, by joining the EMU, progressively increased the prices of their exports without ever being able to devalue the exchange rate. This was particularly serious for the PIIGS countries, which, being particularly prone to inflation, had often resorted to competitive devaluations in the past. On the opposite side of the spectrum, Germany as the 'one' country of the 'n-1' problem, would progressively and constantly increase its competitiveness. This was not only because of a progressively depreciating currency, but also because it would not have to face competitive devaluations by the other members of the EMU ever again.

The imbalances that had characterized the previous attempts at monetary integration in Europe were not only reproduced, but in fact exacerbated by the currency union established at Maastricht. This was characterized by structural asymmetries from the start. Evidence is found in the performance of the purchasing-power parity real exchange rate (RER)[17] of the PIIGS countries in relation to Germany, based on the average consumer price index from 2000–12 (see Figure 3.13 below). On the basis of this data, Italy lost

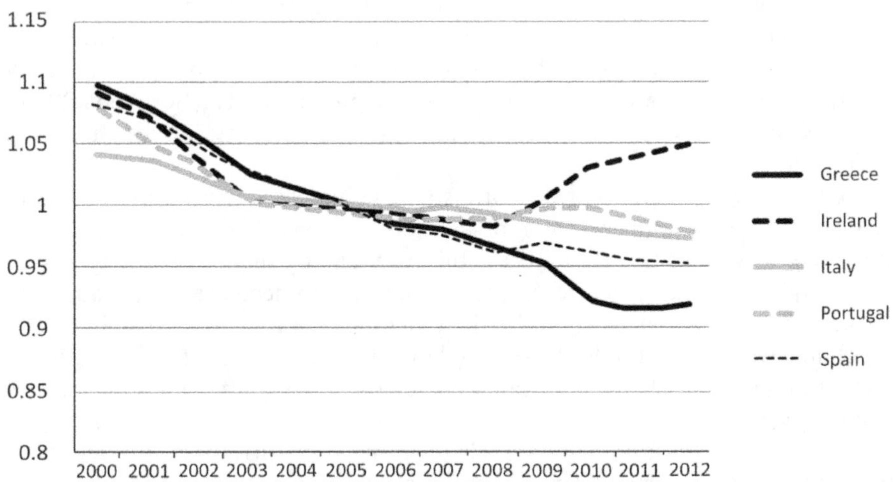

Figure 3.13 PIIGS real exchange rates: 2000–12
Source: International Monetary Fund, World Economic Outlook Database, elaboration of the author.

some 20% of its competitiveness on exports over the course of its permanence in the EMU, and even higher losses were experienced by Greece and Spain.

Overall, by entering the EMU Germany acquired a structural bonus of competitiveness that increased progressively and might well have been one of the main reasons behind the German decision to give up the deutschemark.[18] On the other hand, the rest of the eurozone countries, especially the more inflationary ones, lost competitiveness and were unable to regain it through their previous approach of competitive devaluation (see also Hall 2012; Scharpf 2013). Of course, there is an ongoing debate in the field on whether exchange rate devaluations can be considered an optimal way to achieve competitiveness (Mabbett and Schelkle 2015). More emphasis is often placed on 'internal devaluations', which means increasing competitiveness by reducing labour costs, either reducing wages and/or increasing productivity. On similar grounds both EU institutions and the Greek Government have often proposed increased labour market flexibility, in all its dimensions, as a solution to problems of growth and employment. This characteristically means reducing the power of trade unions, as trade unions have historically and institutionally represented the working class in its fight for more job security and higher wages. Thus, the rigidities of the labour markets were simplistically equated to the strength of the trade unions and, in turn, this had to diminish in order to resolve the problems of competitiveness of the weaker countries of the system. Yet, as we have just seen, these problems were actually structurally embedded in the EMU.

In turn, the fact that it was possible to implement policies aimed at the increasing the flexibility of the labour markets was a consequence of the shift in the balance of power at both the national and transnational level, which had been constitutionalized with the adoption of the specific form of monetary union agreed at Maastricht. This would explain why the only way out of the structural crisis of the eurozone to be identified was the adoption of austerity practices, which were clearly suboptimal, to put it mildly (Bourgeot 2013). More effective would have been to increase productivity, although this is easier said than done.

So, if real wages dynamics do not justify the increases in inflation rates and productivity performances were not so disastrous in the periphery of the eurozone, why were those countries still experiencing higher prices? One suggestion might be that increases in prices unrelated to decreases of productivity or increases of real wages could be the outcome of a process of 'catching up', which in a way was not only foreseeable but had even been greeted by European institutions as one of the main advantages of a monetary union (European Commission 1990).

Whatever the reasons behind such gaps in competitiveness, the reality is that they clearly existed. This precarious equilibrium held until when the markets, with the global financial crisis and the following global economic crisis, realized that the situation was unsustainable. Arghyrou and Kontonikas (2011) argue that the performance of the spreads in the course of the global financial crisis was due to both an international risk factor, measured by the US Stock Market Implied Volatility Index (VIX) and a country specific macro-factor represented by the loss of international competitiveness. In other words, both effects were at play: on one side investors wanted safe havens because of the increased risk following from the global crises. On the other hand, in this riskier environment the macroeconomic and fiscal fundamentals of some countries, especially Greece, that could still be considered acceptable in times of growth, led the markets to believe that betting against the weakest countries of the system was safe. In the face of a lack of available currencies, they started selling the government bonds of the weaker countries, dramatically increasing their spreads.

Similarly, Chang and Leblond (2015) consider the attack to the sovereign debt of 2010/11 as a speculation by financial markets. However, they seem to believe that the speculation from early 2010 onward reflects not only the varying economic fundamentals of individual eurozone Member States but also, and more importantly, the growing concern for the integrity of the euro area itself. Therefore, Mario Draghi's July 2012 'whatever it takes' pledge to save the euro area ultimately calmed bond investors down in a way that bail-outs and the conditionality programmes that accompanied them had not managed to do. Markets sought a large-scale multilateral solution coming from the euro area rather than a unilateral one coming primarily from the debtor countries. Market confidence in the euro area has therefore always rested to a large extent on the expectation of its solidarity (Chang and Leblond 2015: 628).

This interpretation of the motivations behind speculation is untenable: if the problem was mainly the integrity of the euro area, then it should not have been only the weakest countries to be attacked. Also, the reason why the market stopped speculating after the intervention of Draghi in July 2012 was not so much because it signalled to the markets the existence of a eurozone wide solidarity. It was simply because speculation is impossible if there is a lender of last resort, however imperfect it may be, as long as it will basically buy whatever the markets sell. If the ECB buys 'whatever it takes', prices of sovereign debt cannot go down and therefore interest rates cannot increase (see also De Grauwe 2013).

Summing up, more than a shelter against the worst consequences of the global financial and economic crises, the EMU designed at Maastricht and implemented in the following years proved to be a highly asymmetric arrangement, exacerbating the structural problems of the more inflationary prone countries in the system, Greece *in primis*.

Conclusion

To conclude, it is undeniable that the burden of the costs of the global financial crisis was inflicted on the weakest countries of the system, and, within them, on the weakest strata of society. This came through the two related dynamics of the sovereign debt crisis and ensuing austerity programmes, as the case of Greece tragically demonstrates.

The eurozone crisis was eventually resolved by the intervention of the ECB reaffirming the credibility of the currency union despite its asymmetries. However, this is far from configuring increases in solidarity between EU Member States which, as often recalled in the literature, could only be achieved by the establishment of a true federalist fiscal system. At the moment, such a system is not even at the stage of infancy.

On the other hand, a salient feature of the EU approach to crisis management was austerity and 'internal devaluation', with all that this implies in terms of increasing inequalities, both socially and geographically. This disciplinary attitude did provoke some popular discontent, as the result of the Greek bail-out referendum in 2015 shows.[19] However, later events point to the normalization of austerity, even in Greece.

Notes

1 See BBC News, *Markets fall after Irish Republic 85bn euro bail-out*, available at www.bbc.co.uk/news/business-11860879 as accessed on 22 December 2010.
2 See BBC News, *What is the European Stability Mechanism*, available at www.bbc.co.uk/news/business-19870747 as accessed on 9 October 2012.
3 ECB (2010), *Financial Stability Review,* available at www.ecb.int/pub/fsr/html/summary201012.en.html as accessed on 22 December 2010.
4 ECB (2010), *Financial Stability Review*, available at www.ecb.int/pub/fsr/html/summary201012.en.html as accessed on 22 December 2010.
5 ECB (2010), *Financial Stability Review*, available at www.ecb.int/pub/fsr/html/summary201012.en.html as accessed on 22 December 2010.
6 ECB (2010), *Financial Stability Review* available at www.ecb.int/pub/fsr/html/summary201012.en.html as accessed on 22 December 2010.
7 ECB (2010), *Financial Stability Review*, available at www.ecb.int/pub/fsr/html/summary201012.en.html as accessed on 22 December 2010.
8 ECB (2010), *Financial Stability Review*, available at www.ecb.int/pub/fsr/html/summary201012.en.html as accessed on 22 December 2010.
9 See Reuters (2012), *Euro zone agrees to lend Spain up to 100 billion euros*www.reuters.com/article/us-eurozone-idUSBRE8530RL20120610 as accessed on 13 July 2016.
10 See ECB statistics, available at www.ecb.int/stats/gov/html/dashboard.en.html as accessed on 9 October 2012.
11 Ibid.
12 For the debate on the optimum currency area theory and the global financial crisis, see Jones and Underhill (2014); McNamara, K. (2015); Schelkle, W. (2013); Snaith, H. (2013); and Tavlas, G. (2009).
13 See also Ferroni and Klaus (2015) and Willett et al. (2010).
14 In real terms, ULC represents the ratio between total real wage bill and real GDP (or as an equivalent the nominal wage bill and the nominal GDP). Real ULC can therefore be expressed as a share of GDP and not just as a variation or as an index number (unlike nominal ULC). Likewise, it can be calculated as the ratio between the average real compensation and real productivity. Their variations result from the development of real wages and of real productivity (and exclude inflation) (Bourgeot 2013).

15 See Manganelli Wolswijk. (2009) and Arghyrou and Kontonikas (2011). See also Monfort and Renne (2011), Haugh et al. (2009), Gerlach et al. (2010), Attinasi et al. (2009) and Barrios et al. (2009).

16 De Grauwe (1996) had discussed the 'n-1' problem in the context of the Bretton Wood system.

17 The formula for the RER used here is given by: RER = e(P*/P), where e is the nominal exchange rate (1 in the case of the eurozone), P* stands for the international prices index (in this particular case, German prices) and P is national price index. The data was obtained from the World Economic Outlook Database of September 2011, available on the International Monetary Fund's website www.imf.org/external/pubs/ft/weo/2011/02/weodata/index.aspx. Inflation is computed with the average consumer inflation index for all countries. See http://econapproach.blogspot.it/2011/11/real-exchange-rates-and-eurozone-issues.html as accessed on 27 December 2012. For a similar analysis see European Commission, Economic and Financial Affairs (2012), Price and Cost Competitiveness, 1–2/2012, Brussels available at http://ec.europa.eu/economy_finance/publications/pcqr/2012/pdf/pccr_1_2_2012_en.pdf as accessed on 27 December 2012.

18 See Talani (2009); Eichengreen and Frieden (1994); Frieden (1991); Frieden (1994); Frieden and Gros (1998); and Moravcsik (1998).

19 See *The Guardian* web-site https://www.theguardian.com/business/2015/jul/05/greek-referendum-no-vote-signals-huge-challenge-to-eurozone-leaders as accessed on April 3, 2017

References

Ackrill, R.W. (2000), *The Common Agricultural Policy*, Sheffield: Sheffield Academic Press, for the University Association for Contemporary Studies.

Arghyrou, M.G. and Kontonikas, A. (2011), 'The EMU sovereign-debt crisis: Fundamentals, expectations and contagion', Brussels: European Commission, Directorate General for Economic and Financial Affairs, Economic Papers 436, February.

Artis, M. (2009), Assessing the Impact of EMU on Business Cycle Affiliation, in Talani, L.S. (2009), *The future of EMU*, London: Palgrave.

Attinasi, M.G., Checherita, C. and Nickel, C. (2009). 'What explains the surge in euro area sovereign spreads during the financial crisis of 2007–2009?' Brussels, European Central Bank, *Working Paper Series*, 1131.

Barrios, S., Iversen, P., Lewandowska, M. and R. Setzer (2009), 'Determinants of intra-eurozone government bond spreads during the financial crisis', Brussels: European Commission, Directorate General for Economic and Financial Affairs, *Economic Papers* 388.

Bickerton, C., Hodson, D. and Puetter, U. (2015), 'The new intergovernmentalism: European integration in the post-Maastricht period', *Journal of Common Market Studies* 53(4): 702–722.

Bulmer, S. (2015), 'Understanding the New Intergovernmentalism: Pre- and Post-Maastricht EU Studies', in Bickerton, C., Hodson, D. and Puetter, U. (eds), *The New Intergovernmentalism: States and Supranational Actors in the Post-Maastricht Era*, Oxford: Oxford University Press, 289–303.

Bourgeot, R. (2013), Labour Costs and Crisis Management in the Eurozone: A Reinterpretation of Divergences in Competitiveness, available atwww.robert-schuman.eu/en/european-issues/0289-labour-costs-and-crisis-management-in-the-Euro-zone-a-reinterpretation-of-divergences-in as accessed on 12 January 2016.

Caporaso, J. and Kim, M. (2015), 'States Choose but not Under Circumstances of Their Own Making: A New Interpretation of the Integration Debate in Light of the European Financial Crisis' in Caporaso, J. and Rhodes, M. (eds), *The Political and Economic Dynamics of the Eurozone Crisis.* Oxford: Oxford University Press.

Chang, M. and Leblond, P. (2015), 'All in: Market expectations of eurozone integrity in the sovereign debt crisis', *Review of International Political Economy* 22(i3): 626–665.

Culpepper, P. and Regan, A. (2015), 'Why don't governments need trade unions anymore? The death of social pacts in Ireland and Italy', *Transfer: European Review of Labour and Research* 21(2): 131–139.

De Grauwe, P. (1996), *International Money*, Oxford: Oxford University Press.

De Grauwe, P. (2012), Interview available at http://aregan.wordpress.com/2012/03/20/interview-with-paul-de-grauw/, accessed on October 18, 2012.

De Grauwe, P. (2013), 'Foreword', in Marco, M. *The Economics of the Monetary Union and the Eurozone Crisis*, London: Springer.

European Commission (1990), One market, one money, *European Economy* 44, October: 347.

Eichengreen, B. (2014), 'The Eurozone crisis: the theory of optimum currency areas bites back', Berkley, CA, Notenstein Academy, *White Paper Series*, 1–18.

Eichengreen, B. and Frieden, J. (1994), *The political Economy of European Monetary Union*, Boulder, CO: Westview Press.

Ferroni, F. and Klaus, B. (2015), 'Euro area business cycles in turbulent times: convergence or decoupling?', Brussels, the European Central Bank, *Working Paper Series*, no. 1819, June: 1–36.

Frankel, J. and Rose, A. (1998), 'The Endogeneity of the Optimum Currency Area Criteria', *The Economic Journal*, 108(449) (July): 1009–1025.

Frieden, J. (1991), 'Invested interests: the politics of national economic policies in a world of global finance', *International Organization*, 45(4): 425–451.

Frieden, J. (1994), 'The impact of goods and capital market integration on European monetary politics', Preliminary version, August.

Frieden, J. and Gros, D. (1998), *The new political economy of EMU*, Oxford: Rowman and Littlefield.

Gerlach, S., Schulz, A. and G.B. Wolf (2010), 'Banking and sovereign risk in the euro area', London, Centre for Economic Policy Research, *Discussion Paper*, no. 7833.

Giannone, D., Lenza, M., Pill, H. and Reichlin, L. (2011), 'Non-Standard Monetary Policy Measures and Monetary Developments', Brussels: European Central Bank, *Working Paper Series* no. 1290.

Gill, S. (1997), An EMU or an Ostrich?: EMU and neo-liberal globalisation; limits and alternatives, in Minkkinen, P., and Potomaki, H., (1997), *The politics of Economic and monetary Union*, Dordrecht: Kluwer Academic Publishers: 210.

Gros, D. (2011), 'External Versus Domestic Debt in the Euro Crisis', Brussels, Centre for European Policy Studies, *Policy Brief* no. 243, May 2011.

Hall, P. (2012), 'The economics and politics of the Euro-crisis', *German Politics*, 21(4), December: 355–371.

Haugh, D., Ollivaud, P. and Turner, D. (2009), 'What drives sovereign risk premiums? An analysis of recent evidence from the eurozone', Paris: Organisation for Economic Co-operation and Development, *Economics Department Working Papers*, no. 718.

Jones, E. and Underhill, G. (2014), 'Theory of Optimum Financial Areas: Retooling the Debate on the Governance of Global Finance', London: SWIFT Institute, *Working Paper no. 2013-001*: 1–46, November.

Krugman, P. (2012), 'Revenge of the Optimum Currency Area', Cambridge, MA, National Bureau of Economic Research, *Macroeconomics Annual*, 27(1): 439–448.

Mabbett, D. and Schelkle, W. (2015), 'What difference does Euro membership make to stabilization?: the political economy of international monetary systems revisited', *Review of International Political Economy*, 22(3): 508–534.

Manganelli, S. and Wolswijk, G. (2009), 'What drives spreads in the euro area government bond market?', *Economic Policy*, 24: 191–240.

McNamara, K. (2015), 'The Forgotten Problem of Embededness: History Lessons for the Euro', in Matthijs, M. and Blyth, M. (eds) *The Future of the Euro*, Oxford: Oxford University Press: 44–69.

Monfort, A., and Renne, J.-P. (2011), 'Credit and liquidity risks in eurozone sovereign yield curves', Paris, Banque de France, *Working Papers Series*, no. 352.

Moravcsik, A. (1998), *The choice for Europe*, Ithaca, NY: Cornell University Press.

Moravscik, A. (2012), 'Europe after the crisis', *Foreign Affairs*, May/June, available at www.foreignaffairs.com/articles/europe/2012-05-01/europe-after-crisis as accessed on 15 July 2016.

Orlowski, L.T. (2008), 'Stages of the 2007/2008 Global Financial Crisis: Is There a Wandering Asset-Price Bubble?', *Economics Discussion Papers*, no 2008–2043, available at www.economics-ejournal.org/economics/discussionpapers/2008-43 as accessed on 18 May 2009.

Scharpf, F. (2013), 'No Exit from the Euro-Rescuing Trap?', Cologne, Max Plank Institute, *MPIfG Discussion Paper* 14/4, available at www.mpifg.de/pu/mpifg_dp/dp 14-4.pdf as accessed on 15 July 2016.

Schelkle, W. (2013), 'Monetary integration in crisis: how well do existing theories explain the predicament of EMU?' *Transfer: European Review of Labour and Research* 19(1): 37–48.

Schimmelfennig, F. (2014), 'European Integration in the Euro Crisis: The Limits of Postfunctionalism', *Journal of European Integration*, 36(3): 321–337.

Schweiger, C. (2014), 'The EU-25 Fiscal Compact: Differentiated Spillover Effects under Crisis Conditions', *Perspectives on European Politics and Society*, 15(3): 293–304.

Sinn, H.W. (2010), *Casino Capitalism*, Oxford: Oxford University Press: 6.

Snaith, H. (2013), 'Narratives of Optimum Currency Area Theory and Eurozone Governance'. *New Political Economy*: 1–18.

Talani, L.S. (2000), *Betting for and against EMU*, London: Ashgate.

Talani, L.S. (ed.) (2009), *The future of EMU*, London: Palgrave.

Talani, L.S. (ed.) (2010), *The Global Crash: Towards a New Global Financial Regime?*, London: Palgrave.

Tavlas, G. (2009), 'Optimum-Currency-Area Paradoxes', *Review of International Economics*, 17(3): 536–551.

Van Rompuy, H., Barroso, J., Juncker, J.-C. and Draghi, M. (2012), 'Towards a Genuine and Economic Monetary Union', Brussels, *European Council*, 120/12, 26 June 2012.

Walters, A.A. (1990), *Sterling in Danger: The Economic Consequences of Pegged Exchange Rates*, London: Fontana/Collins.

Willett, T., Permpoon, O. and Wihlbore, C. (2010), 'Endogenous OCA Analysis and the Early Euro Experience', *The World Economy*: 851–872.

4 Is There Really a Eurozone Crisis?

Turan Subasat

Although several developed countries have experienced financial crisis since 2008, a special reference has been made to the eurozone countries. Often termed the *eurozone crisis*, this is essentially a current account disequilibrium-based explanation that implies a crisis instigated by the introduction of the euro and the emphasis is placed upon the core and periphery dichotomy.[1] Krugman (2013), for example, argued that 'the creation of the euro was followed by the emergence of huge imbalances, with vast amounts of capital flowing from the core to the periphery', which was followed by a sudden stop and forced the peripheral countries to eliminate their current account deficits. Lapavitsas et al. (2012) also analysed the *eurozone crisis* in terms of the polarization between the core and periphery in an asymmetrical monetary union. In this view, the growing balance-of-payments disequilibrium between the core and periphery has been the main factor behind the crisis.

The above claims, at first glance, appear to be well warranted theoretically and empirically. A monetary union (especially in the absence of fiscal co-ordination) can be subject to asymmetrical shocks and the current account surpluses of the eurozone core (Germany) and the current account deficits of the periphery follow a mirror-image trend since the introduction of the euro in 1999. These arguments are exacerbated by the fact that the eurozone's current account as a whole has been close to balance. A more sophisticated analysis of the eurozone, however, needs to go beyond simple observations as such professed correlations do not prove causality. Establishing causality requires confirming that core's (periphery's) current account surpluses (deficits) are directly linked with the periphery's (core's) current account deficits (surpluses), which can be done by considering the following four issues.

First, the current account experiences of the eurozone countries should establish a clear pattern regarding the core and periphery dichotomy. For example, the core countries should experience improvements in their current account balances whereas the periphery countries should experience deterioration. If some core countries experience deterioration and some periphery countries experience improvement in their current account balances, for example, there would be no evidence for the eurozone core and periphery dichotomy. Second, the experiences of the eurozone countries should establish a distinct pattern compared to the non-eurozone EU, non-EU European and other countries. Comparable results for the eurozone and non-eurozone countries would provide no support for the *eurozone crisis* and imply that the eurozone countries are a part of a wider current account disequilibrium crisis. Third, the impact of the euro over current account disequilibrium would be through its impact on international trade but trade disequilibrium is not the only source of current account disequilibrium. The effect of Income Payments and Unilateral Transfers (which are not influenced by the introduction of the euro) should also be considered. Fourth, the bilateral trade figures should be consistent with the *eurozone crisis* arguments. It is quite possible that the current account surpluses (deficits) of the eurozone core (periphery) countries may have occurred through their trade with countries other than the Eurozone periphery (core).

In short, if some eurozone core and periphery countries experienced similar current account problems, if the eurozone country experiences are not noticeably different from the non-eurozone countries, if factors other than trade played a significant role in their current account disequilibrium and if current account surpluses of the eurozone core are caused by their trade other than the eurozone periphery, there is no evidence for the eurozone core and periphery dichotomy.

It is important to state the objectives of this chapter at the outset clearly. This chapter has a narrow focus. It will investigate whether the introduction of the euro is the main cause of the current account problems in the eurozone. This is a worthy objective since many scholars assume a direct link between the introduction of euro and the current account problems in the eurozone without providing convincing evidence. Other important debates regarding the euro will not be investigated. This chapter, for instance, will not analyse the potential costs and benefits of monetary unions (in general) or the European Monetary Union (EMU), more specifically; it will not consider whether the costs and benefits of the euro are evenly distributed amongst the eurozone members; it will not investigate the contribution of the euro to the stability/instability of the eurozone countries; it will not examine whether exiting the euro would benefit the eurozone periphery;[2] it will not debate about the structural weaknesses of the EMU; it will not review the impacts of austerity policies across the European Union (EU); it will not discuss the alternative policies that could make the euro work better. While these are very important issues, they are beyond the objectives of this chapter. Finally, this paper will not discuss the financial crisis of 2008, its causes and alternative interpretations in detail, except indicating the role of the euro. Similarly, the core-periphery gap in the eurozone is also beyond the limits of this chapter.[3]

This chapter will briefly cover the theoretical and empirical literature and based on the four criteria established above investigate whether there is current account crisis specific to the eurozone countries. If the eurozone countries are a part of a wider current account disequilibrium crisis, it is legitimate to talk about the *crisis in the eurozone* but it is not meaningful to talk about a *eurozone crisis*, which implies that the crisis was instigated by the introduction of the euro.

Alternative explanations of the eurozone crisis

There is a large volume of literature on the *eurozone crisis*, the details of which need not be fully covered in this chapter but here is the gist of the arguments.[4] The mainstream arguments focus on the hampering of international competitiveness due to poor macroeconomic management (excessive fiscal spending resulting from big and inefficient public sector), price rigidities (caused by the structural rigidities in the labour and product markets) and excessive wage growth (inconsistent with the underlying productivity trends), which in turn caused the loss of international competitiveness and current account deficits in the periphery (Biroli et al. 2010, Trichet 2011, Draghi 2012, Jaumotte and Morsy 2012, Sinn and Valentinyi 2013). The proposed solutions, therefore, require the implementation of painful adjustment programmes to restore international competitiveness via fiscal austerity, wage restraint and structural reforms (Uxó et al. 2011). The current account surpluses, by contrast, are considered as the signs of economic efficiency, discreet fiscal policies, wage restraint and high productivity (Uxó et al. 2011).

The credibility of these arguments has been questioned by many writers. Gaulier et al. (2012) and Diaz-Sanchez and Varoudakis (2013), for example, argued that the trade performance of the periphery was far from dismal and the worsening competitiveness and external disequilibrium would be expected in the countries that experienced credit booms. Beck and Peydró (2015) further argued that private over-indebtedness often ends up on governments' balance sheets. The rise in public debt, therefore, is not a cause but a consequence of a financial crisis. Lapavitsas et al. (2012) argued that since the *eurozone crisis* is not primarily a public debt crisis, the reliance of the European policy-making on the fiscal conservatism (austerity policies) is misplaced and will only make things worse. Diaz-Sanchez and Varoudakis (2013) and Comunale and Hessel (2014) argued that the domestic demand boom (instigated by greater financial integration) was the main cause of the current account disequilibrium in the eurozone periphery and the decline in their competitiveness played a negligible role.

An alternative interpretation that counters the above arguments suggests that the German current account surpluses caused problems not only for the eurozone countries but also for the world economy. In this view, Germany is obsessed with fiscal discipline, wage competitiveness and export surpluses, and has adopted beggar-thy-neighbour policies. 'The result has been a structural current account surplus for Germany, mirrored by current account deficits for peripheral countries' (Lapavitsas et al. 2012: 4).[5] Similarly, Uxó et al. (2011) argue that, rather than competitiveness (which should be considered a result not a cause), the focus should be on differential growth rates of domestic demand. The wage restraint and shortage of domestic demand in the eurozone core countries are the main causes of their current account surpluses as well as the excessive domestic demand, wage inflation, external debt, lack of competitiveness and current account deficits of the eurozone periphery. The solution, therefore, requires expansionary policies in the core but not austerity policies in the periphery which can only reduce the aggregate demand and lower their capacity to service debts at due dates. As Mavroudeas (2016: 315) puts it, 'this is the Mainstream argument in reverse: the cause of the problem is the over-prudent North and not the profligate South'.

An important problem with the above arguments is that whether the focus is on 'over-prudence' or 'under-prudence', the deviation in policies needs to be explained in the context of historical developments. In other words, why at a particular juncture in economic history some countries have become over-prudent whereas the others under-prudent itself requires an explanation, which brings us back to the role of euro.

Another popular debate considers the role of the EMU as an Optimal Currency Area and questions whether it is prone to asymmetric shocks (Feldstein 2010 and Krugman 2012). Until the crisis, many commentators considered the temporary current account disequilibrium in the Eurozone as normal (even desirable) and self-correcting in the long run (Blanchard and Giavazzi 2002). In this story, the financial resources would move to the peripheral eurozone countries, cause current account deficits as well as stimulating faster economic growth. Such temporary disequilibrium would eventually be rectified by the convergence process. Inspired by the Lawson doctrine (Blanchard 2006), this view suggests that current account deficits are almost never a problem since they allow countries to invest more than what is possible by using their domestic savings. Higher investment rates, in turn, would boost their economic growth and help them to service their debts.

This argument is problematical since the external resources could be used to boost domestic consumption (rather than investment) and unproductive (even speculative) types of investment. Even when the borrowed resources are invested into socially and economically beneficial sectors (such as health and education), servicing debt could still be problematic if these sectors do not generate foreign currency. Moreover, the large sums of capital inflows are bound to cause overvalued real exchange rates, which in turn hamper exports, make debt servicing more difficult and create the conditions for a speculative attack. Overvalued exchange rates tend to make speculative types of investment more attractive, reduce incentives for productive investments in the trade sector and cause further problems (Subasat 2016b). Another complication arises from the fact that *residential construction*, which tends to over-expand during the economic bubbles, is considered as part of the overall investment. This implies that even rapidly expanding investment rates per se would not ensure enhanced capacity for debt service.

The crisis, however, brought about a more pessimistic interpretation of the current account deficits, which is associated with excessive external borrowing (Jaumotte and Sodsriwiboom 2010). In this view, downplaying the country-specific risks since the introduction euro (which eliminated only the exchange rate risks) also played an important role (Sinn and Valentinyi 2013). Similarly, Milios and Sotiropoulos (2010) focused on the superior growth performance of the periphery countries which increased their imports faster than exports and led to their external imbalances. Higher profit rates in the eurozone periphery also attracted capital from the eurozone core, which helped to finance their current account deficits. Under the monetary union, therefore, periphery countries have been the victims of their own success.[6] Another perspective accentuates the domestic demand boom in the periphery prompted by financialization and the economic convergence expectations that were driven with the introduction of euro (Blanchard and Giavazzi 2002; Lane and Pels 2012). The widening gap between investment and saving rates in the eurozone periphery is considered the supporting evidence for this interpretation.

The solution to the above discussed problems, in this view, is not the abolition of the euro but extending the economic and political unification within the eurozone (De Grauwe 2010 and Lane 2012). An optimal currency area can be accomplished (in addition to the monetary policy) via a common fiscal policy.

A more pessimistic variant of the argument suggests that, through the real exchange rate differentials, the structure of the EMU made the eurozone core more competitive at the expense of the eurozone periphery which led to unsustainable current account deficits in the eurozone periphery (Botta 2012). Many authors in this literature argue that the cause of the *eurozone crisis* was the introduction of euro and the only solution is its abolition (Worstall 2015). They argue that one needs to go beyond some proximate causes of the *Eurozone crisis* and focus on the existence of the euro itself as ultimate cause. Worstall (2015) argues, for example, that a single currency is unlikely to work over such diverse economies and even common fiscal policy would not rectify the problems and lead to an optimal currency area. Similarly, Lapavitsas et al. (2012) argue that the *eurozone crisis* is a crisis of competitiveness in an asymmetrical monetary union. In this view, the growing balance-of-payments disequilibrium between the core and periphery has been the main factor behind the crisis. Due to the asymmetrical functioning of the EMU, the core (periphery) experienced large current account surpluses (current account deficits) and capital account deficits (surpluses) since the introduction of the euro.

In another paper (Subasat 2016b) I have argued that the simultaneous implementation of trade and financial sector deregulation often leads to large and persistent current account disequilibrium and subsequent crisis. This is because current account deficits would be impossible if international borrowing is strictly controlled and policies to ensure current account equilibrium would not lead to excessive international borrowing even under financial deregulation. Countries, however, could borrow from international markets to support their current account deficits for an extensive period of time if trade and financial markets are both deregulated. Severe current account disequilibrium and subsequent crises were experienced by many developing countries during the 1980s and 1990s. Similar current account problems began in several developed countries since the late 1990s and were aggravated by a number of conjunctural factors. First, following several severe financial crises (especially the Asian crisis in 1997), many developing countries (such as Thailand, Indonesia, South Korea and Argentina) pursued policies to acquire current account surpluses and large reserves as a precaution. Second, the oil exporting countries experienced large current account surpluses due to the rapid increase in oil prices since 1998. Third, the People's Republic of China experienced large current account surpluses particularly after its accession to the World Trade Organization in 2001. Finally, Germany pursued mercantilist policies (Weeks 2014) that led to large current account surpluses. These current account surpluses increased the global liquidity and triggered current account deficits mainly in several developed countries some of which were the eurozone countries. As historical experiences reveal, large and persistent current account deficits often create bubble economies, which are destined to collapse.

While the financial crises were experienced by many countries, therefore were not specific to the eurozone, whether the introduction of euro aggravated the problems in the eurozone is a matter of empirical investigation, which will be done in the following section.

Is there a eurozone crisis?

The above theoretical arguments (with the exception of Subasat 2016b) suggest that the introduction of the euro (directly or indirectly) played an important role in the current account deficits and crisis of the eurozone periphery. This is understandably so as the *eurozone crisis* would be meaningless unless a central role in the crisis is given to the euro. In this part, I will argue that the introduction of the euro played no role in the current account disequilibrium, bubbles and subsequent crises in the eurozone countries. The *eurozone crisis*, therefore, does not make analytical sense. The stylized facts associated with the eurozone imbalances do not provide sufficient evidence to disentangle these interpretations. The eurozone countries are a part of a wider current account disequilibrium crisis and there is no crisis specific to the eurozone. There are four reasons to doubt the validity of the *eurozone crisis.*

First, the empirical work by Diaz-Sanchez and Varoudakis (2013) assessed the relative contribution of key factors often associated with external imbalances and concluded that the current account disequilibrium in the eurozone periphery was largely caused by a domestic demand boom triggered by greater financial inflows. While the real interest rate and real GDP growth played an important role, real exchange rate and unit labour cost played a negligible role which implies that the introduction of the euro was not an important factor behind the current account disequilibrium experienced by the eurozone periphery.

Second, the experiences of the eurozone countries regarding current account disequilibrium have been diverse and no clear pattern emerges. Although the eurozone periphery experienced current account deteriorations (Figure 4.1A), whether this is unique to them and caused by the introduction of the euro is questionable. The newcomers into the eurozone such as Slovenia (2007), Cyprus (2008), Malta (2008), the Slovak Republic (2009), Estonia (2011), Latvia (2014) and Lithuania (2015) also experienced deterioration in their current accounts before they entered into the eurozone. (See Figure 4.1B for a selection of these countries.) The adoption of the euro, therefore, cannot be held responsible for the current account problems of these countries. Moreover, the other transition countries (Bulgaria, Croatia, the Czech Republic, Hungary, Poland and Romania) that joined the EU but not the eurozone also experienced similar current account problems. (See Figure 4.1C for a selection of these countries.) This implies that the EU periphery experienced deterioration in their current accounts regardless of their membership of the eurozone.

The issue is equally confusing for the eurozone core countries. Although Austria, Germany and the Netherlands (Figure 4.1D) have experienced significant improvements in their current account balances since 2000, Belgium, Finland, France, Italy and Luxembourg (Figure 4.1E) experienced deteriorations, which contradicts the eurozone core and periphery dichotomy. It is important to note that, these countries did not suffer from large current account deficits before the 2008 crisis (in fact most had significant current account surpluses) but their surpluses declined significantly towards 2008 and became deficits for Italy, France and Belgium. These eurozone core countries, therefore, were not immune to the deterioration of current accounts and they cannot be held responsible for the rapid increase in the current account deficits of the eurozone periphery.

Moreover, Denmark and Sweden are not in the eurozone but have experienced improvements in their current account balances whereas the United Kingdom experienced deterioration (Figure 4.1F). Norway and Switzerland are not in the EU and experienced improvements but Iceland experienced deterioration (Figure 4.1G). Finally, similar trends are observed in other parts of the world. Jamaica, South Africa, Turkey and, most notoriously, the USA experienced rapid increases in their current account deficits since the late 1990s (Figure 4.1H).

The above findings imply that there is no reason to assume that the current account deficits of the eurozone periphery were caused by their membership of the eurozone. Similar current account disequilibrium is observed in eurozone core and non-eurozone countries. Both the eurozone core and periphery dichotomy and *eurozone crisis*, therefore, is problematic.

Third, trade disequilibrium is not the only source of current account disequilibrium in the eurozone periphery. The other components of the current account balance, namely Income Balance (interests, dividends and profits) and Unilateral Transfers (gifts, aid and remittances), which are not directly

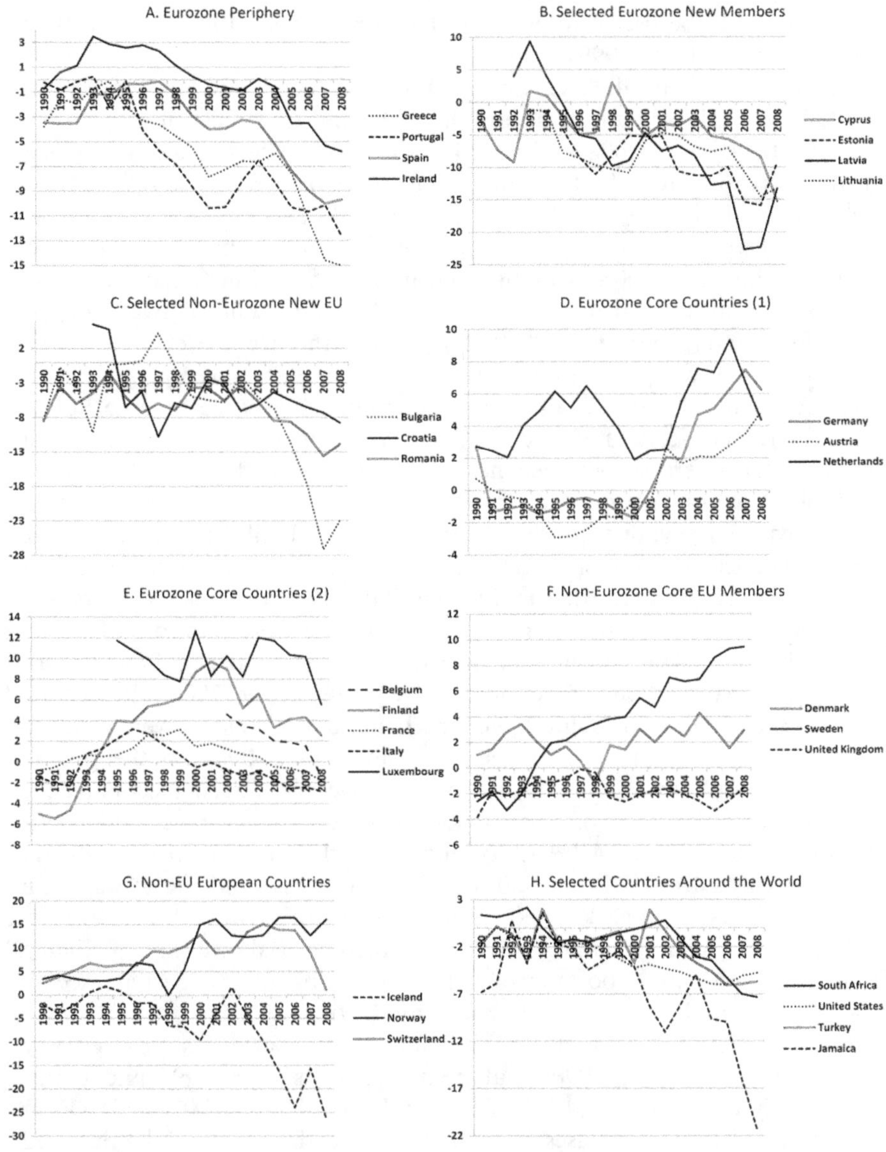

Figure 4.1 Current account balances in selected countries
Source: World Bank, World Development Indicators.

influenced by the introduction of the euro, played a significant role in the eurozone periphery. The eurozone periphery has experienced Income Balance deficits during the entire period under investigation (1990–2011) and were augmented during the 2000s. Initially the net Unilateral Transfers were generally positive but they gradually declined and became negative. To identify the causes of the deterioration in current account balances during the euro period[7] it would be useful to compare the euro period (1999–2008) with the pre-euro period (1990–1999).

For Greece (Figure 4.22A), for example, the Income Balance deficit was 1.3% of the GDP on average during the 1990s but from 2000 it progressively increased to 4.7% in 2008 and was 4.1% in 2011. The Unilateral Transfers surplus increased from 5.1% of the GDP in 1990 to 6.3% in 1993 and has progressively declined since then to 1.2% in 2008 and to 0.3% in 2011. The trade deficit to GDP ratio was large for the entire period but it increased only slightly during the 2000s. Although the trade deficit declined from 9.9% in 2000 to 5.5% in 2004, it increased again to 11.6% in 2008. Between the pre-euro (1990–2001)[8] and euro (2002–08) periods, the average current account deficit increased from 3.5% to 9.7% (a 6.2% increase), the average trade deficit increased from 7.2% to 8.5% (a 1.3% increase), the average Income Balance deficit increased from 1.3% to 2.6% (a 1.3% increase) and the average Unilateral Transfers surplus declined from 5.0% to 1.9% (a 3.1% decline—see Table 4.1). In Greece, therefore, the worsening of the current account balance was largely due to the deterioration of Unilateral Transfers and Income Balance whereas the deterioration of trade played a minor role.[9]

For Spain (Figure 4.2B), the Income Balance and Unilateral Transfers played a lesser but still a significant role in the deterioration of current account balance. The Income Balance deficit was small (1.1% on average) during the 1990s but increased progressively during the 2000s. It increased from 1.3% in 2003 to 3.3% in 2008. The Unilateral Transfers were small but positive until 2002 and became negative since then. Between the pre-euro (1990–1999) and euro (2000–08) periods the average current account deficit increased from 1.8% to 6.2% (a 4.4% increase), the average trade deficit increased from 1.1% to 4.1% (3.0% increase), the average Income Balance deficit increased from 1.1% to 2.0% (a 0.9% increase) and the average Unilateral Transfers surplus declined from 0.4% to −0.2% (a 0.6% decline—see Table4.1). In Spain, therefore, although Income Balance and Unilateral Transfers played an important role, the worsening of the current account balance was mainly due to the deterioration of trade.[10]

Portugal (Figure 4.2C) had small Income Balance surpluses for a few years at the beginning of the 1990s that became deficits since 1994 and became progressively larger. It was 4.6% of the GDP in 2008 and 5.0% in 2011. The Unilateral Transfers surpluses were high during the 1990s (7.4% in 1992). Although remained positive, they declined substantially starting from 1995 (1.4% in 2008). Trade deficit to GDP ratio remained large for the entire period but it did not increase noticeably during the 2000s. Between the pre-euro (1990–99) and euro (2000–08) periods, the average current account deficit increased from 2.9% to 9.7 percent (a 6.8% increase), the average trade deficit increased from 7.8% to 8.8% (1.0% increase), the average Income Balance deficit increased from 0.4% to 2.9% (2.5% increase) and the average Unilateral Transfers surplus declined from 5.3% to 2.0% (3.3% decline—see Table 4.1). In Portugal, therefore, the worsening of the current account

(a)

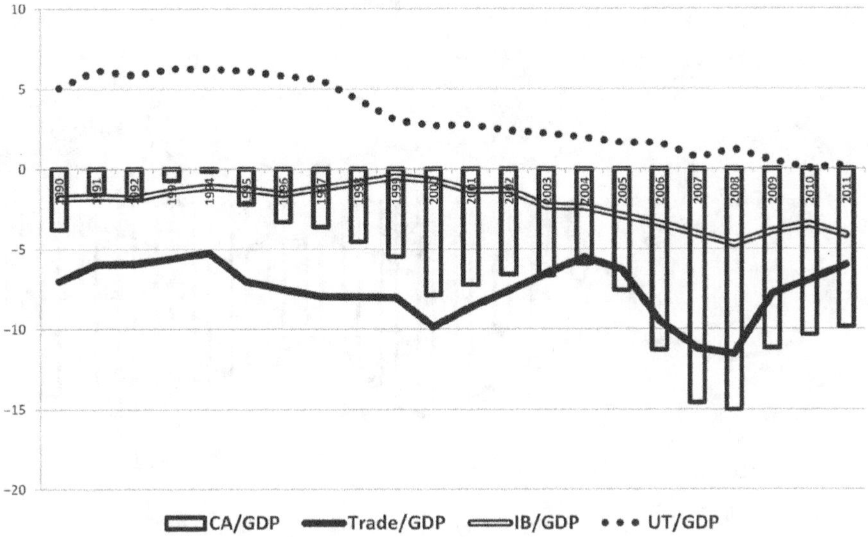

(b)

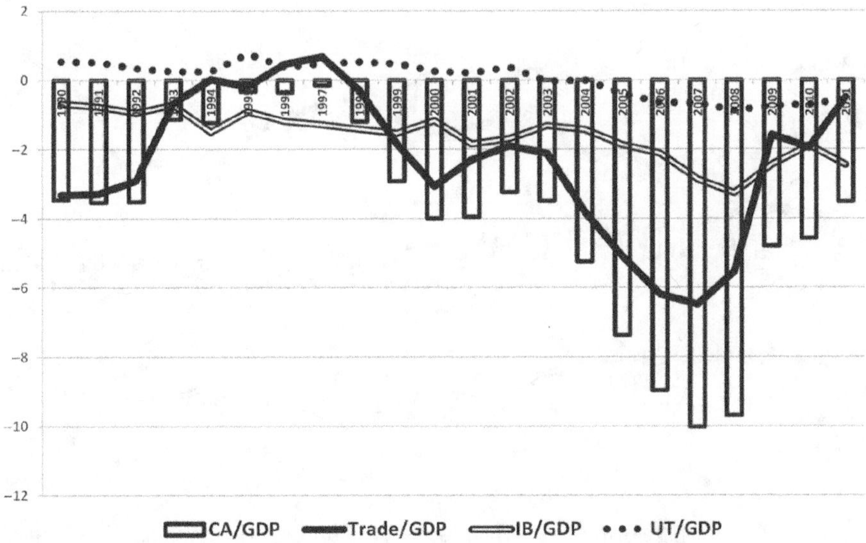

Figure 4.2 The components of the current account balance in the Eurozone Periphery
Note: CA/GDP is the current account balance to GDP ratio, Trade/GDP is the trade balance to GDP ratio, IB/GDP Income Balance to GDP ratio and UT/GDP is the Unilateral Transfers to GDP ratio.
Source: World Bank, World Development Indicators.

(c)

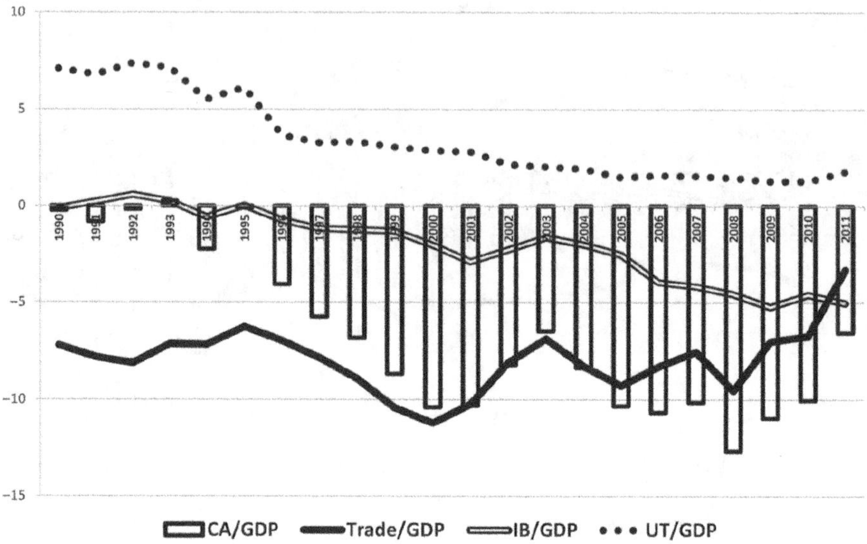

(d)

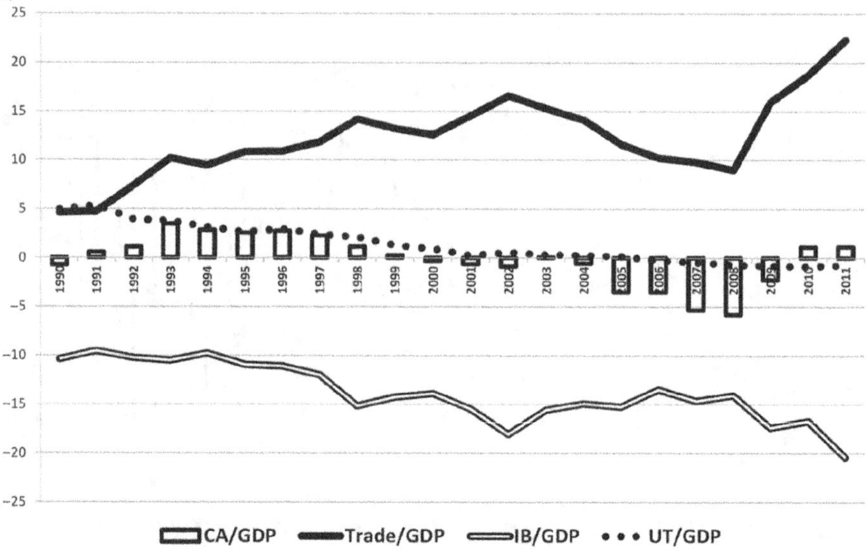

Figure 4.2 (continued)

Table 4.1 The determinants of the current account disequilibrium in the Eurozone periphery

	Greece			*Spain*			*Portugal*			*Ireland*		
	1990–2001	*2002–08*	*Dif*	*1990–99*	*2000–08*	*Dif*	*1990–99*	*2000–08*	*Dif*	*1990–99*	*2000–08*	*Dif*
CA/GDP	–3.5	–9.7	–6.2	–1.8	–6.2	–4.4	–2.9	–9.7	–6.8	1.6	–2.3	–3.9
Trade/GDP	–7.2	–8.5	–1.3	–1.1	–4.1	–3.0	–7.8	–8.8	–1.0	9.7	12.6	2.9
IB/GDP	–1.3	–2.6	–1.3	–1.1	–2.0	–0.9	–0.4	–2.9	–2.5	–11.4	–15.0	–3.6
UT/GDP	5.0	1.9	–3.1	0.4	–0.2	–0.6	5.3	2.0	–3.3	3.3	0.1	–3.2

Source: World Bank, World Development Indicators.

Note: Average figures for the pre-euro (1990–99) and euro (2000–08) periods. CA/GDP is the current account balance to GDP ratio, Trade/GDP is the trade balance to GDP ratio, IB/GDP Income Balance to GDP ratio and UT/GDP is the Unilateral Transfers to GDP ratio.

balance was due to the deterioration of Income Balance and Unilateral Transfers whereas the deterioration of trade played a minor role.[11]

Ireland (Figure 4.2D) had very large Income Balance deficits during the entire period and they became progressively larger. It was 10.4% of the GDP in 1990, 14.1% in 2008 and 20.4% in 2011. Unilateral Transfers surpluses were relatively large during the early 1990s (5.4% in 1991) but progressively declined and became a deficit since 2006. Ireland had very large trade surpluses during the entire period. Between the pre-euro (1990–99) and euro (2000–08) periods the small average current account surplus declined from 1.6% to −2.3% (a 3.9% decline). The average trade surplus increased from 9.7% to 12.6% (a 2.9% increase), the average Income Balance deficit increased from 11.4% to 15.0% (3.6% increase) and the average Unilateral Transfers surplus declined from 3.3% to 0.1% (a 3.2%decline—see Table 4.1). In Ireland, therefore, the worsening of the current account balance was due to the deterioration of Income Balance and Unilateral Transfers whereas trade balance improved.

The above details imply that the worsening of trade balance played a significant role only in Spain, a negligible role in Greece and Portugal and no role in Ireland. This does not mean that trade deficits were small in Greece and Portugal but means that factors other than trade played the main role in the deterioration of the current account balances. These results already cast doubts on the role of euro over the trade and current account disequilibrium in the eurozone periphery but the role of euro (particularly for Spain) could further be investigated by examining the bilateral trade flows between the eurozone core and periphery, which will be done below.

Fourth, the bilateral trade figures (retrieved from the International Trade Centre—ITC) suggest that the eurozone core played no significant role in the trade deficits of the eurozone periphery. This is important because it is very often suggested that the current account deficits of the eurozone periphery are directly caused by their trade deficits against the eurozone core, particularly Germany (Hobza and Zeugner 2013). The French Minister of Finance, Christine Lagarde, for example, suggested that Germany's excessive exports and inadequate imports created problems for the eurozone countries (Poplawski 2013). The same point has been made by Lapavitsas et al. (2012: 2) who argued that '[t]he main source of growth for Germany has been its current account surplus inside the Eurozone'. These arguments can be tested by considering the bilateral trade figures between the eurozone core and periphery.

The developments in trade links between the eurozone core and the periphery do not support the *eurozone crisis* arguments. First, the trade deficits of the eurozone periphery generally increased faster against the rest of the world than the eurozone core. China, Russia and a few other countries played a significant role in this increase. Second, even when the trade deficits increased against the eurozone core increased faster, the eurozone periphery still had large trade deficits against the rest of the world. Third, even when the trade deficits increased faster against the eurozone core, this was often due to a decline in exports to the core rather than an increase in imports, which is inconsistent with the *eurozone crisis* thesis. Membership of the eurozone, therefore, is irrelevant to the aggravated trade deficits in the eurozone periphery.

To substantiate these arguments, this section investigates the influence of the eurozone core on the trade disequilibrium of the eurozone periphery using bilateral trade statistics to reveal whether the increase in trade deficits of the periphery (Greece, Spain, Portugal and Ireland) was due to their trade deficits against the eurozone core (Austria, Belgium, Finland, France, Germany, Italy, Luxembourg and the Netherlands). The role of Austria, Germany and the Netherlands will be investigated separately from the rest of the core since only these core countries experienced significant improvements in their current account surpluses. The other eurozone core countries either experienced a decline in their current account surpluses or experienced deficits.

The total trade defici of Greece increased from US $18,000m. in 2001 to $63,800m. in 2008. The share of Austria, Germany and the Netherlands in the total deficit was 23.7% in 2001, which declined to 19.5% in 2008 (Table 4.2). The same figures for the other eurozone core countries were 27.7% and 23.1%, respectively, and for the rest of the world 48.6% and 57.3%, respectively. In other words, Greece's trade deficit increased faster against the rest of the world than the core countries. China and Russia (and a few other countries such as Libya, Iran, Turkey and India) played an important role in this increase. The share of China increased from 4.4% to 7.5% and that of Russia increased from 7.2% to 9.3%. These figures imply that Greece would have a radical increase in its trade deficit regardless of its euro membership.

The total trade deficits of Spain increased from US $38,800m. in 2001 to $139,500m. in 2008. The share of Austria, Germany and the Netherlands in the total deficit was 33.0% in 2001, which declined to 27.0% in 2008. The same figures for the other eurozone core countries were 25.2% and 7.3%, respectively, and for the rest of the world 41.9% and 65.8%, respectively. In other words, Spain's trade deficit increased faster against the rest of the world than the core countries. China and Russia (and a few other countries such as Portugal, Egypt, Mexico and the UK) played an important role in this increase. The share of China increased from 10.2% to 19.4% and Russia increased from 3.0% to 5.7%. Interestingly, Spain experienced the fastest improvements in its trade balance against France (an 8.4% deficit became a 3.1% surplus) and Germany (a 26.5% deficit declined to a 20.8% deficit). These figures imply that Spain would still have a radical increase in its trade and current account deficits regardless of its euro membership.

The total trade deficits of Portugal increased from US $15,400m. in 2001 to $34,200m. in 2008. The share of Austria, Germany and the Netherlands in the total deficit was 12.4% in 2001, which increased to 17.7% in 2008. The same figures for the other eurozone core countries were 17.4% and 14.2%, respectively, and for the rest of the world 70.2% and 68.1%, respectively. In

Table 4.2 The share of the eurozone core countries in the trade deficits of the eurozone periphery

	Greece			*Spain*			*Portugal*			*Ireland*		
	2001	*2008*	*Dif.*	*2001*	*2008*	*Dif.*	*2001*	*2008*	*Dif.*	*2001*	*2008*	*Dif.*
AGN	23.7	19.5	–4.2	33.0	27.0	–6.0	12.4	17.7	5.3	30.6	6.2	–24.4
OEC	27.7	23.1	–4.6	25.2	7.3	–17.9	17.4	14.2	–3.2	24.2	53.5	29.3
Core total	51.4	42.7	–8.7	58.1	34.2	–23.9	29.8	31.9	2.1	54.9	59.6	4.7
RoW	48.6	57.3	8.7	41.9	65.8	23.9	70.2	68.1	–2.1	45.1	40.4	–4.7

Source: ITC, International trade statistics database.

Note: Positive numbers for 2001 and 2008 indicate trade deficits for Greece, Spain and Portugal and trade surpluses for Ireland. To calculate these figures, the total trade deficits (surpluses for Ireland) and trade deficits against the core countries were calculated separately for each periphery country. Then the share of the core countries in the total trade deficit was determined. For example, the total trade deficit of Greece in 2001 was US $18,000m. and its total trade deficit against Austria ($160m.), Germany ($2,780m.) and the Netherlands ($1,340m.) was $4,270m.. The share of Austria, Germany and the Netherlands in the total trade deficit of Greece, therefore, was 23,7%.

other words, Portugal's trade deficit increased faster against Austria, Germany and the Netherlands than the other eurozone core countries and the rest of the world. China and Libya also played an important role in this increase. The share of China increased from 1.7% to 5.0% and Libya's share increased from 0.4% to 4.2%. The increase in trade deficit with Austria, Germany and the Netherlands requires further investigation. The *eurozone crisis* thesis argues that the eurozone membership hampered the competitiveness of the eurozone periphery, and reduced their exports to and increased their imports from the eurozone core. In the case of Portugal, however, the share of Austria, Germany and the Netherlands in both exports and imports declined radically but the decline in exports exceeded imports, which caused the trade deficit. For example, the share of imports from Austria, Germany and the Netherlands was 19.3% (13.8% for Germany) in 2001, which declined to 16.4% (11.5% for Germany) in 2008. However, the share of exports to the core also declined from 23.7% (19.0% for Germany) in 2001 to 15.6% (12.3% for Germany) in 2008, which caused the trade deficit. The same figures for the other eurozone core countries were 23.1% and 17.4% for exports, and 20.9% and 16.2% for imports. The above figures imply first that Portugal would still have a radical increase in its trade and current account deficits regardless of the euro membership and also that the increase in trade deficit against the core was not due to an increase in imports but due to a faster decline in exports, which is inconsistent with the *eurozone crisis* thesis.

Ireland had large trade surpluses during the entire period. The total trade surplus of Ireland increased from US $31,600m. in 2001 to $42,200m. in 2008. The share of Austria, Germany and the Netherlands in the total trade surplus was 30.6% (for Germany 23.3%) in 2001, which declined to 6.2% (for Germany 5.0%) in 2008. The same figures for the other eurozone core countries were 24.2% and 53.5%, respectively, and for the rest of the world 45.1% and 40.4%, respectively. In other words, Ireland's trade surplus increased faster against the other eurozone core countries than Austria, Germany, the Netherlands and the rest of the world. China and the UK also played an important role. Ireland had a trade deficit against China that increased from 5.4% to 11.9%. The trade balance surplus of 5.4% against the UK became a deficit of −11.9%. Austria, Germany and the Netherlands played a significant role in the decline in trade surplus. The same cannot be said for the entire core countries since the trade balance surplus actually increased.

To recap the third and fourth arguments above (Table 4.3), for the *eurozone crisis* thesis to be accurate, trade must be the main source of current account disequilibrium and the eurozone core must play a significant role in the deterioration of trade balance in the eurozone periphery. The evidence provided above lends no support for the *eurozone crisis* thesis. For Greece, the worsening of trade was not the main source of current account deterioration and the eurozone core played no significant role in the deterioration of the trade. For Spain, although the worsening of trade was the main source of current account deterioration, the eurozone core played no significant role in the

Table 4.3 Recap—Any support for the *eurozone crisis* thesis?

	Greece	*Spain*	*Portugal*	*Ireland*
Was trade the main source of current account disequilibrium in the eurozone periphery?	No	Yes	No	No
Did the eurozone core play a significant role in the deterioration of trade in the eurozone periphery?	No	No	Yes (?)	Yes (?)

deterioration of the trade. For Portugal, trade was not the main source of current account disequilibrium. The eurozone core played an ambiguous role in the deterioration of trade since it was not due to an increase in imports from and decline in exports to the eurozone core but a sharper decline in exports than imports, which is inconsistent with the *eurozone crisis* thesis. For Ireland, although trade surplus radically declined against Austria, Germany and the Netherlands between 2001 and 2008, the trade surplus actually increased and the current account deficits were caused by the deterioration in the Income Balance and Unilateral Transfers. None of the eurozone periphery countries, therefore, provide evidence for the *eurozone crisis* thesis.

Conclusion

This paper argues that, unlike the common perceptions, there is no evidence to support the *eurozone crisis* thesis and the eurozone countries are a part of a wider current account crisis. The Asian crisis of 1997 (which fortified many countries to acquire large reserves), the rapid increase in oil prices since 1998, China's accession to the World Trade Organization in 2001 and Germany's mercantilist policies increased the global liquidity during the 2000s and caused current account deficits in many countries including the eurozone countries. The large and persistent current account deficits created bubble economies, which unsurprisingly collapsed in 2008.

There are several reasons to doubt the *eurozone crisis* thesis. First, the current account experiences of the eurozone countries do not establish a clear pattern regarding the core and periphery dichotomy since many of the eurozone core and non-eurozone countries also experienced acute current account problems. There is nothing, therefore, specific to the eurozone countries.

Second, the introduction of the euro would impact the current account balances of the eurozone countries through its impact on trade balances but trade is not the only source of current account problems. Indeed, amongst the eurozone periphery, only in Spain was trade the main cause of current account problems. In Greece and Portugal, the Income Payments and Unilateral Transfers were the main causes and trade played a negligible role. In Ireland, the worsening of the current account balance was due to the deterioration of Income Balance and Unilateral Transfers whereas trade balance improved.

Third, the bilateral trade figures confirm that the trade deficits of the eurozone periphery were not mainly caused by their trade with the eurozone core. The trade deficits of Greece and Spain increased faster against the rest of the world than the eurozone core. Although Portugal's trade deficit increased faster against the eurozone core, this was due to the decline in exports to the core rather than increase in imports, which is inconsistent with the *eurozone crisis* thesis. Portugal also had sizeable trade deficits against the rest of the world, which suggests that it would have a pervasive increase in its trade deficit regardless of its euro membership. Although Ireland had a radical decline in its trade surplus against Austria, Germany and the Netherlands, it increased its overall trade surplus and improved its trade surplus against the eurozone core countries. Membership of the eurozone, therefore, is irrelevant to the trade and current account deficits in the eurozone periphery and their subsequent crisis.

The *eurozone crisis* thesis implies a crisis specific to eurozone countries instigated by the introduction of the euro. This paper found no evidence to support this thesis. Since there is no evidence to tie the current account problems of the eurozone periphery to their membership of the eurozone, *a crisis in the eurozone* makes analytical sense but a *eurozone crisis* does not.

Notes

1 The core often refers to Germany, France, Belgium and the Netherlands; and the periphery refers to Greece, Ireland, Portugal and Spain. Ireland has a higher per caput gross domestic product (GDP) than many core countries today. Considering Ireland as a periphery country, therefore, is somewhat erroneous.
2 The introduction of euro may not be the underlying cause of the current account problems in the eurozone but exiting it may well contribute to the solution.
3 A good examination of the debates over the causes of financial crisis can be found in Subasat (2016a). See also Brenner (2006) for an interesting debate where the focus is on debt-and-consumption driven growth (asset price Keynesianism).
4 A good discussion of the alternative approaches can be found in Mavroudeas (2016).
5 While Lapavitsas et al. (2012) focused on financialisation, it played a secondary and ambiguous role in their story as the main focus was on the current account disequilibrium.
6 As I argued in another paper (Subasat 2016b), however, this argument is only accurate under very restrictive assumptions, which fail to account for increased export competitiveness due to rapid productivity increase.
7 From the introduction of euro in 1999 to the 2008 crisis.
8 Greece adopted the Euro in 2001.
9 Of the increase in the current account deficit, 50.8% could be explained by Unilateral Transfers, 21.3% could be explained by Income Balance and 21.3% could be explained by trade.
10 Of the increase in the current account deficit, 65.9% could be explained by trade, 20.5% could be explained by Income Balance and 15.9% could be explained by Unilateral Transfers.
11 Of the increase in the current account deficit, 50.7% could be explained by Unilateral Transfers, 36.2% could be explained by Income Balance and 14.5% could be explained by trade.

References

Beck, T. and Peydró, J.-L. (2015), 'Five years of crisis (resolution) – some lessons', available at www.voxeu.org/article/five-years-crisis-resolution-some-lessons.

Biroli, P., Mourre, G. and Turrini, A. (2010), 'Adjustment in the euro area and regulation of product and labour markets: an empirical assessment', London: Centre for Economic Policy Research, Discussion Paper no. 8010.

Blanchard, O. (2006), 'Current Account Deficits in Rich Countries', Paper presented at the 7th Jacques Polak Annual Research Conference Hosted by the International Monetary Fund Washington, DC, November 9–10, available at www.imf.org/external/np/res/seminars/2006/arc/pdf/blan.pdf.

Blanchard, O. and Giavazzi, F. (2002), 'Current Account Deficits in the euro Area: The End of the Feldstein-Horioka Puzzle?', Washington, DC: Brookings Institution Press, *Brookings Papers on Economic Activity*, 2: 147–186.

Botta, A. (2012), 'Conflicting Claims in the Eurozone? Austerity's Myopic Logic and the Need for a European Federal Union in a Post-Keynesian Eurozone Center–Periphery Model', New York: Levy Economics Institute, *Working Paper* no.740.

Brenner, R. (2006), *The Economics of Global Turbulence: The Advanced Capitalist Economies from Long Boom to Long Downturn, 1945–2005*, New York: Verso.

Comunale, M. and Hessel, J. (2014), 'Current account imbalances in the Euro area: Competitiveness or financial cycle?', Amsterdam: Netherlands Central Bank, Working Paper no. 443.

De Grauwe, P. (2010), 'How to embed the Eurozone in a political union', *Centre for Economic Policy Research's Policy Portal*, available at www.voxeu.org/article/eurozone-needs-political-union-or-least-elements-one.

Diaz-Sanchez, J.L. and Varoudakis, A. (2013), 'Growth and competitiveness as factors of Eurozone external imbalances: Evidence and policy implications', Washington, DC: World Bank, *Policy Research Working Paper* no. 6732.

Draghi, M. (2012), 'Competitiveness of the Eurozone and within the Eurozone', Speech at the colloquium 'Les défis de la compétitivité', Paris, 13 March, in Diaz-Sanchez, J.L. and Varoudakis, A. (2014), 'Tracking the causes of Eurozone external imbalances: New evidence', Centre for Economic Policy Research's Policy Portal, available at www.voxeu.org/article/causes-eurozone-external-imbalances.

Epstein, G. (2005), 'Introduction: Financialization and the World Economy' in Epstein, G. (ed.), *Financialization and the World Economy*, Cheltenham and Northampton, MA: Edward Elgar.

Feldstein, M. (2010), 'Let Greece take a holiday from the Eurozone', in *Financial Times*, 17 February.

Gaulier, G., Taglioni, D. and Vicard, V. (2012), 'Tradable sectors in Eurozone periphery countries did not underperform in the 2000s', *Centre for Economic Policy Research's Policy Portal*, available at www.voxeu.org/article/tradable-sectors-eurozone-periphery.

Hobza, A. and Zeugner, S. (2013), 'Current-account surpluses in the Eurozone: Should they be reduced?', *Centre for Economic Policy Research's Policy Portal*, available at www.voxeu.org/article/should-eurozone-current-account-surpluses-be-reduced.

International Trade Centre (2015), International trade statistics database, available at www.intracen.org/itc/market-info-tools/trade-statistics/.

Jaumotte, F. and Morsy, H. (2012), 'Determinants of Inflation in the Euro Area: The Role of Labor and Product Market Institutions', Washington, DC: International Monetary Fund, Working Paper no. 12/37.

Jaumotte, F. and Sodsriwiboom, P. (2010), 'Current Account imbalances in the Southern Euro area', Washington, DC: International Monetary Fund, *Working Paper* no. 10/139.

Krugman, P. (2012), *End This Depression Now*, New York: W.W. Norton & Co.

Krugman, P. (2013), 'The Harm Germany Does, The New York Times', (1 November), available at http://krugman.blogs.nytimes.com/2013/11/01/the-harm-germany-does/?_r=0.

Lane, P. (2012), 'The European Sovereign Debt Crisis', *Journal of Economic Perspectives*, 26(3).

Lane, P.R. and Pels, B. (2012), 'Current Account Imbalances in Europe', Dublin: Institute for International Integration Studies, Discussion Paper no. 397, available at https://www.tcd.ie/iiis/documents/discussion/pdfs/iiisdp397.pdf.

Lapavitsas, C. (2011), 'Theorising Financialization', *Work, Employment and Society*, Vol. 25(4): 611–626.

Lapavitsas, C. *et al.* (2012), *Crisis in the Eurozone*, Verso: London.

Mavroudeas, S.D. (2016), 'The Greek crisis: structural or conjunctural', in Subasat, T. (ed.), *The Great Financial Meltdown: Systemic, Conjunctural or Policy-Created*, Cheltenham and Northampton, MA: Edward Elgar.

Mavroudeas, S.D. and Paitaridis, D. (2014), 'The Greek crisis: a dual crisis of over-accumulation and imperialist exploitation', in Mavroudeas, S. (ed.), *Greek Capitalism in Crisis: Marxist analysis*, New York: Routledge.

Milesi-Ferretti, G.M. and Razin, A. (1996), 'Sustainability of persistent current account deficits', Cambridge, MA: National Bureau of Economic Research, *Working Paper* no. 5467.

Milios, J. and Sotiropoulos, D. (2010), 'Crisis of Greece or crisis of the euro? A view from the European periphery', *Journal of Balkan and Near Eastern Studies*, 12(3).

Poplawski, K. (2013), 'The German Surplus Is Still a Problem for the Euro Area and the World', available at www.ethz.ch/content/specialinterest/gess/cis/center-for-securities-studies/en/services/digital-library/articles/article.html/173816.

Sinn, H.-W. and Valentinyi, A. (2013), 'European imbalances', available at www.voxeu.org/article/european-imbalances.

Subasat, T. (2016a) (ed.), *The Great Financial Meltdown: Systemic, Conjunctural or Policy-Created*, Cheltenham and Northampton, MA: Edward Elgar.

Subasat, T. (2016b), 'Policy-based and conjunctural causes of the 2008 crisis', in Subasat, T. (ed), *The Great Financial Meltdown: Systemic, Conjunctural or Policy-Created*, Cheltenham and Northampton, MA: Edward Elgar.

Trichet, J.-C. (2011), 'Competitiveness and the smooth functioning of EMU', Lecture at the University of Liège, 23 February, available at www.ecb.europa.eu/press/key/date/2011/html/sp110223.en.html.

Uxó, J., Paúl, J. and Febrero, E. (2011), 'Current Account Imbalances in the Monetary Union and the Great Recession: Causes and Policies', *Panoeconomicus*, 5, Special Issue: 571–592.

Weeks, J. (2014), *Economics of the 1%. How mainstream economics serves the rich, obscures reality and distort policy*, London: Anthem Press.

Wolff, R.D. (2012), *Capitalism hits the fan: The global economic meltdown and what to do about it*, Chicago, IL: Haymarket Books.

World Bank (2015), World Development Indicators, available at http://data.worldbank.org/data-catalog/world-development-indicators.

Worstall, T. (2015), 'The Cause Of The Eurozone Crisis Was The Euro: The Solution Is Abolition Of The Euro', *Forbes*, available at www.forbes.com/sites/timworstall/2015/09/08/the-cause-of-the-eurozone-crisis-was-the-euro-the-solution-is-abolition-of-the-euro/#71d942a3686e.

5 Competing Explanations and Strategies for the Greek Crisis and the Question of the Productive Model

Stavros Mavroudeas

Introduction

The Greek crisis that erupted in 2009 is part of the 2007–08 global capitalist crisis. The latter is the first major crisis of the 21st century and, because of its structural nature, it has long-term repercussions. Its structural nature is expressed in the feeble recovery after the crisis, the 'double dip' that followed and the fears for a future return of the recession. Another crucial repercussion is the eruption of several regional crises of which the crisis of the eurozone (with Greece at its centre) is the most significant.

The Greek crisis was expressed as a debt crisis (that is a disequilibrium in the sphere of circulation) although, as this paper will argue, its causes are deeper and lay in the sphere of production. In any case, and irrespective of different explanations, it is nowadays unquestionable that this crisis goes hand in hand with destructive processes in the sphere of production. It is evident that the current Greek productive model—with the shrinkage of the primary sector, the growing deindustrialization and the bubble of services—has failed and it is not sustainable. Thus, all competing strategies for surpassing the crisis have offered proposals about restructuring the Greek production model. Notwithstanding, these proposals differ widely as they represent different understandings of the Greek crisis and they reflect different socio-economic interests. In each of these strategies productive restructuring holds a different role. For example, those explanations that consider the Greek case simply as a debt crisis, that is a crisis in the sphere of circulation alone that only subsequently affected the sphere of production, attribute to productive restructuring a secondary role behind the primary role of securing debt viability. They, more or less, purport that if the latter is solved then productive restructuring would follow suit. On the contrary, if the causes of the crisis are posited in the sphere of production, as Marxist approaches that focus on the tendency of the rate of profit to fall maintain, then productive restructuring assumes the primary role.

The next section presents the main competing explanations of the Greek crisis and how they confront the problem of the productive model. The third section analyses the strategies that emanate from them the strategies and what role has productive restructuring within them. Its last sub-section acts as conclusions by proposing a strategy of disengagement from the European Union (EU).

Competing explanations of the Greek crisis

In Mavroudeas (2015c) explanations of the Greek crisis were classified into three major theoretical trends: (a) Mainstream or Orthodox, (b) Heterodox, and (c) Marxist.

Orthodoxy is the dominant stream within state institutions and universities. Unlike journalistic parlance, it is not purely neoliberal. Neoliberalism is a good ideological tool for the ruling class but an extremely ineffective tool for economic policy because of its unrealistic assumptions (e.g. perfect information, rational expectations). Thus, Mainstream is currently dominated by a more down-to-the-earth mix of soft neoliberal approaches and New Keynesianism (a highly conservative version) branded as Macroeconomics of the New Consensus (Arestis 2009).

Heterodoxy is composed of currents that share most of the fundamental analytical and methodological framework of Orthodoxy but question some critical assumptions (e.g. perfect markets). Today, its main body is made up of post-Keynesianism (a radical version of its parent current) and of Radical Political Economy (various mixes of neo-Marxist and post-Keynesianism).

Marxist Political Economy is a radically different approach, differing methodologically and analytically from the two previous trends. What differentiates it even from Marxisant Heterodox streams is its emphasis on the specific Marxist analytical (e.g. Labour Value Theory, centrality of profitability) as opposed to selective and eclectic references to Marxism.

Mainstream explanations

Orthodoxy has an extremely weak crisis theory precisely because it is based on the belief that capitalism—both in the long- and the short-term—is a perfect system. Thus, all markets (labour, products, money, etc.) are balanced (i.e. supply equals demand) more or less automatically and endogenously. Imbalances (i.e. crises) arise only from external factors or if some economic agents behave irregularly. So, imbalances (because even the word ‘crisis’ is avoided) do not arise from endogenous and therefore structural causes of the system but from conjuncture. This thesis is problematic. Firstly, it cannot explain why crises are a recurring phenomenon. Secondly, it does not help to deal with them as it implies that if ‘irregular’ behaviours appear then the market will eliminate them on its own. Thus, economic policy is almost redundant. In order to overcome this deficiency, Orthodoxy resorts to stratagems. Thus, the New Macroeconomic Consensus recognizes in the short-term the potential for imbalances and therefore some discrete policies, while in the long-term it accepts the natural tendency for balance. In addition, Orthodoxy focuses mainly on the sphere of exchange and neglects a serious analysis of the sphere of production (which is the primary one according to the Classical and the Marxist Political Economy). It therefore seeks to interpret almost all phenomena as market processes.

Mainstream interpretations of the Greek crisis follow the general path. They attribute it not to structural problems but to short-term policy errors. Consequently, they consider it simply a debt crisis caused by a high fiscal deficit. Therefore, it is not, at least in principle, related to the failure of the country's productive model (that is, a matter directly related to the sphere of production). They are sub-divided into three streams, with different analytical and political endowments each.

a The first stream regards the Greek case as a special national case: a 'Greek disease'.
b The second stream considers that the 'Greek disease' was exacerbated by the structural weaknesses of the eurozone (i.e. its non-optimal currency area nature) that cannot be corrected.
c The third stream is taking an intermediate position: there is a 'Greek disease' and this has been exacerbated by the eurozone's structural weaknesses, but they can be repaired.

Additionally, all Mainstream interpretations are based on the Twin Deficit Hypothesis (TDH). TDH argues that an exorbitant fiscal deficit (FD) causes a current account deficit (CAD). This is a neo-Keynesian view (in contrast to the neoliberal Ricardian Equivalence Hypothesis) whose empirical validity is highly debatable. For example, Katrakilidis and Trachanas (2011) show that this hypothesis holds for the pre-Economic and Monetary Union (EMU) period (1960–80) but is reversed (the CAD aggravates the FD) in the subsequent period (1981–2007).

The almost unanimous acceptance of TDH has obvious class causes. Thus, the responsibility of the crisis is attributed to the public sector and therefore fiscal austerity is justified. The next step is to attribute FD to wage increases. It is purported that, because of clientelism, excessive wage increases in the public sector that exacerbated FD and in the private sector reduced competitiveness (and therefore the trade deficit—TD). The combined effect was an acute CAD crisis as the country borrowed from abroad and after the 2008 crisis the sustainability of this debt was questioned. The typical Mainstream argument is that Greek nominal unit labour costs (NULCs) grew faster than that those of other EMU members. This explanation is faulty.

1 Competitiveness does not depend only on cost but also on structural factors. Moreover, wages are not the only cost factor. Profit margins are even more significant. Thus, despite reducing wages at around 35%, exports did not increase because (among other reasons) capitalists increased their profit margins.

2 Kaldor's (1978) paradox emphasizes the significance of structural factors by showing that countries with high competitiveness are not low wage ones.
3 Greek wage increases systematically lag behind productivity increases. Thus, the real unit labour costs (RULCs) declined almost continuously for several decades.
4 Wage reduction as a means for improving competitiveness requires that competitors do not resort to a similar policy (that is there is no 'race to the bottom'). If there is—as happens extensively today—then a wages reduction policy is almost useless.

However, Mainstream explanations have also serious analytical deficiencies (Mavroudeas and Paitaridis 2015a). Firstly, they underestimate the role of the 2007–08 global capitalist crisis by considering it simply a financial one and neglecting its deep roots in the production sphere. Secondly, they believe that the Greek crisis is independent of the global crisis. Typically, most international and national studies in 2008 claimed that the Greek economy is immunized against the global crisis. Only later, the global crisis of 2007–08 was added but as a mere exogenous factor: the 2007–08 crisis did not directly concern Greece but it worsened the international environment. Therefore, Orthodox interpretations fail to recognize the fundamental structural dimensions of the Greek problem and instead point to cyclical economic policy errors and institutional features. The first Mainstream sub-current attributes the Greek crisis to national peculiarities that led to erroneous economic policies. The second sub-current considers the EMU a faulty economic institution that produces problematic economic policies. However, the institutional distortion concerns mainly the circulation sphere and geopolitical issues and not at all with the production sphere. The third sub-current attributes the EMU's problematic structure to neoliberalism and its faulty policies; thus, whatever institutional and 'weak' structural problems are recognized they are products of the circulation sphere.

Consequently, there is no recognition in principle of any problem in the productive structure of the Greek economy and therefore the concept of 'productive restructuring' is missing from Mainstream strategies. Besides, accepting the critical role of the failure of Greek productive model of production would put the blame squarely at the hands of the Greek bourgeoisie; something that Mainstream analyses vehemently despise. Only belatedly, and after the systematic failures of Economic Adjustment Programmes (EAPs) devised by the EU-European Central Bank-International Monetary Fund (IMF) troika, there were some limited Mainstream references to Greece's problematic productive model. However, the main problems recognized are entrepreneurial unfriendliness and excessive regulation. No attention is being paid to the problematic sectoral structure of the Greek economy (i.e. widespread de-industrialization, shrinking primary sector and oversized tertiary sector) apart from a vaguely defined need to boost exporting branches. Accordingly, no active industrial policy is proposed.

Heterodox explanations

Heterodox explanations differ from Mainstream ones on the following issues.

1 They do not consider capitalism as a perfect system; hence the possibility of crisis is always present. However, in contrast to older Heterodoxy (and traditional Keynesianism), they attribute the causes of the crisis to middle-range (that is historically conjunctural) institutional factors and policies rather than to systemic features of capitalism, accepting that the capitalist system is not a perfect mechanism but is endogenously prone to crises and disequilibria.
2 They focus their criticism on neoliberalism and especially the EMU's architecture. Nevertheless, they usually leave behind criticisms of capitalism as such and those of them that refer to Marxism do so in a rather eclectic manner and usually in hybrid versions applying instruments from Institutionalism and variants of post-Keynesianism. Consequently, they differ from the Marxist tradition in several crucial issues.

   a) The profit rate, which is the defining Marxist variable, is either completely absent or is a mere appendage playing no substantive part in their analyses. In its place, there is a Keynesian emphasis on the lack of effective demand and on neo-mercantilist international relations.
   b) Their policy proposals avoid any significant reference to socialist transition and merely propose some progressive reforms within the remit of the capitalist system.

There are several Heterodox interpretations of the Greek crisis. They all concur with Mainstream explanations that the Greek crisis is simply a debt crisis (that is without roots in the production sphere and in capital's profitability). They differ regarding the mechanisms of that caused CAD. In Mavroudeas (2015c) they were classified into four sub-currents.

1 Stathakis (2010) argues that CAD is caused by FD, which is attributed to big capital's tax avoidance and middle-classes' tax evasion.
2 Argitis (2012) argues that CAD is caused by a Minskian financial instability mechanism (i.e. a special version of the financialization thesis).
3 Lapavitsas et al. (2010) argue that CAD is caused by the TD and not the FD. TD is attributed to German neo-mercantilist policies, the EMU's problematic nature and the new global form of financialized capitalism.
4 Milios and Sotiropoulos (2010) attribute the debt crisis to class struggle and financialization.

Almost all sub-currents follow the *financialization* thesis. This is a popular post-Keynesian and Radical theory (see Mavroudeas 2015b). It claims, in a nutshell, that modern capitalism muted in a new type of system, since money capital not only dominates other capitalist activities (productive and commercial capital) but also acquires an independent channel of labour exploitation. Hence, its profit derives not only from a redistribution of surplus value expropriated by productive capital from labourers in production, as Marxism argues, but also from the direct exploitation of the latter through usurious practices mainly of the banking sector. Despite its popularity, the financialization thesis rests on problematic analytical and empirical foundations. The view that there is a new financialized capitalism implies either that there are two capitalist classes (in post-Keynesianism) or that there is a new undefined hybrid (in Marxisant versions). Both versions are analytically and empirically unsustainable. Moreover, modelling capitalism as a system based on usury (hence on unequal exchange) is equally erroneous and cannot grasp its inner function that rests on equivalent exchange. Additionally, these theories neglect completely the production sphere and end up as *economics of circulation*, not very different from Mainstream ones. Thus, their monetary theories cannot grasp the intricate relationships that link fictitious capital with production and resort to its complete isolation. Consequently, similarly with Mainstream analyses, they consider the 2007–08 crisis as a mere financial one where the profit rate plays no role. Respectively, they argue that the Greek crisis has nothing to do with declining profitability.

Heterodoxy's wider problems are exacerbated in their Greek analyses. They almost totally neglect Greece's productive structure and reject without consideration the evidence of a profitability crisis. They also neglect that Greece is not a 'financialized' capitalist country, simply because its crucial elements are not there: it was always bank-based (that is, stock exchange and 'shadow banking' do not play any significant role) and household debt is very low compared to that of Western capitalist economies. Therefore, the Greek crisis cannot be attributed to a financial bubble.

Apart from their general deficiencies, each Radical explanation of the Greek crisis has its own errors. Lapavitsas et al. (2010) and Milios and Sotiropoulos (2010) are typical examples.

Lapavitsas et al. (2010) argue that the Greek crisis stems from financialization and the EMU's structural deficiencies: the former triggered the 2007–08 crisis and thus dismantled the weak foundations of the EMU; the latter favours German neo-mercantilist policies that produce trade surpluses at the expense of trade deficits in euro-peripheral economies. In arguing so, Lapavitsas et al. (2010) accept the problematic Mainstream explanation of falling competitiveness (that attributes it to NULCs and wage increase) and simply myopically reverse it: the eurozone crisis was not caused by excessive Greek wage increases but by excessive German wage stagnation. This reverse idol argument is both analytically and politically unsustainable (see Mavroudeas 2015b). Within the eurozone this argument is self-defeating: if Germany does not reverse its wage restraint policy then there is no other solution but the reduction of Greek wages. Of, course, Lapavitsas et al. (2010) argue that Greece has to exit the eurozone in order to rectify its CAD through exchange rate devaluation and import substitution that would remedy its TD. This proposal is also unsustainable as they totally neglect Greece's problematic productive structure (exports dependent upon imports, etc.) and also the inability for an active industrial policy for productive restructuring within the constraints of the European Common Market. This would require the total disengagement from the EU (not just exit from the eurozone), but Lapavitsas explicitly rejects it.

In this explanation, productive restructuring is a distant accessory as the crisis does not come from the production sphere. It is weakly situated within a stabilization period that is supposedly based on the current productive structure and exchange devaluation generating import substitution (Lapavitsas et al. 2017). Given the constraints of the Common Market, whatever restructuring takes place during this period relies excessively upon private initiative; which is a well-trodden slippery road, as Greek private capitals traditionally avoid taking long-term restructuring risks, particularly in times of recession. Moreover, essentially little actual productive restructuring takes place during this purported period as all prioritized key sectors belong to the old and failed productive model. Even this weakly designed stabilization period succeeds—which implicitly but crucially depends upon an amicable and mutually beneficial divorce with the eurozone that is totally impossible—then a more active productive restructuring is also impossible due to the Common Market constraints.

Unlike Lapavitsas, Milios and Sotiropoulos (2010) argue that neither declining competitiveness nor the EMU is responsible for Greek over-indebtedness. On the contrary, the EMU facilitated capital investment from the most developed (and with lower growth rates and profitability) to the least developed economies, augmenting the growth of the European periphery. Thus, they agree with Mainstream accounts that Greece's 1990s high growth rates were not a 'bubble' and also about the benevolent nature of foreign capital. They argue that this idyllic picture was disrupted by financialization (with the creation of financial bubbles and excessive leverage) that led to the 2007–08 global financial crisis (understood also as merely a financial crisis). The latter derailed the hitherto benign deficits of the less developed EU economies. To support the faltering capital accumulation, FDs increased dramatically resulting in the debt crisis. The EMU has played only a peripheral role in this debacle because of its neoliberal dominance and for not being an optimal currency area. However, Milios and Sotiropoulos (2010) believe that this can be rectified through the creation of a 'social Europe'.

This second Radical explanation is also problematic. Apart from accepting the Mainstream fairy tales about foreign capital's benevolence and the 1990s 'strong Greece', they totally neglect the production sphere and its deep structural problems (to a large extent created by the integration in the Common Market subsequently exacerbated by participation in the EMU). For them, relations of economic exploitation between EU economies do not exist. Lastly, they explicitly consider productive reconstruction as a misleading inter-class proposal that goes against a pan-European working-class front and leads to the dangerous path of economic nationalism.

Marxist explanations

Marxist explanations propose a strong structural interpretation of the Greek crisis by placing its roots in the production sphere and discerning there a falling profitability trend (Mavroudeas 2016). Thus, financialization and neoliberalism are considered conjunctural by-products of these deep structural tendencies. Moreover, they consider the Greek case as part of the 2007–08 global crisis, which is also understood to be an à-la-Marx crisis (i.e. caused by the tendency of the rate of profit to fall—TRPF). Consequently, the issue of the productive model and its restructuring strategies is at the core of Marxist explanations.

Mavroudeas (2015c) discerns three sub-currents:

1 Maniatis and Passas (2015) attribute the Greek crisis to a long-term TRPF that was expressed in the 1973 crisis and the inability of subsequent capitalist restructurings to sufficiently rectify this fall.
2 Economakis et al. (2015) argue that the Greek crisis has its roots in the 1973 profitability crisis and the subsequent inadequate recuperation of the profit rate. Then participation in the European integration aggravated structural conditions and led to falling competitiveness that led to the current crisis. The latter was subsequently aggravated further because of the under-consumption caused by the austerity policies.
3 Mavroudeas and Paitaridis (2015b) argue that the Greek crisis is caused by TRPF (also deriving from the profit rate's incomplete recuperation from the 1973 crisis) and was aggravated further by the imperialist exploitation from the euro-core economies.

According to the last sub-current the Greek situation is a crisis of over-accumulation that has two key structural dimensions:

1 The *internal dimension* derives from the falling profitability caused by the long-term increase of the organic composition of capital (OCC).
2 The *external dimension* derives from the imperialist economic exploitation that less developed EU economies (Greece among them) suffer from more than developed ones.

Mavroudeas and Paitaridis (2015b) argue that the current Greek crisis stems from the 1973 profitability crisis, which was doubly onerous for Greek capitalism. Similarly to the West, it terminated the post-war 'golden age', which—in contrast to the West—was based on wage repression and the lack of a robust welfare system. The onset of the 1973 crisis coincided with the fall of the military dictatorship that led to a re-emergence of labour militancy and social struggle, forcing capital to make serious concessions to the former. Thus, Keynesian income distribution policies that were not applied in Greece after World War Two (contrary to the West) were introduced after 1973 (exactly when the West abandoned them). These policies overburdened the already declining capitalist profitability. They succeeded in containing popular radicalism but failed to solve the over-accumulation crisis.

Therefore, a realignment with the West began after 1985, which was assisted by Greece's participation in the process of European integration. There were successive waves of capitalist restructuring with the adoption first of conservative Keynesian and then of neoliberal policies. These, however, failed to rectify sufficiently both the falling profitability and the over-accumulation aspects of the crisis. Then, from the end of the 1990s there was a leap forward as the financial system fuelled liquidity into the system and helped create investment and consumption through the creation of fictitious capital (that is, through the uncertain betting on future surplus-value extraction). This financially created boom postponed, but at the same time augmented, the existing over-accumulation problems. It was accompanied by additional anti-labour measures (e.g. long hours and increased unpaid overtime) that increased the rate of exploitation of labour. However, these counteracting to the TRPF processes were not sufficient in solving Greek capitalism's problems. Thus, in 2007–08, similarly to the West as Greece had realigned with it to a great extent, these processes could not keep their necessary pace in order to avoid the eruption of the profitability crisis and the latter burst.

Greece's participation in the process of European integration played a crucial role in the aforementioned evolution. After 1973 it helped Greek capitalism to stabilize itself against popular radicalism. Additionally, Greek capital hoped that it would gain both economically and geopolitically by becoming even a junior partner with the more developed Western European capitals. However, this project carried with it serious costs. The participation in the European Common Market led to the dismantling of protectionist structures and exposed Greek capital to competition from the more developed Western European capitals. Greek capital was in no position to stand against this. Thus, after making progress through the imposition of anti-labour austerity from 1985 onwards, it retreated to the services sector. There, thanks also to crony relations with the political system, it could enjoy a quasi-protectionism. This led to a significant shrinkage of the agricultural sector and an extensive deindustrialization because foreign capitals conquered large swathes of these markets through imports rather than through direct investment (which remained insignificant). Greek capital was compensated, for a period after the 1990s, by reaping economic imperialist profits through its expansion in the less developed Balkan economies. Accession to the EMU aggravated these problems further as the Greek capital lost the ability to navigate monetary policy according to its specific needs.

The outbreak of the crisis put an end to this game. The profitability crisis re-emerged and its Balkan imperialist 'subsidies' collapsed as intensified intra-imperialist antagonisms pushed Greek capital aside. Then the profitability problems took the form of 'twin deficits' (FD and CAD). With the outbreak of the crisis all developed economies abandoned the neoliberal doctrines and employed conservative Keynesian anti-cyclical policies (expansionary fiscal and accommodative monetary policies). Therefore, from 2008 government deficits soared and, in many cases, foreign debt followed suit (as finance for the FDs). However, contrary to the Mainstream mantras, these augmented FDs were not caused by unrestrained wage increases but by the subsidization of capital's falling profitability. This was the case in Greece with some additional characteristics. Greek capitalism is historically characterized by relatively high FDs. This is not unusual for developing economies where the state as a collective capitalist necessarily plays a significant role in capital accumulation. Thus, falling profitability led to the increased FD.

On the balance of payments side, Greek capital had existing problems as it retreated—facing Western competition—to the services sector. The deteriorating competitiveness was caused by exorbitant wage increases but was mainly due to structural reasons. Greek capital could not enjoy sufficient economies of scale (due to the small size of the economy) and also preferred to keep its profit margins high. This led to a worsening of the TD. Additionally, since the accession to the EMU, public borrowing was channelled towards international markets on the pretext that the euro offered cheaper interest rates. This, on the one hand, facilitated Greek banks in expanding in more profitable areas as they were not obliged to buy, at the same extent, public debt. On the other hand, it aggravated CAD as public debt became external. By the same token, it became less controllable than internal debt; a change that was paid for dearly with the eruption of the crisis. Thus, falling profitability plus the EU's structural constraints led to the worsening of CAD.

Antagonistic strategies for overcoming the crisis and the issue of productive restructuring

The above outlined competing explanations of the Greek crisis dictate different and antagonistic strategies for overcoming it. For Marxist analysis the issue of productive restructuring should be at the centre of any strategy as the current Greek productive model is non-viable. However, different class interests imply different productive restructuring policies.

There is a pivotal question regarding crisis overcoming strategies that concerns European integration, which imposes widespread and very tight constraints on the Greek economy. Hence, it is a critical choice whether a strategy would be applied within or outside the EU constraints. Needless to say, answers to this dilemma reflect completely opposite class interests.

Consequently, two basic strategies exist. The first suggests the restructuring of the Greek economy according to the prerogatives and the constraints of European integration. The second proposes the restructuring of the Greek economy outside the framework of the EU. Moreover, the first strategy is subdivided into two versions. The first version is the pro-cyclical austerity policy of the Greek EAPs. The second version proposes a renegotiation of the EAPs that keeps the bail-out loans and aspects of the fiscal consolidation and structural reorganization but adds some anti-cyclical elements together with a pause in the austerity policies (through some form of neo-Keynesian policy mix). The second basic scenario is also sub-divided in two versions. The first version suggests exiting from only the EMU. The second version deems as necessary the complete disengagement from both the EMU and the EU.

The EAPs' strategy

This strategy is the Mainstream choice and expresses an unequal compromise between the euro-core economies and the USA (through the IMF) on the one hand and the Greek bourgeoisie on the other (see Mavroudeas 2017). As later became evident, there are serious conflicts between the two major partners of this strategy (the EU and the USA). The junior partner (the Greek bourgeoisie) has limited clout as its modern 'Great Idea' of participating in the European integration failed utterly and is leading to an acute downgrading in the international division of labour. Nevertheless, it is significantly weakened and also tightly tied to the EU, and does not even consider the case of disengaging from it.

The EAPs' analytical and policy origins lay in the Washington Consensus and the blueprint of IMF's Structural Adjustment Programmes (SAPs) that were devised in the 1990s in order to face the crises of the 'globalization' era. Their basic pillars are: (a) opening the economy to international capital, (b) bolstering the private sector vis-à-vis the public sector, and (c) changing towards an export-led growth productive structure. SAPs, particularly after the adoption of the *expansionary austerity* doctrine (see Giavazzi and Pagano 1990) are heavily pro-cyclical (i.e. they hold the belief that you must enter more deeply into the crisis in order to exit faster from it). Their main pillars are:

1 fiscal austerity;
2 pro-business reforms (deregulation of labour market, external relations and product markets) and facilitation of foreign capital influx;
3 devaluation; and
4 debt restructuring.

The Greek EAPs are special modifications of the IMF's SAPs, imposed by the EU, that made them even more problematic than their prototype. The third pillar is missing (due to the EMU), the fourth was added belatedly and unsuccessfully (after the failure of the first EAP). They are also frontloaded. This increases their austerity effect (as restructuring must rely heavily on 'internal devaluation'). The result is that they plunged Greece into an uncontrollable and long-lasting recession that derailed all the EPAs' milestones and projections (debt to GDP ratio, growth rate, etc.).

The EAPs' strategical aims are twofold: (a) in the short-term make debt viable, and (b) in the mid-term transform Greek capitalism structurally. This is an overambitious strategy riddled with contradictions and—even today—failing to achieve its aims. Additionally, it is a risky strategy as its structural transformations disrupt the entire post-war architecture of Greek capitalism (e.g. proletarization of the middle strata) and foment social and political unrest. However, there is no alternative for the EU and the Greek bourgeoisie (see Mavroudeas 2017).

Productive restructuring has an ambiguous position in the EAPs. It is not explicitly mentioned because it would be tantamount to accepting the failure of the European integration class strategy. Moreover, contemporary Mainstream theory rejects activist industrial policies. It is implicitly put into the structural reforms dictated by the EAPs. However, these do not constitute an industrial policy per se but simply the pro-entrepreneurial transformation of the institutional framework. A clearer indication of sectoral and branch priorities is offered by some pivotal Mainstream lobby studies (e.g. by McKinsey) that have been incorporated into the EU's National Strategic Reference Framework (NSRF). However, these sectoral and branch priorities are essentially a continuation of the previous failed Greek productive model. This denotes that for the EU that it is a strategic choice to transform Greece into a peripheral 'special economic zone' with a low cost, low wages, low value added, cheap assets and low technology economy that is the appendage of pan-European value chains. This economy would operate as a services- and low-cost goods export hub for European multinationals.

Redesigning the EAPs with anti-cyclical and debt-relieving measures

This strategy is proposed by mainly Heterodox but also by some Mainstream perspectives. After the eruption of conflicts with the EU, the IMF put its weight behind it. This strategy does not dispute the EAPs' strategic aims but suggests a more balanced policy mix. It proposes a new debt restructuring (either through debt haircut or through reprofiling) and some discreet anti-cyclical counter-measures. The latter include developmental aid (through the NSRF and the dubious Juncker plan) or, in more grandiose versions, a European Marshal plan and EU fiscal unification. They also include a less frontloaded time schedule with lower primary surpluses, etc.

This is not a self-sustained strategy but simply a variation of the EAPs. It is contradictory as it wants to blend an inherently pro-cyclical programme with elements of its opposite. The logic of the former is completely opposite to that of the latter. Anti-cyclical restructuring requires more time and is inconclusive. In contrast, the pre-cyclical restructuring reflects both the deeper logic of the capitalist system but also the dominant interests of the euro-core. Also, anti-cyclical restructuring was tested in Greece after the crisis of 1973 and it failed. The main reason for this failure was that in a capitalist over-accumulation crisis anti-labour austerity should be accompanied by devalorization of capital; otherwise, the crisis cannot be surpassed. The only possibility for the policy mix this strategy suggests is if pro-cyclical restructuring has been largely successful so some counter-measures can be afforded.

The strategy also does not have an alternative proposal regarding productive restructuring. While some lone voices lament the 'third-worldization' of Greece, they cannot offer a coherent alternative industrial policy. Thus, they suffice to follow the dominant blueprint and simply try to amend some of its more barbaric aspects.

Exit from the Euro-zone while remaining in the EU

This strategy that proposes exiting from the EMU while remaining in the EU stems from some of the Radical explanations of the Greek crisis. It is subdivided into a variant that supports the confrontational exit and another that supports the consensual exit.

The rationale behind this proposal is solitary. It considers that the exit from EMU would restore the tools of monetary and exchange rate policy in the country. Then, through competitive devaluation, Greek competitiveness would be improved and, consequently, both TD and CAD will be rectified. This strategy has a productive restructuring corollary as it argues that the devaluation would initiate an import substitution process and, thus, a regeneration of several productive activities.

The first part of this strategy (improving competitiveness through devaluation) is extremely vulnerable. A competitive devaluation might give some short-term increase in competitiveness, assuming that competitors do not respond in kind. However, long-lasting competition advantages require profound changes in the production structure of the economy and need time. This is particularly significant for Greece, as its exports depend overwhelmingly upon the import of intermediate goods. In this case a competitive devaluation without significant productive restructuring is almost useless.

However, the second part of this strategy is equally problematic. If a fast and frontloaded productive restructuring is required—without which even stabilization is not possible—then this necessitates an activist industrial policy that can only be applied by the public sector. However, no such policy is permitted within the European Common Market.

Therefore, the main weakness of this strategy is that it ignores the deep structural problems of the Greek economy and tries to cope indirectly through the monetary arm. In its consensual version it stumbles upon the EU's institutional barriers. In its confrontational variant it necessarily requires the total disengagement from the EU from the very beginning of the policy.

Disengagement from the EU

This is the only coherent alternative strategy to that of the EAPs and it is proposed by Marxist approaches. It starts with the recognition of the deep structural problems of the Greek economy and the particular form they have acquired due to its participation in the process of European integration. It argues that the only pro-labour solution to the crisis requires the productive restructuring of the Greek economy outside the process of European integration and towards a socialist transition. This process should be organized as a *transitional programme* whose intermediate priority is disengagement from the EU. This is a model for a self-centred (but not closed) economy with emphasis on the development of a coherent net of inter-branch linkages that would sustain the economy. This would be supported by a discreet and highly regulated foreign economic policy. Productive restructuring is at the centre of this strategy and needs to be frontloaded and extensive. It will be organized through five-year plans that would cover both the public and the private sector and would be compulsory.

This transitional programme would pass through several distinctive phases.

1 An initial 'special period' marked by intense conflict with the EU and the West and heavy handed emergency measures to address immediate needs.
2 A stabilization period whose central feature would be the consolidation of a state-capitalist economy with a private but also a growing public sector with socialist characteristics.
3 A period of socialist transition through a balanced and sustainable strengthening of the socialist sector and the corresponding reduction of other sectors.

The 'special period' policies should be organized along short- and long-term priorities. Short-term priorities are:

1 disengagement from the EU;
2 rejection of foreign debt;
3 capital controls in the economy;
4 nationalization of the financial system and the creation of special-purpose financial facilities;
5 a strongly progressive tax system;
6 controlled management of the exchange rate of the new currency (possibly through a multiple exchange rate system or a short-term dual currency system); and
7 an extensive price-control system.

The most crucial but long-term parameter of this programme is the planned productive restructuring of the economy based on the public sector (that is the social ownership and control of at least the strategic economic sectors). This implies the democratic elaboration of five-year plans for the whole economy. Their focus should be on the development of the productive sectors of the economy by regenerating the primary sector and with particular emphasis on rapid reindustrialization. This restructuring cannot be based solely on the existing productive structure of production (as expressed through the relevant multipliers) but should move proactively to build new branches that are necessary. Full employment is another central goal of this programme. Monetary and fiscal policy would follow the needs of this strategy but within the objective constraints. This alternative strategy, pivoting on the disengagement from the EU, is the only way to overcome the crisis in favour of the great social majority of working people.

References

Arestis, P. (2009), 'New Consensus Macroeconomics: A Critical Appraisal', New York, Levy Economics Institute, Working Paper no. 564.

Argitis, G. (2012), *Bankruptcy and economic crisis: Failure and breakdown of the Greek model of capitalism*, Athens: Alexandreia [in Greek].

Economakis, G., Androulakis, G. and Markaki, M. (2015), 'Profitability and crisis in the Greek economy (1960–2012): an investigation' in Mavroudeas, S. (ed.), *Greek capitalism in crisis: Marxist Analyses*, London: Routledge.

Giavazzi, F. and Pagano, M. (1990), 'Can Severe Fiscal Contractions Be Expansionary? Tales of Two Small European Countries', Cambridge, MA: National Bureau of Economic Research, *Macroeconomics Annual* 5.

Kaldor, N. (1978), 'The Effect of Devaluations on Trade in Manufactures', in Kaldor, N., *Further Essays on Applied Economics*, London: Duckworth.

Katrakilidis, C. and Trachanas, E. (2011), 'Has the Accession of Greece in the EU Influenced the Dynamics of the Country's "Twin Deficits"? An Empirical Investigation', *European Research Studies* XIV(1).

Lapavitsas, C., Kaltenbrunner, A., Lindo, D., Michell, J., Painceira, J.-P., Pires, E., Powell, J., Stenfors, A. and Teles, N. (2010), 'Eurozone Crisis: Beggar Thyself and Thy Neighbour', *Journal of Balkan and Near Eastern Studies*, 12(4).

Lapavitsas, C., Mariolis, T. and Gavrielides, C. (2017), 'Eurozone failure, German policies and a new path for Greece', Berlin, Rosa Luxemburg Stiftung, available atwww.rosalux.de/en/publication/id/14546/eurozone-failure-german-policies-and-a-new-path-for-greece.

Maniatis, T. and Passas, C. (2015), 'The Law of the Falling Rate of Profit in the post-war Greek Economy' in Mavroudeas, S. (ed.), *Greek capitalism in crisis: Marxist Analyses*, London: Routledge.

Mavroudeas, S. (ed.) (2015a), *Greek capitalism in crisis: Marxist Analyses*, London: Routledge.

Mavroudeas, S. (2015b), '"Financialization" and the Greek case' in Mavroudeas, S. (ed.), *Greek capitalism in crisis: Marxist Analyses*, London: Routledge.

Mavroudeas, S. (2015c), 'The Greek saga: Competing explanations of the Greek crisis', Kingston University London, Economics Discussion Paper Series 2015–2011.

Mavroudeas, S. (2016), 'The Greek crisis: a structural or a conjunctural crisis?' in Subasat, T. (ed.), *The Great Financial Meltdown: Systemic, Conjunctural or Policy-Created? New Directions in Modern Economics*, Cheltenham and Nottingham, MA: Edward Elgar.

Mavroudeas, S. (2017), 'Troika's Economic Adjustment Programmes for Greece: Why do they Systematically Fail' in Marangos, J., (ed.), *The Internal Impact and External Influence of the Greek Financial Crisis*, New York: Palgrave Macmillan.

Mavroudeas, S. and Paitaridis, D. (2015a), 'Mainstream accounts of the Greek crisis: more heat than light?' in Mavroudeas, S. (ed.), *Greek capitalism in crisis: Marxist Analyses*, London: Routledge.

Mavroudeas, S. and Paitaridis, D. (2015b), 'The Greek crisis: a dual crisis of over-accumulation and imperialist exploitation' in Mavroudeas, S. (ed.), *Greek capitalism in crisis: Marxist Analyses*, London: Routledge.

Milios, J. and Sotiropoulos, D. (2010), 'Crisis of Greece or Crisis of the Euro? A View from the European Periphery', *Journal of Balkan and Near Eastern Studies*, 12(3).

Stathakis, G. (2010), 'The Fiscal Crisis of the Greek Economy', Paper presented at the 1st Annual International Initiative for Promoting Political Economy conference, 10–12 September, University of Crete.

6 Internal Devaluation and Hegemonic Crisis (2010–16)

Elias Ioakimoglou

Introduction

Nine years after the beginning of the crisis and seven years since the first Memorandum of Understanding,[1] which imposed a programme of fiscal and structural adjustment to the economy, Greece remains in a state of economic depression deeper and longer than the American Great Depression of the 1930s. The course of the Greek long depression corresponds to a well thought strategy, *internal devaluation*,[2] which aims at decreasing domestic prices relative to competitor prices and thus improve competitiveness, boost growth and increase employment. The strategy has been implemented in Greece in its pure form and in a harsh way.

What have we learned from the Greek experiment of internal devaluation? Firstly, the Greek depression shows that what mainstream economics dubbed *internal devaluation* was simply forced devaluation of wage labour by means of massive unemployment and structural reform in the labour market modifying radically the balance of power between firms and workers. Secondly, as Greece is a wage-led economy, the steep fall in the purchasing power of wages reduces consumption drastically, then gross domestic product (GDP) and employment, then capacity utilization and investment, without having any noticeable effect on export prices or export volumes. Thus, the strategy of internal devaluation led to economic depression. Thirdly, economic depression gives rise to a crisis in the reproduction of the dominated social classes, a *social reproduction crisis,* which opens the way to political destabilisation.

It is argued in this chapter that political destabilization in Greece is best described by the term of *hegemonic crisis*[3] referring to the ability of the dominant classes to 'represent the general interest vis-à-vis the dominated classes' (Poulantzas 1978 [1968]). Put in a more detailed way, as accumulation of people adjusts to the accumulation of capital, the employment losses due to imperfect, disrupted capital accumulation in Greece, combined with fierce austerity, debt and deconstruction of the welfare state, trigger a variety of processes of destruction of the existing *social reproduction regime* leading possibly to a crisis in the political hegemony of the ruling class and thus opening a window of opportunity to radical change. Hegemonic crisis does not lead automatically to radical change since accompanied by a *counter-tendency* to passivity and submission emanating from the misery and despair that social reproduction crisis produces.

The rest of the chapter is organized as follows: section one describes concisely the implementation of the strategy of internal devaluation as a macroeconomic disaster that plummeted Greece into a long depression and the popular classes in material deprivation and poverty. Section two shows in what ways the social consequences of the strategy turn into a *crisis of social reproduction*, and section three how social reproduction crisis generates a *tendency to hegemonic crisis* and its counter-tendency to passivity.

Internal Devaluation and Economic Depression

The Greek Depression is not an accident, nor the outcome of wrong policies or mistaken ideas; it is the outcome of a meticulously elaborated strategy, namely *internal devaluation* (a radicalized form of *competitive disinflation*). The strategy of internal devaluation has been fiercely applied in Greece for eight consecutive years (2010–16). According to its authors, its objective is to improve competitiveness and transform Greece into an export-led economy able to repay its debt. GDP and employment growth would follow naturally.

In order to achieve its objectives, the strategy of internal devaluation focuses on the relation between labour costs and price competitiveness: lower wages would presumably lead to lower prices and thus to higher export performance. Hence, in the battle for income between firms and workers, the latter are constantly asked, in the name of the general interest, to reduce their claims, while government intervention is oriented towards making wages more flexible, which is making workers more vulnerable to unemployment by means of structural reform of the labour market.

Since the implementation of the first Memorandum of Understanding, which was agreed between the troika and the Greek Government in 2010, the economic and social indicators have deteriorated dramatically (Institute of Labour GSEE, 2014, 2015, 2016, Alexiou and Nellis 2013). Using the tools of fiscal adjustment, structural reform in the labour market, and policy-induced unemployment, the strategy of internal devaluation results in a radical and continuous change in the balance of power between workers and firms, labour and capital, and substantially reduces labour income in all its forms (wage, social public expenditure, etc.). Still, this strategy of redistribution of income from labour to capital did not fulfil any of its officially stated objectives: eight years of prodigious fiscal effort, draconian wage cuts, ferocious structural reform in the labour market, and the dismantling of the social state, produced devastating results on GDP (–23%)[4] and employment (–17%) without any observable improvement in the contribution of exports of goods and services to the increase of GDP.

At the core of this macroeconomic fiasco, there is mainstream economists' perception of the relation between wages and consumption, and the relation between prices and labour cost. For mainstream economic theory, the propensities to consume out of profits and out of wages are equal and thus changes in real wages have no impact on consumption. However, in Greece as well as in several other countries (Onaran and Galanis 2013) the propensity to consume out of wages is higher than the propensity to consume out of profits, i.e. wage earners spend a larger share of their income than profit recipients. Consequently, increases in real wages that shift income distribution in favour of labour, induce an increase in consumption demand and therefore an increase in GDP. On the other hand, this favourable effect of wage rises on GDP can be counter-balanced by the negative effect of wage increases on profits and therefore on fixed capital investment and GDP. It follows that aggregate demand may rise or fall depending on the relative magnitude of the two contradictory effects of wage increases on GDP: a higher real wage reduces fixed capital investment but increases private consumption. Furthermore, one must take into account international trade and exports since increased wages can harm competitiveness and reduce GDP. Taking into account all factors, it is estimated that in Greece an increase in the wage share leads to an increase in aggregate private demand, i.e. the sum of private consumption, private fixed capital investment and net exports (Marsellou 2013, Onaran and Obst 2015). In other words, the beneficial effect of wage rises on consumption exceeds the detrimental effect on investment and exports. Summing up, Greece is in a *wage-led demand regime* (Lavoie and Stockhammer 2013) and the steep fall in the purchasing power of wages leads Greece to economic depression that is massive unemployment, disinvestment, a huge loss in productive capacity seen only in times of war, material deprivation and rising poverty, obsolescence of infrastructure, deconstruction of social services, increasing public debt, and surging numbers of non-performing loans. The Greek Depression is now registered as deeper and longer than the American Depression of the 1930s.

The macroeconomic fiasco of internal devaluation is due also to the way mainstream economists see the relation between prices and labour cost. They expected that prices would follow decreasing wages and unit labour cost while there is no statistically significant relation between the two variables (Storm and Naastepad 2007, Storm and Nasstepad 2012, Storm and Naastepad 2015; Felipe and Kumar 2011). Moreover, changes in relative unit labour costs do not affect changes in the current account balance in a statistically significant way (Diaz-Sanchez and Varoudakis 2013, Gabrisch and Staehr 2013). What actually happened in Greece was a dramatic decline in the purchasing power of the average wage and in unit labour cost which did not feed into important price decreases. The abrupt decline in real wages and unit labour cost (–12,0%) during the first seven years of internal devaluation is not followed by an equivalent fall in prices as predicted by mainstream theory but by a meagre decrease (–4,4%, although prices of imported raw materials had decreased by 11% since 2013). This resulted in upsurge of profit margins[5] (as both manufacturing and services industries operate in non-competitive conditions, see Polemis 2014) and in income redistribution of four percentage points of GDP from labour to capital (Institute of Labour GSEE, 2014, 2015, 2016).

Income redistribution in favour of profits is fostered by successive waves of structural change in the labour market (Kapsalis and Kouzis 2013, Dimoulas 2014), which makes workers more vulnerable towards unemployment, so that for the same unemployment rate, they can now obtain lower wages than before. The main labour market reforms are as follows:

1 Collective bargaining structures have been dismantled and reduced to a minor institutional status, almost a detail in the operation of the labour market.
2 The determination of minimum wages has been removed from the general national collective agreement between the Greek General Confederation of Workers and employers' organizations. It is now determined by decree by the Ministry of Employment. It has been reduced from €751 monthly gross earnings to €586 in a single stroke in 2013 and its change has affected the average wage since the minimum wage is a reference for the determination of pay in the business sector.
3 Compulsory arbitration, implemented in the 1980s, used to give weak unions backing from public authorities in settling their disputes with powerful employers. The abolition of compulsory arbitration now diminishes the bargaining power of the workers.
4 Employee compensation for layoffs has been dramatically reduced.
5 It is expected that in 2017, with the application of the third adjustment programme, the protection of workers against mass dismissals and the protection of trade-unionists will be greatly weakened if not abolished.
6 The downsizing of the public sector organized by the troika and the governments in office, mostly during the first adjustment program (2010–11), reduced the number of workers in secure jobs as well as their wages. Between 2009 and 2016, the wage bill of public servants decreased by approximately one-third. The dismantling of the public sector is leading the national health system, social security, public education and social care into disaster. It also changed the overall balance of power between capital and labour as trade-unionism has some of its bastions in the public sector. Furthermore, relatively higher wages in the public sector were affecting positively the target wage in collective bargaining in the business sector.

The strategy of internal devaluation is complemented by massive tax increases imposed to supposedly transform Greece into a country able to repay its debt. Taxes add their burden to primary redistribution of income and contribute to GDP decreases (Institute of Labour GSEE 2014, 2015).

Furthermore, during the Greek Depression, debt, a powerful tool of dispossession of property, also became an important factor. Higher debt of middle- and working-class households (mostly mortgages) has been used by households during 1995–2008, when the economy was booming, to meet social reproduction needs (in the case of the working classes) and to keep up with rapidly rising standards of living, n the case of middle classes (Pastrapa and Apostolopoulos 2014). During the depression, as disposable income of households collapsed, the debt/income ratio soared and depressed demand further as households struggled to repay their debt while their income decreased.

Taken all together, income distribution reducing labour earnings, rising taxes, reduced welfare expenditure, rising debt/income ratios, constitute a mechanism of economic depression (Ioakimoglou 2012b) and redistribution of income and wealth, which deprives the dominated classes from important means of life. That leads to a *social reproduction crisis.*

Social Reproduction Crisis

From the point of view of the social reproduction crisis we can distinguish three broad segments of the dominated classes in Greece: Firstly, *employees* working in continuously deteriorating conditions (with the exception of executives and a fraction of highly skilled employees). Secondly, *relative surplus population*, i.e. labour reserves readily available for capital's use as required. Thirdly, a *population of paupers* caused by total, permanent exclusion from the world of capitalist work.

Concerning employees, they are severely deprived of means of reproduction and their ability to sustain themselves has been reduced extremely. The average real wage declined by 19% during the years of internal devaluation under the pressure of massive policy-induced unemployment (25% in 2016 as opposed to 8% in 2008). During the third quarter of 2015, monthly gross earnings for one in five employees was less than the minimum wage of €586, whereas gross earnings of 50% of employees were lower than €1,100. The number of precarious workers is soaring and a process of diffusion of precariousness is underway in segments of the Greek labour market, which, until recently, had been considered immune to it. New flexible forms of employment are introduced in the workplace even in some sectors of the upper echelons of the labour market, and new forms of duality appear inside the modern sector of the economy. Concerning the duration of the contracts, firms prefer fixed-term contracts and part-time employment instead of open-ended contracts (permanent full-time employment). As for pay practices, the majority of employers consider that given the current situation of the labour market (high unemployment rates, especially for the young, surging precariousness, rapid extension of part-time work, trade union weakness, etc) the new minimum wage of €586 including employer and employee contributions to social security funds, is a fair wage for semi-skilled and unskilled workers (while executives' earnings are now on average higher than in 2008). It is estimated that almost 1m. employees (approximately one-third of wage labour) are paid with a delay of one to 12 months. Overtime is unpaid or underpaid in three times out of four.[6].

The outcome is that between 2010 and 2016, employees as a whole lost at least 40% of their purchasing power (as a result of lower real wages, unemployment and increased fiscal burden). Put another way, reproduction expenditure of employees and their families is now reduced to less than 2/3 of the corresponding expenditure in 2008.

The reproduction of labour power also involves public expenditure and production of public goods (health care, education, etc.) and a vast array of state policies (de Brunhoff 1976). In order to secure the reproduction of current and future supplies of labour power, the capitalist state establishes institutions and exercises bio-power (Foucault 1978)[7] through which it controls, at least partly, biological, material, educational, ideological (Althusser 2014) reproduction. As market-driven adjustment of population to accumulation is not sufficient, the state acts possibly as a mediator and a policy-driven adjustment can be made active. During the Greek Depression, the state abandoned its role of mediator between capital accumulation and social reproduction giving absolute priority to the immediate valorization of capital in conditions of economic collapse. Working-class households are deprived of affordable services that previously alleviated their burden regarding social reproduction, including health care, education, care for the elderly, child care, etc. (Burgi 2013).

On top of that, non-performing loans of households and firms in 2016 reached almost one-third of total loans (40% if restructured loans are taken into account). Since July 2016, dispossession of houses by the banks is greatly facilitated by new legislation removing almost entirely the protection of the main residence. Important characteristics related to household bankruptcy are income or/and job loss, family breakup and being a woman with children (Marsellou and Bassiakos 2015). Still, bankruptcy is not a phenomenon restricted to the very poor.

As a result, in 2016, working-class households, and to a lesser degree some fractions of the middle classes (to be more precise, of the *new petty bourgeoisie*[8]) are clearly in a situation in which their reproduction is partial, incomplete, painful, threatening identities previously constituted in relation to 'normal' life in social spaces of work and family. Disrupted capital accumulation, disintegration of the welfare state, increased taxes, debt captivity and property dispossession, produce deconstructing effects on the existing *social reproduction regime,* which in Greece has been constituted during a 40-year long process, from the mid-1970s to 2008. (This includes the male breadwinner to the shared-responsibility dual-earner household, increasing female participation to the labour market, restructuring of domestic labour processes on the basis of commodities produced by the capitalist sector and social services produced by the state, fading domestic production of use-values such as food, apparel, etc., outsourcing of child-care, care of the elderly and educational/recreational activities, use of larger domestic spaces, increasing use of individual means of transport, disintegration of traditional public spaces of socialisation and relative withdrawal in individualistic spaces of reproduction). Deprivation of basic goods such as electricity and heating, reducing medication and other health expenditure putting health at risk, downgrading of food quality, going into a never-ending debt spiral, moving to smaller and cheaper housing or into the parents' house, sharing housing with non-family persons, going without a telephone, avoiding transportation, giving up social activities outside the home entailing social isolation, were forms of deprivation already reported before the crisis for a small fraction of the population. During the depression, all kinds of material deprivation is reported for large social groups. Currently, 36% of the population is under the poverty threshold.[9] However, the poverty threshold actually is set at €4,500 in annual income compared to €7,200 in 2005. When current income is compared to the poverty threshold of 2005, we find that with 2005 standards almost 45% of the population is below the threshold of poverty, compared to 12% percent in 2005. Some 41% of the economically active population and 44% of children are now facing material deprivation. One in five employees is classed as working poor (by 2015 standards). While only 4% of the population was unable to pay for medical examinations and treatment in 2009, the corresponding figure for 2015 was 16%. Some 42% of the households are facing housing costs exceeding 40% of their total disposable income. Last, but not least, the deconstruction of the existing regime of social reproduction during the depression is so deep that implies changes in fundamental socialization processes and tends to uproot people from their previous personal, social, cultural and familial environment and introduces them brutally into new life practices without the old maps that had guided them until recently. As a result, the crude birth rate (i.e. the ratio of the number of live births during the year to the average population in that year) declined from 10.6% in 2010 to 8.5% in 2015.

Nevertheless, employees are not all equally affected. The inner divisions of work in capitalist mode of production (Coriat 1976, Coriat 1984, Coriat 1994; Poulantzas 1975: 225–50) between skilled intellectual work/less-skilled and unskilled work, supervisors/supervised employees, workers of high/low professional experience, generate (along with particular characteristics of the Greek social formation and its historical contingencies) a dual-segment wage-labour structure (Ioakimoglou 2016a, Ioakimoglou 2016b): one in five employees are in the primary segment of the *business sector*, which concentrates skilled and intellectual workers educated to tertiary level (among them approximately 5% are executives and 15% are scientific personnel and highly skilled technicians). Four in five employees are in the secondary segment, which concentrates unskilled and semi-skilled workers educated to primary or secondary level. Leaving executives aside, all other segments of employees are suffering losses in income and employment, although at different degrees. Scientific personnel and highly skilled technicians (which altogether form the new petty bourgeoisie of the private sector) are less affected than other workers who form the core of the working classes.[10] Among workers, those with long professional experience are more protected than younger workers. It is thus working-class employees and young workers who bare most of the burden of depression, unemployment and structural adjustment induced by the strategy of internal devaluation.

An important feature of the condition of working-class households is that they are locked in material deprivation. As they are dependent on the market for goods and services that can no longer be produced at home, i.e. their reproduction is based mainly on commodities produced by the business sector[11] and sold to the market, workers are compelled to return incessantly to the labour market as vendors of their labour power (their only potential source of income) to meet capitalists as buyers. Workers 'cannot get free of capital', according to Karl Marx, and their work and their lives adjust to the existence, to the *raison d'être* of capital that is valorization of capital. Their lives are internalized in the movement of capital, in a *wage-labour trap,* which is also a factor of workers' discipline at work and at home.

In the context of the Greek Depression, valorization of capital imposes austerity, not as a choice but as a necessary policy of the capitalist class to tackle falling profitability of over-accumulated capital (Milios 2015). The resulting lower wages (and corresponding skyrocketing profit margins) determine the boundaries enclosing the economic space that capital leaves to social reproduction. Long-standing austerity sustains a social reproduction crisis for a long time, and the resulting transformations culminate, possibly, in a new *social reproduction regime.*

Employees are locked in reproduction crisis also by the fact they are caught in an *additional-worker*[12] *trap.* As working-class families' earnings are becoming smaller than the minimum consumption level necessary to sustain themselves, to produce a new generation of workers, to take part in social life and to be accepted and respected by the community, they are forced to work more hours and accept multiple jobs. Female participation in waged work increases even during the crisis. Thus, the supply of labour remains high in the face of low labour demand, and the resulting unemployment keeps real wages low: unemployment feeds into labour supply increases and vice versa.

The second fraction of the dominated classes is the *relative surplus population,* composed of the unemployed and the underemployed: precarious, unprotected, casual, informal, undocumented, discouraged and migrant workers, all of them moving in and out the labour market. The exclusion of relative surplus population from the capitalist production process is partial or temporary, and knowledge and skills of labour reserves are preserved, at least partly. The number of unemployed increased by approximately 800,000 during the crisis (from 8% to 25%). From the point of view of social reproduction, the condition of the relative surplus population does not differ substantially from the condition of working-class employees, except in magnitude of poverty and intensity of material deprivation, and most important, by the fact that the larger fraction of unemployed are stuck in a *long-term unemployment trap*: the long-term unemployed might not find themselves in employment again as their professional knowledge and skills erode after long spans of time out of work. The trap is as deep as long-term unemployment is high: during the Greek Depression it exceeds 70% of total unemployment.

The material basis for the existence of a *population of paupers* generated by total, permanent exclusion from the world of capitalist work, the population of those without wages and without the hope of wages, is found in the relation of labour power to capital. Although from a general point of view, labour power is the capacity for labour, the mental, physical and social capabilities that are necessary to produce a use-value that is a useful thing, which by its properties satisfies human wants, from the capitalist point of view the utility of labour power is to valorize capital. Valorization of capital (extraction of surplus value) is obtained by the productive consumption of labour power[13] in the capitalist production process. Labour power is incorporated into constant capital (fixed capital, intermediate consumption of raw materials and services used by the firm) to act as its means of valorization. Therefore labour power can be sold only under the condition that it preserves the value of the means of production, it reproduces the cost of its own maintenance, and provides unpaid labour as a source of capitalist profit *of a size compatible with capitalists' claims.* It is only under these conditions that labour power is socially recognized as useful in its capacity to produce useful things (use-values). Workers who are not needed for valorization of existing capital are unable to sell their labour power and their reproduction becomes imperfect, incomplete, since they lose their sole or main income. In that case, where the reproduction of capital is unable to include in its movement the reproduction of fractions of the working classes, they are excluded from the world of work, partially or totally, temporarily or permanently. When there is prolonged disinvestment (negative rates of capital accumulation), as in the case of Greece since 2010, the quantity of wage labour needed to valorize capital decreases dramatically; accumulation of people adjusts to accumulation of capital[14] to a low level of employment *structurally defined by capital's profitability aspirations* (Ioakimoglou 2012, Sotiropoulos et al. 2013). During the Greek Depression, 8% of fixed capital has been destroyed, potential GDP has plummeted by 17%, long-term projections of GDP growth do not exceed 1.25% annually[15] (IMF 2016) and the linkage between output growth and unemployment reduction is rather weak (Koutroulis et al. 2016). As a result, in the juncture of economic rebound, Greece might face a serious risk of jobless recovery. According to IMF projections (IMF 2016), Greece will continue to struggle with high unemployment rates for decades to come.

The depression leads fractions of the population to permanent exclusion from the world of capitalist work and tends to generate a redundant, superfluous population, *a population of paupers,* which is the third segment of wage labour in Greece. Emigration becomes an exit from this condition: More than 200,000 Greek citizens, of which a large fraction are young educated people without the hope of a wage (or self-employment), left Greece during the depression years mostly for northern European destinations. Other redundant, superfluous populations, the less educated, are excluded from normal social reproduction, and the correspondence between the mode of their survival and the capitalist production process fades and gradually disappears as their capacity to work in capitalist production processes (i.e. all the forms of knowledge, skill and social aptitude they have been acquiring in the past, vanish in the course of their impoverishment in idleness). They become 'the dead weight of the industrial reserve army' as Marx put it; they are in a *trap of self-sustained misery.* These populations are to be found in the 4.4m. persons in poverty by 2005 standards (in a country of 10.8m. inhabitants), the 2.2m. people in the condition of severe material deprivation, in the 800,000 long-term unemployed, the 3m. who are unable to keep their homes adequately warm, the 3.7m. who have arrears on utility bills, the 14% of children (aged 0–17) living in a dwelling with a leaking roof, damp walls, floors or foundation, or rot in window frames or the floor.[16] The most educated, especially 25–29 year-olds who are suffering high unemployment rates (Bell and Blanchflower 2015), will emigrate and those who will be able to rescue their labour power, at least partly, will return to the world of wage-earners in the rather improbable event of Greek economy returning to a path of sustainable rapid growth. The others will live in social spaces of *internal social exile.*[17] Until now, with the exception of immigrant camps, populations of paupers in Greece are not yet highly concentrated in closed spaces but diffused in the porosity of 'normal' still-decaying neighbourhoods in cities, blurring the contours of the three segments of wage labour (working-class employees, relative surplus population, population of paupers). In any case, from the point of view of *social reproduction* there is now, in Greece, a continuum from working-class employees to relative surplus population and from there to the population of paupers (Denning 2010). Wage-earners and the unemployed constitute the *proletariat,* those who are constrained to sell their labour-power in order to live. The proletariat thus includes working-class employees as well as the unemployed, both being the result of a unique process of metamorphosis in which the accumulation of capital reconfigures incessantly the working class by successive movements of attraction and repulsion of labour forces in and out of the production process. There is also a continuum from relative surplus population to the population of paupers: When unemployment is massive, the periods involved grow longer and longer, and an increasing number of long-term unemployed are being turned into paupers. During the Greek Depression, pauperism extends also to retirees, the workers of the past, who fall below the poverty threshold and they join the ranks of the paupers, at least when deprived of property or protection from their families.

The social relations in which the three segments of the working classes live and try to sustain themselves in Greece constitute a device of discipline and submission of wage labour (both at the level of production and social reproduction) to the priorities of capital valorization, to the profit aspirations of the capitalist power bloc. This *workers' discipline device* is composed of structural characteristics of the capitalist mode of production and contingent elements imposed by neoliberalism, such as welfare restructuring and reprivatization of social reproduction (Gill and Bakker 2003: 67–82), individual reproduction strategies, labour-market reform and institutionalization of priorities of capital over material life (LeBaron 2010). As LeBaron and Roberts (2010: 24) put it, 'state and market forces have created a carceral matrix that contains and manages tensions and contradictions and that locks people's current and future life choices and possibilities into unequal and unfree capitalist social relations as well as limits their social and physical mobility within these relations'.

Political Hegemony Crisis

Piketty makes the observation that when Marx published *The Communist Manifesto,* in 1848, while the first communist and socialist movements developed, his argument was that in spite of half a century of prodigious industrial growth and technological innovation, the condition of the masses was as miserable as before (Piketty 2014). Marx explains the inner logic of the argument: the bourgeoisie 'is unfit to rule because it is incompetent to assure an existence to its slave within his slavery'. He establishes, although in a rather implicit way, a causal relationship between the ability of the dominant class to assure the conditions of reproduction of the dominated classes on the one hand and political power on the other.

This relationship described by Marx is not a mechanical causality, it does not possess the form of a linear causality (or of a linear law); disrupted, incomplete reproduction of the dominated classes is not the 'cause' of political instability, but it creates objective conditions that make political instability probable. If there is disrupted reproduction of wage-labouring classes, it will create historical conditions threatening political stability and possibly opening the way to political crisis. *Disrupted, imperfect reproduction of wage-labouring classes will create a tendency to political crisis.* Whether this tendency will eventually result in a political crisis depends on contingent factors (factors that may or may not exist depending on the country and the historical moment).[18]

Put in a more detailed way, the concept of *tendency,* preferred by Marx to describe this kind of causality, implies that before there is a political crisis, all the conditions of that crisis already exist in isolation; before there is political crisis, there exists absolutely nothing that is formed. The concept of tendency indicates thus the existence of an absence, of a void leaving pending the formation of a political crisis. The void is filled by contingency: the tendency can result in a political crisis under the impact of an *encounter*[19] with contingent historical conditions. Without encounter, there is nothing but isolated conditions lacking consistency.

The Marxian concept of tendency includes also the idea of *counter-tendencies* (Duménil 1978), indicating counteracting factors that can delay or weaken the absolute realization of the main tendency. These counter-tendencies, although in contradiction with the main tendency, have the same source with it: 'Marx defines the terms between which there is a contradiction as the contradictory effects of a single cause' (Balibar 1968). In this theoretical schema, where economic depression leads to disrupted reproduction of labour power, the *tendency to political crisis* would be the main tendency and the disorganizing effects of massive unemployment and material deprivation on militancy would be a *counter-tendency,* both tendencies emanating from the same single cause that is disrupted, defective reproduction of wage-labouring classes. Still a question is pending: what is there in the nature of political power that opens the possibility of destabilization in times of social reproduction crisis?

The idea of *hegemony* is at least as old as Sun Tsu, the great Chinese strategist, for whom one of the five factors of the art of war is the Moral Law: 'The Moral Law causes the people to be in complete accord with their ruler, so that they will follow him regardless of their lives, undismayed by any danger' (Sun 1910). The same idea is central to Machiavelli's *The Prince* in which the prince must gain the people's friendship in order to form an alliance with the people against the nobility (Machiavelli 1532 [1910]: 38–42); he uses consent and coercion to form a people who fear him but do not hate him. 'It is essential for a Prince to be on a friendly footing with his people, since, otherwise, he will have no resource in adversity.' However, it was Gramsci that transformed the idea of hegemony into a concept, although in a theoretical schema full of contradictions (Anderson 1976, Althusser 2006). These contradictions have been largely rectified by Nicos Poulantzas in *Political Power and Social Classes.* Poulantzas (1978) drew heavily upon Marx's political writings to formulate abstract structural determinations of capitalist power and to explore in what exact way these are articulated with contingent factors in the tangible reality of *capitalist social formations.* In a nutshell, in his theoretical schema the concept of hegemony is understood in the following way: 'The concept of hegemony indicates how … the political interests of these [dominant] classes are constituted as representing the "general interest" of the body politic i.e. the "people-nation"' (Poulantzas 1978: 13–141). It follows that a hegemonic project of the dominant classes can obtain active consent of the dominated classes if they recognize the 'general interest' in the economic and/or political programme of the dominant classes.

The concept of hegemony in the work of Poulantzas is also used in another sense: 'The capitalist state and the specific characteristics of the class struggle in a capitalist formation make it possible for a "power bloc" composed of several politically dominant classes or fractions to function. Amongst these dominant classes and fractions one of them holds a particular dominant role, which can be characterised as a hegemonic role' (Poulantzas 1978: 141). In other words, the fractions of the dominant classes and their allies, are united under the leadership of a hegemonic fraction in a 'power bloc' because they recognize their particular interest in the political and economic project proposed by the hegemonic fraction. Thus, hegemony has a double function: to create active consent of the ensemble of society to a political and/or economic strategy on the one hand, and to secure the unity of dominant classes and fractions by means of this strategy on the other.

Departures from this schema of hegemony can give rise to several political regimes of partial, incomplete, imperfect hegemony. In some cases, passivity takes the place of active consent, when large fractions of the popular classes do not recognize their own interest in the political and/or economic strategy proposed by the power bloc but simultaneously their organised forces, defeated and confused, are unable to formulate an alternative strategy, such as in the case of Thatcherism where the dominant strategy has prevailed as a *There-Is-No-Alternative* strategy confining the dominated classes into passivity.[20]

Hence, in times of structural economic crisis, such as economic depression, political hegemony requires:

1 the formulation of a strategy for a new capital accumulation regime or a model of growth whose successful implementation ends the crisis and opens a new era of sustained growth and low unemployment;
2 the formation of a power bloc unifying most of the dominant classes or fractions under the strategy; and
3 the active consent of the dominated classes recognising the general interest of the ensemble of society in the strategy of accumulation proposed, or passivity obtained by an efficient there-is-no-alternative argument.

If conditions one or two are not met, then a hegemonic crisis is unfolding leading eventually to political destabilization and making radical change a discernible possibility. The above sketch of the theory of political hegemony à-la Poulantzas is essential in its simplicity for the interpretation of the actual historical moment in Greece:

Concerning the first element of political hegemony, the ruling class in collaboration with the troika of international organizations proposed the strategy of internal devaluation as a strategy that would supposedly end the crisis by turning Greece into an export-led prosperous economy able to repay its external debt. The theory behind the strategy was coined during the first half of the 1990s starting with the publication of *Unemployment. Macroeconomic Performance and the Labour Market* by Layard et al. (1991), a Copernican revolution in mainstream labour economics, followed by the Organisation for Economic Co-operation and Development's 1994 *Jobs Study* and hundreds of empirical academic papers. It is a theoretical schema in which the existence of social conflict is recognized in the form of a battle for income between firms and workers, and in which workers must always reduce their claims on GDP in the name of the general interest. Therefore, government intervention to make wages more flexible is justified, and *structural reform* of the labour market appears as the spearhead of every policy aimed at reducing unemployment, increasing competitiveness, and boosting exports, investment and growth. The strategy of internal devaluation is an application of this theoretical schema, still dominant today despite its repeated failure to fit reality in its conceptual corset.[21] The strategy was proposed in Greece in order to unify the dominant classes in a power bloc, to restore endangered alliances with petty bourgeoisie fractions and to obtain the active consent or the passivity of the dominated classes. It was thus a strategy with hegemonic vocations, proposing a different, difficult, but unavoidable future to the people-nation.

Concerning the second element of political hegemony, a power bloc has been rapidly constituted unifying most of the dominant classes or fractions under the strategy: big capital, bankers, industrialists and shareholders, executives of big corporations and financial firms, small business owners and rentiers. Establishing alliances with the traditional petty bourgeoisie (shop-keepers and high income professionals), but also with some fractions of the new petty bourgeoisie (academics and big media journalists, high-ranking public sector bureaucrats, neoliberal intellectuals and artists), the power-bloc quickly grew into a powerful social alliance.

Although the first two conditions of political hegemony under the strategy of internal devaluation have been fulfilled already during 2010, the third condition that is the active consent or at least the passivity of the dominated classes has never been fulfilled. The dominated classes did not recognize general interest in the strategy of the power bloc because right from the beginning it became obvious that the strategy, was not only in a conflict of unprecedented harshness with social reproduction, but was also plunging the economy into a depression much deeper and longer than predicted by Greek governments and international institutions. Hence, in the absence of a hegemonic narrative of the ruling classes, their strategy is delegitimized, and a crisis in political hegemony has been unfolding since 2010. Resistance to the strategy of the ruling classes followed naturally. It grew mainly in three domains: the street, the neighbourhood and the central political scene.

During 2011 and 2012, general strikes declared by trade-unions have been the largest and most combative of the past 40 years. In massive demonstrations workers expressed their anger and demands, giving to the usually peaceful demonstrations during strikes the characteristics of a direct conflict with the political establishment.

Resistance in the neighbourhoods has woven horizontal social relations based on solidarity, collaboration, equality and direct democracy, thus acquiring relative autonomy vis-à-vis capital and the state. In this context, important aspects of social reproduction (such as health, care, services for providing food, etc.) have been reconstructed on alternative material, political and cultural bases (Broumas et al. 2016; Rakopoulos 2014; Rakopoulos 2015).

What happened in the streets and in neighbourhoods, combined to struggles in the central political scene (in parliament, mass media, municipalities, etc.), fuelled the rise of Syriza (the Greek Coalition of the Radical Left) and opened a window of opportunity to radical change. Underneath the surface of the turbulent political life and the rise of Syriza, a long process of formation of a unified social bloc of the working classes was in progress. The formation of this bloc started in 2010 with the implementation of the first economic adjustment programme and culminated a few days before the referendum of July 2015 when the dominated social classes organized massive demonstrations of historical size and energy and voted 'no' against all the warnings for the risk of being fired, impoverished and thrown into the misery of a country outcast from the supposedly prosperous, stable and secure economic environment of the eurozone. The absence of hegemonic narrative and the visibility of naked self-interest of the power bloc precipitated the long process of the formation of a unified resistant social bloc, including working-class employees, relative surplus population, a population of paupers, radicalized youth and important fractions of the new petty bourgeoisie.

Great expectations about Syriza being able and willing to apply an anti-austerity economic programme dragging the economy out of recession, lowering unemployment and reducing income inequalities, were subverted in one night, when Prime Minister Alexis Tsipras capitulated, instead of dramatically increasing the risk of a major crisis for the eurozone by bringing back to the agenda Syriza's programmatic commitments to redistributing income, wealth and power in favour of the dominated social classes, so as to change the balance of power in the negotiations. Since July 2015, the dominated classes have been facing new waves of measures reducing their income and property, their security and social rights, and the economy remains in a state of stagnation.

Politically, Greece is now in a volatile situation: there is a strong anti-austerity social bloc of conscious, politicized workers, unemployed, young people, poor people and militants who have acquired precious political skills during six years of social conflict and political struggle, yet there is no political party or organization able to represent it.

Uncertainty and Social Conflict

It is generally understood though that Greek Depression will not last forever. A new capital accumulation regime emerges, gradually and painfully, as the result of 'creative destruction'. Its main features are already apparent: first, a smaller productive system composed of bigger 'leaner and meaner' firms that survived the crisis, leaving behind, in the ruins of the depression, myriad small and microenterprises and a rather large number of corporations; second, a low-wage, unprotected, labour force deprived of rights and made docile through insecurity; third, a miserable social state, shorn of its essential protective functions; fourth, a society in which two-thirds of the population is in a state of precariousness, material deprivation or in danger of poverty; and fifth, a permanent social reproduction crisis pushing at the margin large masses of the population excluded from the world of work.

In such a regime, fixed capital stock would have to rest at a low level in order to keep unemployment high as a condition to keep wages low and profit margins at levels compatible with the exorbitant claims of owners of capital. Moreover, the Greek economy is also locked in at a low level of fixed capital by the priority of sustainable external balance of goods and services (imposed by the golden rule of finance: *credibility, confidence, consistency*).

In these conditions, the existence of a large relative surplus population, high unemployment and underemployment, and precarious and discouraged workers, is central to the accumulation regime as a discipline device. To be more precise, at the heart of this accumulation regime we find two discipline devices, one based on labour markets and one on capital markets and finance.

Capital markets are central to the organization of capitalist exploitation since finance supervises individual capitals, sets targets for profitability in the form of high financial value and punishes firms diverging from the target (Sotiropoulos et al. 2013). These functions constitute a *financial discipline device* imposing intensive exploitation of labour and high profitability in the form of a *there-is-no-alternative* policy. At this point, workers are confronted by the *workers' discipline device* (described above), which imposes the following dilemma: acquiesce to capital despotism, 'function as an efficient, disciplined labourer…or face the dire consequences: unemployment, poverty, and the insecurity, ill health, and hardship these entail' as David McNally (2011) put it in *Global Slump*.

Still, this emerging *disciplinary neoliberal regime*, rapidly evolving towards its final ideal form in Greece, incorporates as an element embedded in his structure, as an original sin, the conflictive relationship between the exorbitant claims of unleashed capital on the one hand, and social reproduction in forms acceptable by the dominated classes on the other. This conflict makes the regime inherently unstable politically since It will be a regime in permanent social production crisis raising the question of political hegemony. A *tendency to hegemonic crisis* is thus a structural feature of the disciplinary neoliberal regime.

Then again, this tendency is accompanied by a *counter-tendency to passivity* of the working classes emanating from the disorganizing effects of massive unemployment and material deprivation on militancy and politicization, both tendencies stemming from the same single cause: disrupted, defective reproduction of wage-labouring classes, a genuine social reproduction crisis also producing conflict and passivity. Which tendency will prevail is uncertain and the void will be filled by social conflict and political struggle.

Notes

1 Signed by the Greek Government and the 'troika' (the International Monetary Fund—IMF, the European Central Bank and the European Commission) in 2010.

2 Formerly known as *competitive disinflation.*

3 There are approaches that consider the Greek crisis in a broader imperialist context on the basis of core-periphery theories (see Fouskas and Dimoulas 2013 as a recent example). The author does not follow the core-periphery theoretical tradition and Greek capitalism is considered in this chapter as a secondary link in the imperialist chain of countries in the Leninist sense of the term. Consequently, the bail-out agreements are not considered a direct imposition of the troika but a

common strategy of the *power bloc* (Poulantzas 1978 [1968]) in Greece and its allied European bourgeoisies under the hegemony of the latter.

4 Stockhammer and Sotiropoulos (2014) estimated that to balance current accounts in Greece, Ireland, Italy, Portugal and Spain a 47% reduction in GDP was needed (or 23% if estimation is based on recession years data). The actual outcome for Greece was 28%.

5 Profit margin is equivalent to the profits/wages ratio.

6 All data and information on the labour market in this paragraph are from the *Institute of Labour* (Greek General Confederation of Workers), Athens.

7 'The adjustment of the accumulation of men to that of capital, the joining of the growth of human groups to the expansion of productive forces and the differential allocation of profit, were made possible in part by the exercise of bio-power in its many forms and modes of application', Michel Foucault (1978).

8 Poulantzas describes the new petty bourgeoisie in the following way: 'The first fraction of non-productive workers with an objectively proletarian polarisation includes (i) the great majority of lower-level workers in the commercial sector (shop assistants, etc.) (…); (ii) employees who are affected by the introduction of machinery actually within the non-productive sector, and acutely so by the mechanisation of labour (…); (iii) those employed in certain parts of the service sector: workers in restaurants, cafes, theatres, cinemas, as well as lower-level health workers (e.g. hospital orderlies), etc. (…). The second fraction of the new petty bourgeoisie with an objectively proletarian polarisation is that of the subaltern agents of the public and private bureaucratised sectors; this is where the various types of "office workers" among others, are located. (…) The third and last fraction of the new petty bourgeoisie with an objectively proletarian polarisation is that of the technicians and subaltern engineers directly involved in productive labour, the production of surplus-value' (Poulantzas 1975[1974]: 300–27).

9 See detailed data on the Eurostat database.

10 Large fractions of the new petty bourgeoisie of wage earners tend to ally with the anti-neoliberal stance of the working classes.

11 The reproduction of the labour force is internalized to the movement of capital only in advanced capitalism, where the production of *relative surplus value* prevails over the production of absolute surplus value. Throughout the 19th century, workers' consumption was subsistence consumption based mostly on exchange values produced by non-capitalist agriculture, and on use-values produced domestically (Engels 1845 [1987], Meillasoux 1981, Cambridge University Press. See also Palloix 1978: 105).

12 The propensity of the spouse to participate in the labour market is bolstered when her husband is or is expected to be unemployed or paid a lower wage.

13 From a general point of view, labour-power is the capacity for labour, the mental, physical and social capabilities which are necessary to produce a use-value that is a useful thing, which by its properties satisfies human wants. From the capitalist point of view, its use-value is to valorise capital..

14 'Capital itself regulates this production of labour power, the production of the mass of men it intends to exploit according to its own needs. Hence capital not only produces capital, it produces a growing mass of men, the material through which alone it can function as additional capital' Marx 1867 [1990]: 1061.

15 With the exception of the first four years of recovery that will succeed depression, when the average GDP annual growth rate is expected to be 2.5% on average.

16 Eurostat data on Material Deprivation and Economic Strain.

17 Historical forms of *internal exile* are slums (Roy 2011), decaying neighbourhoods in cities (Amin 2013), areas such as the Parisian *banlieus* (Dell'Umbria 2006), Latin American areas behind walls ostracising paupers, incarceration, concentration camps of refugees and migrants, etc.

18 This logical schema embedded in the Marxian concept of *tendency* draws heavily on the physical philosophy of Epicurus and Democritus (Marx 1841) in which contingency plays an important role.

19 The idea of *encounter* refers to the Epicurian idea of unpredictable swerve of atoms (known also under the Latin name of *clinamen)* triggering a process of creation of a world.

20 It is quite different when passivity of popular classes is obtained by brutal force, as in the case of dictatorial regimes, such as the Greek military dictatorship (1967–1974) when the dominant classes formed a power bloc and strong alliances with important fractions of the petty bourgeoisie but remained isolated from the popular masses and above all from the working classes (Poulantzas 1978).

21 Heterodox economists have produced extended literature of critical review highlighting the flaws of the mainstream labour market theories.

References

Alexiou, C. and Nellis, J.G. (2013), 'Challenging the Raison d'être of internal devaluation in the context of the Greek economy', *Panoeconomicus*, 60(6): 813–836.

Althusser, L. (2014), *On the Reproduction of Capitalism. Ideology and Ideological State Apparatuses*, London: Verso Books.

Althusser, L. (2006) 'Marx in his Limits', in Althusser, L. *Philosophy of the Encounter*, London: Verso Books: 139–162.

Amin, A. (2013), 'Telescopic urbanism and the poor', *City*, 17(4): 476–492.

Anderson, P. (1976) 'The Antinomies of Antonio Gramsci', *New Left Review* 100(43).

Balibar, E. (1968 [1970]), 'Elements for a Theory of Transition' in Althusser, L. and Balibar, E. *Reading Capital*, London: Verso Books, 289.

Bell, D. and Blanchflower, D.G. (2015), 'Youth unemployment in Greece: measuring the challenge', *IZA Journal of European Labor Studies* 4(1).

Broumas, A., Ioakimoglou, E. and Haritakis, K. (2016), 'Greece: Grassroots Labour Struggles in a Crisis-ridden Country', in Azzellini, D. and Kraft, M.G. (eds) *The Class Strikes Back: Self-Organised Workers' Struggles in the 21st Century*, Leiden: Brill.

Burgi, N. (2013), 'Démantèlement de la santé, destruction de la société', in Burgi, N. *La Grande Regression. La Grèce et l'avenir de l'Europe*, Lormont: Editions Le Bord de l'Eau.

Camarero, M., D'Adamo, G. and Tamarit, C. (2016), 'Wage leadership models. A country-by-country analysis of the EMU' *Economic Modelling*, 1–10 (in print).

Coriat, B. (1976), *Science, Technique et Capital*, Paris: Editions du Seuil.

Coriat, B. (1984), *La Robotique*, Paris: La Découverte.

Coriat, B. (1994), *L'atelier et le robot*, Paris: Editions Christian Bourgois.

de Brunhoff, S. (1976), *Etat et Capital*, Grenoble: Presses Universitaires de Grenoble.

Dell'Umbria, A. (2006), *C'est de la racaille! Eh bien j'en suis. A propos de la révolte de l'automne 2005*, Paris: Editions de l'Echappée.

Denning, M. (2010), 'Wageless life', *New Left Review* no. 66: 79–97.

Diaz-Sanchez, J.L. and Varoudakis, A. (2013), 'Growth and Competitiveness as Factors of Eurozone External Imbalances', *World Bank, Policy Research Working Paper* 6732.

Dimoulas, C. (2014), 'Exploring the impact of employment policy measures in the context of crisis: The case of Greece', *International Social Security Review*, 67(2): 49–65.

Duménil, G. (1978), *Le concept de loi économique dans le capital*, Paris: La Découverte.

Engels, F. (1845 [1987]), *The condition of the English working class*, London: Penguin Books.

Felipe, J. and Kumar, U. (2011), 'Unit Labor Costs in the Eurozone: The Competitiveness Debate Again', *Levy Economics Institute of Bard College, Working Paper*no. 651.

Foucault, M. (1978), *The History of Sexuality. Volume I: An Introduction*, New York: Pantheon Books.

Fouskas, V. and Dimoulas, C. (2013), *Greece, Financialization and the EU*, New York: Springer.

Gabrisch, H. and Staehr, K. (2013), 'The Euro Plus Pact: competitiveness and cross-border capital flows in the EU countries', *Mimeo*, available at www.foreurope.eu/fileadmin/documents/pdf/Hubert_Gabrisch_Paper.pdf.

Gill, S. and Bakker, I. (2003), *Power, Production and Social Reproduction*, New York: Springer.

International Monetary Fund (2016), Preliminary Debt Sustainability Analysis – Updated Estimates and Further Considerations, *Country Report* 16/130.

Institute of Labour GSEE (2014, 2015, 2016), *Economic and Employment Outlook* (in Greek).

Ioakimoglou, E. (2012a), Internal Devaluation and Capital Accumulation, *Institute of Labour, Greek General Confederation of Workers* (in Greek).

Ioakimoglou, E. (2012b), 'How Internal Devaluation Increased the Profit / Wages ratio and dragged the economy into depression', Slideshare infographic, available at www.slideshare.net/ioakimoglou/greece-how-policy-decisions-dragged-the-economy-into-depression.

Ioakimoglou, E. (2016a), 'The Gender Pay Gap in Greece, Cyprus and Portugal. 2014 compared with 2008. Bridging the Gender Pay Gap Programme' *Cyprus Labour Institute PEO*, (in print).

Ioakimoglou, E. (2016b), 'A small portrait of wage labour in the greek business sector (2014Q3)', Slidshare inforgraphic, available at www.slideshare.net/ioakimoglou/a-small-portrait-of-wage-labour-in-the-greek-business-sector-4-printing.

Kapsalis, A. and Kouzis, Y. (2013), '*Le travail, la crise et les memorandums", in La Grande Regression. La Grèce et l'avenir de l'Europe*', Paris: Editions Le Bord de l'Eau.

Koutroulis, A., Panagopoulos, Y. and Tsouma, E. (2016), 'Asymmetry in the response of unemployment to output changes in Greece', *The Journal of Economic Asymmetries*, 13(C): 81–88.

Layard, R., Nickell, S. and Jackman, R. (1991), *Unemployment. Macroeconomic Performance and the Labour Market*, Oxford: Oxford University Press.

Lavoie, M. and Stockhammer, E. (eds) (2013), *Wage-led Growth*, London: Palgrave Macmillan.

LeBaron, G. (2010), 'The political economy of the household: Neoliberal restructuring, enclosures, and daily life', *Review of International Political Economy*, 17(5):889–912.

LeBaron, G. and Roberts, A. (2010), 'Toward a feminist political economy of capitalism and carcerality', *Signs*, 36(1): 19–44.

McNally, D. (2011), *Global slump: The economics and politics of crisis and resistance*, Oakland, CA: PM Press.

Meillasoux, C. (1981), *Maidens, Meal and Money*, Cambridge: Cambridge University Press.

Machiavelli, N. (1532 [1910]), *The Prince (The Harvard Classics)*, New York: PF Collier & son Company.

Marsellou, E.G. (2013), 'The effect of functional income distribution on aggregate demand in Greece', *Institute of Labour, Greek General Confederation of Workers* (in Greek).

Marsellou, E.G. and Bassiakos, Y.C. (2015), 'Bankrupt Households and Economic Crisis. Evidence from the Greek Courts', *Journal of Consumer Policy* 39(1): 41–62.

Marx, K. (1841 [2010]), 'Difference Between the Democritean and Epicurean Philosophy of Nature' ,in *Marx & Engels Collected Works, Volume I*, Chadwell Heath: Lawrence & Wishart, 25–107.

Marx, K. (1867 [1990]), 'Results of the Immediate Process of Production', Appendix in *Capital (Penguin Classics), Volume 3*, London: Penguin: 1061.

Marx, K. (1867 [1990]), *Capital (Penguin Classics)*, London: Penguin Books.

Marx, K. and Engels, F. (1848), *The Communist Manifesto*, with an introduction by David Harvey, London: Pluto.

Milios, J. (2015), 'Austerity Isn't Irrational', *Jacobin Magazine*, available at www.jacobinmag.com/2015/06/syriza-greece-austerity-neoliberalism-tsipras, 6 September 2015.

Organisation for Economic Co-operation and Development (1994), *Jobs Study.*

Organisation for Economic Co-operation and Development (2016), *Economic Survey: Greece 2016.*

Onaran, Ö. and Galanis, G. (2013), 'Is Aggregate Demand Wage-led or Profit-led? A Global Model', in Lavoie, M. and Stockhammer, E. (eds), *Wage-led Growth*, London: Palgrave Macmillan, 71–99.

Onaran, Ö. and Obst, T. (2015), 'Wage-led growth in the EU15 member states', *Foundation for European Progressive Studies,* Post_Keynesian Economics Study Group Working Paper 1602.

Palloix, C. (1978), *Travail et Production*, Paris: La Découverte: 105

Pastrapa, E., and Apostolopoulos, C. (2014), 'Estimating Determinants of Borrowing: Evidence from Greece', *Journal of Family and Economic Issues*, 36(2): 210–223.

Piketty, T. (2014), *Capital in the Twenty-First Century*, Cambridge, MA: Harvard University Press.

Polemis, M.L. (2014), 'Measuring market power in the Greek manufacturing and services industries', *International Review of Applied Economics*, 28(6): 742–766.

Poulantzas, N. (1978 [1968]), *Political power and social classes*, London: Verso Books.

Poulantzas, N. (1975 [1974]), *Classes in Contemporary Capitalism*, London: NLB.

Poulantzas, N. (1975 [1976]), *The crisis of the dictatorships. Portugal, Greece, Spain*, London: NLB.

Rakopoulos, T. (2015), 'Solidarity's Tensions: Informality, Sociality, and the Greek Crisis', *Social Analysis*, 59(3): 85–104.

Rakopoulos, T. (2014), 'Resonance of Solidarity: Meanings of a Local Concept in Anti-austerity Greece', *Journal of Modern Greek Studies* 32(2): 313–337.

Roy, A. (2011) 'Slumdog Cities', *International Journal of Urban and Regional Research*, 35(2): 223–238.

Sotiropoulos, D.P., Milios, J. and Lapatsioras, S. (2013), *A Political Economy of Contemporary Capitalism and its Crisis*, Abingdon: Routledge.

Stockhammer, E. and Sotiropoulos, D.P. (2014), 'Rebalancing the Euro Area: The Costs of Internal Devaluation' *Review of Political Economy*, 26(2): 210–233.

Storm, S. and Naastepad, C.W.M. (2007), 'OECD demand regimes (1960–2000)', *Journal of Post Keynesian Economics* 29(2): 211–246.

Storm, S. and Naastepad, C.W.M. (2012), *Macroeconomics beyond the NAIRU*, Cambridge, MA: Harvard University Press.

Storm, S. and Naastepad, C.W.M. (2015), 'Europe's Hunger Games: Income Distribution, Cost Competitiveness and Crisis', *Cambridge Journal of Economics* 39(3): 959–986.

SunTzu (1910 [2009]), *The Art of War*, Pax Librorum Publishing House.

7 The 'Politics of Fulfilment' as Preliminary for the Making of a Precarious State in Greece

Maria Markantonatou

Introduction

From the mid-1980s up to the outbreak of the crisis in 2008 there was an accelerating convergence of different national socio-economic models in relation to such processes as the globalization of the economy, and the deregulation and expansion of the finance-led growth pattern. As a result, common policies of liberalization were implemented in a number of different European countries, as well as in the USA. Whatever the country-to-country variations in the speed with which these policies were implemented, and indeed in their consequences, there were notable common features, such as privatizations, pension systems underwritten by private capital, corporate governance reforms benefiting shareholders, liberalization of the banking sector, weakening of labour protection, cutbacks in expenditure on public health and education, and reform of public administration on the basis of private sector priorities (Höpner et al. 2014). Notwithstanding the convergence factor of liberalization, after the outbreak of the crisis in the eurozone, significance was once again attributed to differences between national socio-economic models, even to the extent that they were sometimes perceived as themselves having produced the crisis. They furthermore soon became part of a discussion on the advantages and disadvantages of exiting the eurozone, mainly for Greece, but also for other countries (e.g. for Portugal, see Louçã 2012, and for Finland, see Rosendahl 2015).

At the political level, since the beginning of the crisis there had already been emphasis on how the Greek economy differed from those of the other eurozone countries, with George Papandreou, for example, having been one of the first to speak of how the crisis was the product of Greece-specific problems such as clientelism, state inefficiency and corruption,[1] and with many other European leaders rapidly following his example. At the academic level, though little research prior to the crisis had detected in Greece signs of a 'divergent capitalism' (Björn and Terizakis 2009), after the outbreak of the crisis there was a rapid increase in the number of publications identifying Greece as a problem *sui generis.* Behaviouristic analyses, which soon went mainstream, explained the Greek divergence on the basis of assumed rent-seeking behaviour of actors who simply pursued their short-term demands or interests in the fields of politics and public administration, generating struggles over privileges, and were unconcerned with the long-term economic and social consequences of their behaviour. The role of the state according to this analysis was merely that of satisfying its own electorate and clientele. Its unwillingness or inability to change the abovementioned attitudes in fact paved the way for the crisis. The Memoranda would therefore have the salutary function of eliminating these rent-seeking behaviours, so contributing to the modernization of both economy and state.[2]

This article discusses such political assumptions, by-products of the debate on the divergences of the Greek socio-economic model. It pays particular attention to Francis Fukuyama's perspective on Greece, this being one of the most characteristic intellectual justifications of the policies implemented since 2010 in the name of what might be called the 'divergence thesis', a body of arguments that ascribes the crisis in Greece to endogenous factors, country-specific peculiarities and Greek deviations from norms attributed to other specific European states, or to imagined and idealized notions of Europeanness. In his most recent book, entitled *Political Order and Political Decay: From the Industrial Revolution to the Globalisation of Democracy*, Fukuyama (2015) outlines a version of modernization theory that pushes to its limits the 'divergence thesis' on Greece, enlisting a Weberian perspective on the state and integrating this with a behaviouristic and historical analysis to present a stark exposure of the thesis' political consequences.

Before embarking on a discussion of Fukuyama's approach, some convergences and divergences of the Greek model should be noted. Streeck's (2011) periodization of the various regulatory models employed throughout the post-war decades up to the time of the current crisis relevant: from Keynesian regulation to the crisis of the 1970s, from the increasing public debt of the 1980s to the enhanced private indebtedness of the 1990s and finally to the crisis of 2008.[3] According to Streeck, as growth rates started to decline in the 1970s, governments that had hitherto been implementing *inflation-tolerant policies* were set the task of coping with intensification of the capital-labour conflict, necessitating a move away from their previous Keynesian orientations and concomitant policies of full employment. As capitalists reacted to stagnating growth by disinvesting (resulting in rising unemployment), governments in the 1980s turned to policies of monetary stability in conjunction with increasing *public debt.* Debt replaced inflation as a tool for bridging the gap between the economic demands of society and the needs of the market. As dependence on borrowing increased, creditors began to require tighter fiscal discipline and neoliberalization deepened. A policy favouring *private indebtedness* (mortgage loans for low-economic-status groups, credit liberalization, etc.) came into operation from the 1990s onwards, together with reduced taxation for entrepreneurs, until in 2008 the crisis broke out. The period starting in 2008 was characterized by new reductions in social spending and bail-outs for banks, i.e. an attempt to convert private debt into public debt. Citizens were required to fund it, while at the same time tolerating an ever-shrinking welfare state.

So four phases are to be distinguished for post-war Greece: a post-Civil-War period of reconstruction under authoritarian rule; a brief Greek interlude of quasi-Keynesian regulation following the fall of the military dictatorship; a period of finance-led growth and partial neoliberalization from the mid-1990s onward; and, since 2010, today's regime of 'structural adjustment' programmes. The first two periods are periods of divergence from Streeck's ideal-typical periodization. In the third period, some degree of convergence can be detected. However, any convergence that has taken place since the mid-1990s has been abruptly interrupted. The fourth period has been a period of crisis and of consecutive austerity agreements.

In the next section, we present an overview of some Greek divergences and convergences, followed by an outline of Fukuyama's approach, with a focus on the theoretical link he posits between the 'divergence thesis' and the policies implemented since 2010. As we shall see in the course of this analysis, supposed state modernization through the Memoranda has laid the foundations for a new, idiosyncratic form of *Erfüllungspolitik* ('politics of fulfilment') and generated a 'precarious state' in Greece, leading to what Polanyi has described as the separation of economy and society and to dedication to the Hayekian 'good money' project, overriding democracy in favour of market liberalism.

Convergences and divergences in the Greek socioeconomic model

Greece's first divergence from developments in other European countries dates from the post-war period. The post-war period in Europe has been characterized as capitalism's 'golden age', but the same hardly applies to Greece, for these were years of recuperation from the Civil War. In Greece its salient characteristics were authoritarian rule and a 'dual society' comprising the winners and losers of the Civil War. The state offered jobs and subsidies to the former and repudiated and excluded the latter (Katrougalos 1996: 48). For the state the first priority was to incorporate the shattered rural social strata and the displaced peasants, the unemployed in the urban centres and the literate members of the petty bourgeoisie. The aim of this integration policy was to restore the political function and class role formerly served and played by these groups, for the purpose of securing social cohesion and compliance with the regime (Tsoukalas 2005: 24). The economic survival of these groups would in this way be safeguarded, whereas the losers of the Civil War would be marginalized—a crucial point, given the political instability of the immediate post-Civil War period. This strategy of patronizing selected parts of the population, so as to reconstruct a relatively well paid middle class, would also provide the regime with the appropriate intellectuals and public administration with loyal personnel (ibid.).

On the basis of similar political criteria, the state additionally pursued an alliance with a class of small-scale proprietors and medium-sized business owners. This policy generated a segmented market model of private economy and small or familistic firms, characterized by low wages, uninsured work and the absence of social security contributions (Karamessini 2009: 224). As elsewhere in Europe, so too in Greece the state was expanded considerably in the post-war period, but in the Greek case expansion was due to the state's role as employer and co-ordinator of the Marshall Plan funds, without any significant steps in the direction of the welfare state. In contrast to the situation in Western Europe, in Greece the welfare state remained residual, never achieving coverage in any way comparable to the Northern European norm (Crouch 2004: 9).

Greece also diverged from the Northern and Western European model in its adoption and abandonment of Keynesian policies, which occurred with a time lag. Due to stagnating growth, falling profits for capital, inflation, and changes in the balance of social forces, policies of deregulation were implemented in Europe in the 1970s. This did not occur in Greece after the fall of the military dictatorship. The political Right was strengthened in countries of Northern Europe in this period, by contrast, in the Mediterranean it was the social democratic parties that became significant (ibid.). Thus, in Greece, PASOK (Panhellenic Socialist Movement) campaigned pre-electorally against Greece's admission to the European Economic Community, considering Greek interests to be different from those of the core countries of Europe and advocating 'self-generating development' for Greece. However, this stance was gradually to be abandoned. As economic conditions deteriorated, PASOK's attitude became progressively more pro-European. Greek and foreign industrial investment was diminishing and there were numerous bankruptcies in manufacturing, food processing and the metal industry (Louri and Pepelasi-Minoglou 2002: 335). In the period of PASOK's greatest electoral success, prior to the mid-1980s, a variety of rhetorical tropes were deployed ranging from the 'socialization' of strategic enterprises to the 'social state' and even the 'path to socialism'. However, a succession of impediments emerged, reflecting the fragile balance of power between industrialists, trade unions and the Government. In conjunction with economic stagnation, they had the effect of weakening the Government's quasi-Keynesian policies. The state accordingly resorted to external borrowing to finance a democratic-capitalist settlement. Apart from the burden of the ailing firms that had been created in the context of a plan, drafted in 1983, to restructure and nationalize them, the public debt increased as a side-effect of efforts to cope with underinvestment, while at the same time preserving the social alliance with the middle classes, sections of the working class and the family-centred petty bourgeois strata that comprised PASOK's electorate.

Policies up to the early 1990s can be understood within the historical-political framework of the post-dictatorship period. The motivation behind them was, in part at least, to cope with the increased democratic demands of working-class and lower middle-class groups. This abbreviated Greek version of Keynesianism, implemented against a background of longer-term application in other countries, aimed at promoting a form of class compromise with the potential to foster capitalist development and democratic stabilization through, on the one hand, integrating the lower social strata into the new conjuncture and, on the other, satisfying upper-class demands. As happened elsewhere in Southern Europe, attempts after the fall of dictatorship to establish a welfare state coincided chronologically, more or less, with the introduction of neoliberal policies (Jessop 2002: 145). In 1985, for example, an austerity campaign was implemented in Greece, rendering the working-class optimism of a few years prior a 'brief interlude' (Crouch 2004: 9).

Policy since the mid-1990s is marked by a degree of convergence with developments in Europe: financialization, labour precarization, entrepreneurial-friendly governance, and managerialism. In Greece such processes coincided with a Europeanization agenda and the strategic goal of admission to the Economic and Monetary Union. Social state rhetoric was displaced by the economic directives of the 'Convergence Programme', in the framework of what came to be known, under the PASOK administration, as 'modernization'. The change of priorities, by comparison with the 1980s, was remarkable. The period between 1995 and 2008 was one of high growth, characterized by credit liberalization, investment in public infrastructure, a booming market in real estate, tourism, services and shipping, the contracting-out of public services to private firms, and privatization. It was a type of growth predicated on favourable interest rates that made possible extended borrowing and gave impetus to a finance-led economy (Fouskas and Dimoulas 2012: 12). Its concomitant was on the one hand an ever expanding banking sector, and on the other a disproportionate level of activity on the stock market, accompanied by increases in labour productivity.[4] While there was a decline in the share of gross domestic product (GDP) accounted for by agriculture and manufacturing, the level of capital mobility remained high as Greek enterprises, lured by the cheap labour and flexible working conditions that were widespread there, found investment opportunities in the Balkans (Slaveski and Nedanovski 2002).

The decades of the 1990s and 2000s saw increasing promotion of labour flexibilization and flexicurity. Typical of the first decade of the new century were an increasing disproportionality between wages and hours actually worked (Organisation for Economic Co-operation and Development 2010), the expansion of uninsured labour, and the shrinkage of social and legal protection for employees. Entrepreneurial-friendly policies were reflected in asymmetries between taxation on labour income and on profit income, resulting in an ever-greater disparity between taxation requirements and taxation revenue.[5] Tax avoidance and tax evasion made their own additional contribution to economic deterioration and the country's indebtedness, as did other tax privileges for banks, for shipping capital, the Church and, after 2000, high income earners generally.[6] Public expenditure in Greece fluctuated around levels close to or lower than the European average,[7] with the defence sector standing out as an exception.

The period after the outbreak of the 2008 crisis in the USA, which spread to the eurozone and soon hit Greece, is marked by great divergence between this country and other eurozone member states, especially those of the North. The agreements signed between Greece and its international creditors were aimed at securing rescue loans, on condition of strict austerity, shrinkage of the public sector, wage cuts, and the privatization of remaining state assets. Internal devaluation, whose ostensible purpose was to make the Greek economy more competitive, initiated a phase of radical slashing of wages, pensions and social benefits, along with abrupt dismissals of thousands of people in both the public and private sector, which within five years have transformed Greece beyond recognition. The quality of public services in the fields of health, education and local administration deteriorated as a by-product of downsizing policies and drastic budget cuts. The labour market was thoroughly deregulated with the imposition of enterprise-level and individual bargaining to override sectoral and national collective agreements. The GDP fell at a rate without recent historical precedent, and domestic demand was drastically reduced, with thousands of small and medium-sized enterprises closing down as a result of emergency taxes and lack of liquidity, and with unemployment reaching unprecedented levels. (For an overview of the effects of the austerity programmes see Markantonatou 2013.)

To the Memorandum, via Max Weber

Developments since 2010 in Greece have triggered different forms of social resistance. Strikes by various trade unions, hundreds of social protests and political gatherings, not to mention other forms of resistance (e.g. the 'movement of the squares', occupations of public spaces, social initiatives to obtain relief from the effects of austerity, etc.). All these represented, as suggested elsewhere (Markantonatou 2013), efforts on the part of society to protect itself from the wave of liberalization and austerity. They correspond to Polanyi's (2001: 79) notion of the 'double movement', by virtue of which some forms of social resistance to marketization in the 19th century succeeded in securing protectionist measures. However, social resistance failed to obstruct austerity in today's Greece, and the same is true of the electoral aspect of this resistance, which transformed the political system of the last few decades and since 2015 has made Syriza (Coalition of the Radical Left) the main party of government.

The argumentation that linked the crisis in Greece to the architecture of the eurozone or the *modus operandi* of today's global finance-led capitalism was gradually weakened. Especially after the conclusion of a new Memorandum (European Commission 2015) under the Syriza-ANEL (Independent Greeks) Government, the *there-is-no-alternative* doctrine gained momentum. The defeat, following the third Memorandum, of anti-austerity demands and programmes, along with the related political forces, validated the narrative that austerity policies are in the final analysis unavoidable, not only because of the emergency economic situation, but also because of certain facts about the state. Apart from the Memoranda, *there is no alternative* also because the Greek state, which for the last few decades has remained unmodernized, inefficient and clientelistic, must be held accountable for the dire straits in which the country now finds itself. Social and political distortions, clientelism, cronyism and corruption, have made economic and political supervision by creditors an inevitable necessity.

This view is put forward succinctly by Fukuyama in *The End of History and the Last Man*. In his latest book, Fukuyama has recourse to the Weberian notion of the state as wielder of the monopoly of legitimate force within a specific territorial area. He proceeds to examine whether each of a number of states can be regarded as covered by this definition and identify which of them approximate it more closely. He lists a series of countries ranging from sovereign and (from a Weberian viewpoint) functional states such as Germany, the USA and the United Kingdom, to 'fragile', 'semi-failed' or 'failed' states such as Nigeria and Sierra Leone (Fukuyama 2015: 299). Obviously, in his typology, the first group of states corresponds most closely to the Weberian definition, whereas the second comes nowhere near it. Countries such as Greece and (Southern) Italy constitute a third category, that of somewhat economically developed countries that, nevertheless, suffer from bureaucratic inefficiency, a patronage system and clientelism.

In a special chapter on Greece entitled 'The birthplace of democracy', Fukuyama (ibid.: 94) designates the Greek model as 'clientelistic', with 'low quality government' and a 'low trust society'. He opposes what he understands as being the mainstream view, namely that the reasons for the conflicts in the eurozone after 2010 have concerned cultural and religious differences between Protestant and Catholic/Orthodox political actors. The 'real division', according to Fukuyama (ibid.: 96), is that between 'a clientelistic and non-clientelistic Europe'. Elaborating on the Greek case, he further argues that urbanization in Greece in the early 20th century was not the 'by-product of industrialization' as it was in the UK, Belgium and Germany. It was instead driven, as in the Balkans and the Middle East, 'by the movement of entire villages to cities, preserving *Gemeinschaft* intact' (ibid.: 99). Cities operated as administrative and cultural centres rather than as sources of industrial labour. The state never acquired an impersonal character and a modern bureaucratic form; it remained far removed from the Weberian ideal-type and never effaced clientelism (ibid.: 99–105).

The construction of an effective state, for Fukuyama, is also contingent on the order in which the institutions of the state and of democracy are established. Thus, another reason for the problems of the Greek state is 'the early arrival of electoral democracy, before a modern state had an opportunity to coalesce' (ibid.). Outside interventions became necessary, initially for the liberation from the Ottomans. Moreover, 'foreigners continued to dominate Greek politics long after it achieved formal independence' (ibid.: 101–02). In general, the 'combination of a weak state dominated by foreigners, the absence of a strong entrepreneurial capitalist class, and the early opening of the franchise and democratic contestation laid the groundwork for Greece's pervasive clientelism' (ibid.: 101).

The key theoretical point is the link Fukuyama posits between his interpretations of certain historical conjunctures and the reality of today's programmes of supervised austerity, as if these programmes were a natural or even predictable outcome of Greece's history. By explaining Greece's much debated clientelistic state through supposedly objective factors or historically and culturally unchangeable features, even today's crisis management is finally reduced to them and, thus, justified: 'In a way, the struggle among the EU, the [International Monetary Fund] IMF and the Greek government over the financial crisis early in the twenty-first century is only the latest version of this ongoing story [of foreign interventions]' (ibid.: 212).

By establishing a causal link between the policies of the last five years and features assumedly intrinsic to the Greek state and perennially present throughout its modern history, Fukuyama pre-empts criticism of the neoliberal austerity programmes, their governing principles and their effects. They become simply the predictable and more or less natural continuation of a long story of imposed modernization. The Weberian notion of the state functions in this connection not as an ideal type but rather as a practical yardstick, something like a technical tool for measuring the efficiency of the state and/or the enormity of its failure. Starting from the assertion that Greece 'never developed a strong, Prussian-style state', Fukuyama, an advocate of the country's exit from the eurozone, comes to the conclusion that the imposition of technocratic government (under Lucas Papademos) was an 'effort to force such changes [of state modernization] by outside powers' (Fukuyama 2012).

To the Europeanization of the Memoranda, via Greece

If the programmes were nothing more than part of Greece's political fate—a natural vulnerability to foreign intervention attributable to the historically unalterable inefficiency of the Greek state, as implied by Fukuyama—then there would be no reason for the principles underlying the Memoranda to be promoted elsewhere too. The structural adjustment programmes would correct Greek distortions, cure Greek ailments and hardly concern other countries. However, this is not the case because most governments of the eurozone member states promote neoliberal and entrepreneur-friendly reforms: policies of competitiveness, labour precarization and fiscal discipline, precisely in the rationale of the Memoranda.

The 'Five Presidents' Report' (Juncker, Tusk, Draghi, Dijsselbloem and Schultz 2015) is indicative. They call for 'sound policies' and for 'sharing more sovereignty' in order to achieve 'economic convergence', which, in turn, would require that member states 'accept increasingly joint decision-making on elements of their respective national budgets and economic policies' (ibid.: 5). As regards wages, so called Competitiveness Authorities are recommended in order to 'harmonise practices and institutions in charge of wage formation across borders', and remove 'national preferences and legal traditions' (ibid.: 8). Moreover, within the fiscal union, an 'automatic stabilization' mechanism is proposed as a means of protection from crises, but its aim would 'not be to actively fine-tune the economic cycle', for the eurozone is regarded as the terrain of a self-regulating market (ibid.). It is also suggested that the European Fund for Strategic Investments should operate as a financial reservoir, but under specific conditions: 'it should undermine neither the incentives for sound fiscal policy-making at the national level, nor the incentives to address national structural weaknesses' and 'it should not lead to permanent transfers between countries or to transfers in one direction only …' (ibid.: 15).

In addition, there is no reference to any form of debt mutualization or fiscal easing for countries in need, so that even analysts friendly to the report see a 'danger…that the Five Presidents' ideas will be seen … as offering no way out of the prevailing austerity narrative' (Begg 2015). The priority of 'economic convergence' is repeatedly stressed, but on the other hand, it is also emphasized that this 'should not be conceived as a way to equalize incomes between Member States' (Juncker et al. 2015: 15). Thus, while national asymmetries and income inequalities between member states are deepening, 'economic convergence' is becoming a synonym for a common course of liberalization, beyond the peculiarities and distinctive features of different countries. Even if such peculiarities are not irrelevant to the crisis, the prevalence of neoliberal principles in different countries shows that such programmes are not Greece-specific, nor are they a response to the lack of state modernization in Greece particularly, as suggested by Fukuyama and other supporters of the 'divergence thesis'.

This is also shown by an International Labour Organization (2015) analysis of the latest IMF expenditure projections for 187 countries, which speaks of a new 'adjustment shock' in the coming years. Specifically, it is expected that by 2020:

a 'civil service reforms', in both high-income and developing countries, will result in wage reduction or erosion, payments falling into arrears, freezes on recruitment, retrenchment of workers and employees;
b 'rationalization of spending' on safety nets and welfare benefits, through revision of eligibility criteria to focus only on the poorest, will bring about a net shrinkage of social protection coverage;
c pension systems will be 'reformed' by raising contribution rates, increasing eligibility periods, lifting the retirement age and lowering benefits;
d there will be an intensification of 'labour flexibilization', with revisions to the minimum wage, tailoring of salary adjustments to cost-of-living benchmarks, decentralization of collective bargaining, and the easing of firing and compensation arrangements at the enterprise level;
e a further 'reform' of healthcare systems will proceed, with higher fees and the introduction of co-payments and cost-saving measures in public health centres; and

f increased consumption taxes on goods and services and a raising of value-added tax or sales tax rates.

Most of these reforms, which have been already undertaken by Greek governments of various ideological orientations since 2010, are also on the table for a series of European countries. Culturalist analyses of the crisis, such as that of Fukuyama, tend to overlook the way that this doctrine of fiscal discipline has become generalized throughout the eurozone. Fukuyama further idealizes what he perceives to be the Western state as the final, ultimate or highest stage of political development. For instance, he uses the phrase 'getting to Denmark', to imply not the actual country Denmark, but an imaginary state, which 'would have all three sets of political institutions in perfect balance: a competent state, strong rule of law, and democratic accountability' (Fukuyama 2015: 25). Behind 'Denmark' lies the Weberian notion of the state, which Fukuyama believes is the motivation behind the foreign forces' political project. 'The international community would like to turn Afghanistan, Somalia, Libya and Haiti into idealized places like "Denmark", but it doesn't have the slightest idea of how to bring this about' (ibid.).

In the same spirit, he puts forward the idea that the 'foreign intervention' is there to correct Greek distortions and contribute to modernization of the state. However, this does not explain why, even in Weberian terms and employing analytic categories such as that of the 'fragile states', Greece's course since 2010 has not been towards 'Denmark' but rather towards Africa or the Middle East. Indeed, in the Fund for Peace's Fragile States Index for 2014, Greece is classified among the 'less stable' and 'most-worsened' states for the period 2009–14 together, with Libya, Syria, Mali and Tunisia (Haken et al. 2014: 13). Greece is further characterized as 'the only Western nation' in the grouping of countries with a 'significant worsening' over the last decade, together with Mozambique, Kenya, Eritrea, etc. Some of the criteria cited are 'external intervention' (foreign assistance, credit ratings), or 'poverty and economic decline' (government debt, unemployment, youth unemployment, purchasing power, GDP growth), 'state legitimacy' (political participation, level of democracy, corruption) and 'human flight and brain drain' (ibid.: 10). All of these criteria employed in the characterization of 'fragile states' serve as reminders of the dramatic consequences of the policies chosen for Greece after 2010. They are policies that disorient or even block the route to 'Denmark' rather than paving the way to it.

Politics of Fulfilment and Self-fulfilling prophecies

As a result of this type of crisis management and the creditors' persistence in pursuing punitive austerity and fiscal discipline, what has emerged is a kind of 'politics of fulfilment'. The term *Erfüllungspolitik* was used to denote German governmental efforts in the interwar period to fulfil the terms on war preparations and a number of territorial issues set by the victors of the Great

War in the context of the Versailles Treaty (Winkler 2000: 418). Policies in Greece since 2010 constitute a new, peculiar variety of the politics of fulfilment. Although what is at stake is obviously not war reparations or disarmament, the conditions resemble those that, according to Polanyi, debtor countries suffered in the context of the gold standard, when they were obliged to fulfil terms set by creditors as proof of 'good behavior':

> 'Loans, and the renewal of loans, hinged upon credit, and credit upon good behavior. Since under constitutional government (unconstitutional ones were severely frowned upon) behavior is reflected in the budget and the external value of the currency cannot be detached from the appreciation of the budget, debtor governments were well advised to watch their exchanges carefully and to avoid policies which might reflect upon the soundness of the budgetary position.'
>
> (Polanyi 2001: 14)

'Good behaviour' and the 'politics of fulfilment' towards creditors have become the main ways of staying in government for a number of parties and governmental coalitions since 2010 and even a safe strategy for state modernization and Europeanization in accordance with creditors' criteria. If 'unconstitutional governments were frowned upon' in the era of the gold standard, as mentioned by Polanyi in the above quote, the same is true of today's 'unmodernized' ones. However, the effects of the politics of fulfilment in Greece, which are difficult to reconcile with the ideal type of the modernized state, have come to be regarded as inevitable, even in relation to the most vulnerable social groups. Child poverty, for instance, according to a 2014 report by the United Nations Children's Fund (UNICEF), rose from 20.08% in 2008 to 40.5% in 2012. In this report Greece is included among the countries 'most severely affected by recession', in terms of the risks for children and the capacity of families to reduce such risks (UNICEF 2014). Unemployment, reductions in family income and deterioration of public services for health and education mean material deprivation for children, risks related to nutrition, safety, mental health, school performance, social stigmatization and exclusion (ibid.). Children with disabilities face similar problems, and schools, due to budget cuts, are deprived of basic infrastructure and resources to support them and their families (Papanikolaou 2014).

Supporters of the 'divergence thesis' display little interest in these effects of the politics of fulfilment or of the finance-led model of capitalist growth and the neoliberal guiding principles of the eurozone, which led to drastic economic and political peripheralization of Southern European countries, particularly Greece (Önaran 2012). The orientations and interests of creditors, political conflicts and class struggles are all dismissed for the sake of a culturalistic theory of the state, which, in the final analysis, confines itself to justifying the decisions taken by the élites of the eurozone, and even idealizing them as modernizing operations.

However, a point made by Fukuyama in the afterword to his book is worth noting: 'Belief that the state was uncomfortable became a self-fulfilling prophecy; it was easier simply to work around it', he writes about the USA (Fukuyama 2015: 555). What Fukuyama has in mind with this reference to 'self-fulfilling prophecy', is that what started as a diagnosis of the 'political decay' of the state (ibid.: 552), mutated into a mainstream idea that the state was no longer reformable. Privatizations and downsizing of the public sector have become so widespread over the last few decades that even Fukuyama considers this liberalization excessive. The number of outsourced employees working in the public sector in the USA now exceeds the number of public servants (ibid.: 553), while problems of transparency and accountability are particularly serious in the case of private military companies. 'As more services, functions, and people exited the state, what remained of state functions did not necessarily improve in quality', Fukuyama explains (ibid.: 555).

Though he does not apply this analysis to the Greek case, something that would probably appear incompatible with his own conclusions, the same self-fulfilling prophecy mechanism he identifies in the USA has also operated in Greece. It is surely no accident that the country was described after the first Memorandum as 'a failed state that must become a European protectorate' (Straubhaar 2012). After the third Memorandum, which emerged from a Government basing its electoral success on an anti-austerity campaign, Greece was characterized as an 'economic protectorate' in the frame of rising European 'neoliberal colonialism' (Rasmus 2015), and even as the 'third European protectorate together with Kosovo and Bosnia-Herzegovina' (Zielonka 2015).[8]

From three analytical fields, namely state-economy, state-society and state-administration, Fukuyama chooses to focus on the third, specifically sidelining the first. However, even in relation to the state-administration field, a suggestion that the Memoranda policies contributed to modernization cannot be substantiated. What is involved is transition to a managerial model, which, in conformity with the Memoranda agreements, implants in Greek public administration a series of international actors and organizations such as the European Commission, the IMF, the Organisation for Economic Co-operation and Development (OECD) and certain corporations that have been assigned tasks in various fields (for this implantation of different experts, organizations and stakeholders, see Task Force for Greece 2014). However, what the transition has fostered is more a process of standardization of public administration in accordance with the dubious criteria favoured by these organizations than any real adaptation to existing conditions, any upgrading of services provided to users, or any improvement in long-term economic efficiency.

Analyses of state efficiency in terms of the standards of the Weberian ideal type end up more justifying mainstream policies than contributing to disengagement from the vicious circles of Memorandum/recession/Memorandum and intervention/state fragility/intervention. The more austerity measures are implemented for deregulation of the labour market, shrinkage of the tasks of the state, promotion of privatizations, etc., the more fragile the state becomes, making new interventions appear necessary and justified. The self-fulfilling prophecy set in motion by the politics of fulfilment has generated a precarious state in Greece, with characteristics to be overviewed in the next section.

The precarious state

Mainstream analyses interpret precarization as being part of a broader biopolitical project of constructing 'obedient subjects' or 'disciplined bodies' through 'modes of subjectification' and 'governmentality'. Such analyses understand precarization to be a kind of insecurity, which remains, however, in the realm or at the threshold of social peace and neoliberal social reproduction.[9] Analysis of this kind is crucial in discussion of precarization, especially in developed neoliberal economies, but, in the light of the current ongoing crisis in Greece and elsewhere, to see precarization as something mild, or as a subterranean and not glaringly conspicuous process, is insufficient. The crisis has instilled new urgency into the concept of precarization, making it more dramatic and heightening the relevance of perspectives centred on the economy. One such perspective is provided by Polanyi, for whom the crisis of the 1930s was the end product of a system with 'precarious foundations'. He used the term 'precarious' to denote the general project of market liberalism, including the gold standard, whose breakdown resulted in the collapse of capitalism:

> 'The breakdown of the international gold standard was the invisible link between the disintegration of world economy … and the transformation of a whole civilization in the thirties. Unless the vital importance of this factor is realized, it is not possible to see rightly either the mechanism which railroaded Europe to its doom, or the circumstances which accounted for the astounding fact that the forms and contents of a civilization should rest on so *precarious foundations*.'
>
> (Polanyi 2001: 21)

Today's crisis is often compared to that of the 1930s and the eurozone to the gold standard. For instance, Streeck (2015a) describes the eurozone as a '*de facto* gold standard' and Pettifor (2015) argues that 'today's Eurozone … is not different … from the "fetters" or "corset" that was the gold standard'. Though the gold standard was based on a fixed exchange rate mechanism between different national currencies to promote international trade and the euro is 'the money of a fixed exchange mechanism with a common currency' rather than the 'money of a currency union' (Münchau 2015), the commonalities are striking: hard currency policies benefiting marketization, deflation, the degradation of labour, expansion of the banking sector and what Polanyi (2001: 10) named 'haute finance', not to mention supremacy of economic and technical priorities over social ones.

For Greece, these requirements have laid the foundations for a precarious state. The precarious state has as its corollary the 'precarious society' cited by von Holdt (2012), or by Dörre (2015: 12), who speaks of 'a type of society previously unknown in continental Europe'. Dörre in particular, describes 'Greece, along with other crisis-ridden states', as 'a precarious society of capitalist slump' in which 'not only gainful employment, but indeed more or less *all* basic social institutions have become unstable' (ibid.). The precarious state can be further understood as being the result of what Polanyi would have described as the separation of the economic from the political sphere. In today's conditions it is beset by a tension between the democratic demands put forward in the framework of national democracies, especially those severely hit by the crisis and hard currency policies, and the priorities of fiscal discipline as set by the eurozone's élites.

> 'Politically, what in Polanyi's case was a split between political power and economic power became, in the Eurozone case, a split between nationally organized political power and transnational economic power channeled by the [European Central Bank] ECB, again with severe consequences for democracy.'
>
> (Woodruff 2014: 6)

This split has also been described as a process of 'depoliticization' (Radice 2014: 323) that has been underway since 2010 in Greece and potentially at the European level, for example through institutionalizing austerity by means of the Fiscal Compact.[10] Market liberalism and depoliticization, in the sense of de-democratization, have in turn been fostered by state intervention. Rather than being a contradiction in terms, this has in fact always been the case throughout the history of liberalism, as explained by Polanyi, who never tired of stressing that the market system had from the beginning been the result of state intervention rather than something spontaneously created, as was suggested by his contemporary liberals.[11]

In the Greek case, depoliticization meant a tendency to disassociate social and democratic demands from economic priorities. Everyday life examples of the phenomenon include the intensive demonization of elections as factors damaging 'market confidence', dictation to Greek voters from a number of representatives of creditors what they should vote for and what they should reject, threats by creditors against deviations from implementation of the program, etc. Meanwhile, democratic tools were deprived of any effectiveness that might be ascribed to them, as in the case of referenda cancelled or treated as cancelled, something that became typical of the crisis period. Indeed, in 2011 the announcement of a referendum triggered the fall of the PASOK Government, and the imposition of a non-elected 'technocratic government'. In 2015, when a second referendum was finally allowed to take place, it was actually treated, or interpreted, as if it had not occurred.

As a result, the democratic capacity to influence politics has atrophied, so that whatever the vote, whatever the party in power, right-wing or left-wing, whatever the governmental coalitions, the forced austerity policies, the emergency parliamentary procedures and the neo-colonial dimension all remain unaltered. The neo-colonial dimension of the precarious state is reflected, to cite one recent example much discussed in newspapers, in the obligation, officially imposed on any Greek Government regardless of their political priorities or pre-electoral assurances, to do the bidding of the creditors: 'The Government commits to consult and agree with the European Commission, the ECB and the IMF on all actions...of the Memorandum before these are finalized and legally adopted' (European Commission 2015).[12]

This arrangement has been described as 'sado-liberalism' (Dale 2016), or it can also be understood as being the realization of an idea formulated by German Chancellor Angela Merkel in 2011 as 'market-conforming democracy' (*marktkonforme Demokratie*), namely a national democracy devoted to sending the 'right signals to the markets' and shaping parliamentary procedures so as to respect what is assumed to be the will of the market, the creditors and the investors will.[13] That no political force in Greece has been able to challenge the predominance of this market-conforming democracy means that the state has begun to acquire the profile of a precarious and reformatory state, whose mission is to tailor politics to a series of criteria set by representatives of creditors, international financial institutions and ad hoc commissions of economic control. This precarious state corresponds to the Hayekian vision of total disassociation of fiscal and currency policy from social demands, which Hayek baptized 'special interests' and accordingly rejected, thereby more or less openly rejecting democracy.

> 'A good money, like good law, must operate without regard to the effects that decisions of the issuer will have on known groups or individuals. A benevolent dictator might conceivably disregard these effects; no democratic government dependent on special interests can possibly do so.'
>
> (Hayek 1976: 117–118)

Dedication, in accordance with the Hayekian prescription, to 'good money', indifferent to the social consequences of such a policy, has become the hallmark of governments in Greece. It has been in Greece that the 'good money' perspective has, in the framework of the 'divergence thesis' in its various guises, found its most rigorous operatives. Perceiving rent-seeking, clientelism and the special interests of different social groups as the basic cause of the crisis, they apply themselves to curing the malady by means of forced austerity under international supervision.

Final Remarks

In order to elaborate a sociological analysis of the crisis, rather than drawing, like Fukuyama, on Weber's analysis of the state, Streeck adopts Weber's perspective on money. Streeck's (2015b: 6–11) point of departure is that while Adam Smith saw money as a neutral medium for determining the value of objects and replacing direct by indirect exchange, and similarly saw monetary systems simply as the product of participants' need to expand trade relations, Weber, for whom money was not just a representation of purchasing power but a state-intermediated 'weapon' in the 'struggle of man against man' (Weber, cited in Streeck 2015b: 5), drew distinctions between monetary systems and understood them to be not self-regulating and neutral, but vehicles for competing social interests: a reflection of power relations.

For Streeck, discussing the eurozone as a 'monetary system' in Weber's sense means differentiating between two socio-economic growth models. Domestic-demand-driven growth supported if necessary by inflation, and demand driven by budget deficits, are according to Streeck (ibid.: 15), typical of the European South. The Northern economies, by contrast, are export-based and inflation-averse and, thus, not necessarily in need of the option of devaluation. He stresses that these models are not equally served by staying in the eurozone, but he also sees the eurozone's neoliberal orientations as being maintained for as long as they are in the interest of the strongest economies and for as long as no other option appears for the debtor countries other than to adhere to the rules set by the creditors.

> 'In the debates about the "correct" interpretation of the single currency, the current German government and its allies still have the upper hand … . If this continues, the Southerners will have no choice but to adapt their political and economic institutions to the neoliberal version of the European monetary regime as interpreted by the North.'
>
> (Streeck 2015b: 20–21)

This assumption is confirmed by events since 2010 and especially since the third Memorandum programme, which gave the *there-is-no-alternative*-doctrine a new impetus.

However, the fact that the right of the strongest has been predominant since the beginning of the crisis also shows that it is the political articulation of forces and the political rather than the economic dimension of the crisis that is more important than the divergences and peculiarities of the Greek (or any other) socio-economic model. Perhaps this is why in the crisis years, instead of contributing to the development of more social and economic justice as the 'divergence thesis' perhaps intended, the model has provided austerity advocates with arguments and has become assimilated into the project of European neoliberalism, with all the concomitant shrinkage of democracy through the politics of fulfilment.

This does not mean that the distortions addressed by the various versions of the 'divergence thesis' are irrelevant to the crisis in Greece. However,, in a time when global capitalism is perhaps more speculative, unstable, rent-seeking and predatory than ever before in its history, the Greek divergences are not sufficient to explain the dramatic situation the country has been living through since 2010. Furthermore, the critique of perspectives such as

Fukuyama's does not of course imply that no modernization is necessary. If nothing else, state modernization is one of the few demands that has received such a broad social acceptance and forged a consensus between different class groups, public actors, and political parties of various ideological persuasions. However, demands for democratization are not identical with demands for marketization and liberalization.

As Polanyi (2001: 157) has related, as early as the 19th century if the self-regulating market did not function, failed or entered a phase of crisis, this, according to its advocates, was simply because specific social groups opposed it. Similar arguments were to be heard in the Greek case, attributing the crisis to internal factors and divergences of different kinds, making a recital of culturalist precepts rather than an investigation of monetary systems as social systems, the mainstream explanation. For instance, according to John McGinnis, an admirer of Fukuyama's thesis on the 'End of History':

> 'The Euro was the monetary representation of history's end. … But the currency union fatally assumed that all cultures of European nations resembled those of the Last Man: market-oriented with accountable democratic government. But Greece does not share in the sober Protestant culture of the nation states of Northern Europe. … And while Greece no doubt diverges more greatly from the Northern European culture than any other nation in the Euro, other Mediterranean nations … also look very different. Thus, culture is making a comeback, both as an obstacle to ending history and as an explanation of social reality.'
>
> (McGinnis 2015)

However, rather than just 'culture' it is a series of culturalized conflicts over monetary and currency issues that is making a comeback, resembling the conflicts of the interwar period described by Polanyi, who devoted a great part of his analyses to unmasking the *modi operandi* of the gold standard. It is to be expected that conflicts around such issues will intensify, along with fears of once again living a '1930s moment', as Christine Lagarde, Managing Director of the IMF, put it, namely 'a moment where trust and co-operation break down and countries turn inward'.[14] Far from being 'the monetary representation of history's end' (McGinnis 2015) the eurozone, along with the forces currently dominant in it, is tending to transform—through national divergences, but also above and beyond them—fiscal discipline, the politics of fulfilment and the precarious state, into generalizable patterns, leaving democracy defenceless.

Notes

1 In the World Economic Forum at Davos in 2010, Papandreou, Prime Minister at that time, described Greece as a country dominated by corruption and clientelism (see Elliott 2010).

2 According to Kazakos (2011: 248), 'despite the reservations concerning particular measures, the wide and ambitious reform program implies, in its entirety, the transition from a rent-seeking society with extended micro-corruption to a society wherein diametrically opposite values are restored'. Others considered that the loans to Greece perpetuate the country's role as a rent-seeker. According to Ott (2011: 40), Greece's bail-out reproduced such a situation and, thus, solidarity to Greece meant to refuse the financial transfers that boost 'rent grabbing'. For the role of explanations based on the rent-seeking approach see Markantonatou (2013).

3 These are the phases that characterize the period of 'democratic capitalism', namely 'a political economy ruled by two conflicting regimes of resource allocation: one operating according to marginal productivity, or what is revealed as merit by a "free play of market forces", and the other based on social need or entitlement, as certified by the collective choices of democratic politics' (Streeck 2011: 7). Democracy and capitalism are considered to constitute potentially conflicting poles due to the dialectical, conflictual and materially manifested dynamics of their interplay.

4 Labour productivity rose between 1995 and 2004 by 30%, one of the highest rates among the 18 more advanced European Union countries (Ioakimoglou 2011: 13).

5 Public revenues decreased from 43% of GDP in 2000 to 37.3% in 2007 (Karamessini 2012: 164).

6 Public debt followed an upward path, from 97% of the GDP in 1995 to 107.4% in 2007, (Eurostat 2012).

7 For example, from 2001 to 2009, health expenditure equalled 5.1% of GDP (compared to an EU average of 6.7%), education expenditure was a mere 3.8%, lower than the EU average of 5.3%, whereas social protection spending amounted to 16.8%, compared with an EU average of 18.6% (Eurostat 2012).

8 Though comparison with Kosovo and Bosnia seems overstated, Zielonka's (2015) description is in fact reminiscent of the situation in Greece. 'Cheating is the rule of the game in protectorates. The metropolis cannot admit its failure, and it therefore pretends that things are moving forward. The periphery cannot do without external help, but implementing imposed policies is not practical either. Even the most euro-enthusiastic observers stop short of arguing that EU policies in Kosovo, Bosnia-Herzegovina and now Greece are successful, but an exit strategy is feared even more than an ongoing stalemate.'

9 For instance, according to such a perspective, 'the way that precarization has become an instrument of government also means that its extent must not pass a certain threshold, such that it seriously endangers the existing order: in particular, it must not lead to insurrection. Managing this threshold is what makes up the art of governing today (Lorey 2015: 8).

10 Radice (2014: 323) argues that an '*ad hoc* example of depoliticisation is the assumption of troika control in the Eurozone periphery, under which the IMF, the ECB and the European Commission … took powers of veto over national fiscal policy as a condition for providing loans'.

11 'Strictly, economic liberalism is the organizing principle of a society in which industry is based on the institution of a self-regulating market. True, once such a system is approximately achieved, less intervention of one type is needed. … [A]s long as that system [of market liberalism] is not established, economic liberals must and will unhesitatingly call for the intervention of the state in order to establish it, and once established, in order to maintain it. The economic liberal can, therefore, without any inconsistency call upon the state to use the force of law; he can even appeal to the violent forces of civil war to set up the preconditions of a self-regulating market' (Polanyi 2001: 155).

12 The same obligation concerns privatizations in the framework of 'prior actions': 'the Government commits to facilitate the privatization process and complete all

needed Government actions to allow tenders to be successfully executed' (European Commission 2015).

13 For Merkel's full comments, see her press statement, *Blätter für deutsche und internationale Politik*, dated 1 September 2011, available at www.blaetter.de/aktuell/dokumente/%C2%BBwir-werden-wege-finden-die-parlamentarische-mitbestimmung-so-zu-gestalten-dass-si.

14 For more of Lagarde's comments, see BBC News article 'IMF's Christine Lagarde warns of "1930s moment"', dated 23 January 2012, available at www.bbc.co.uk/news/business-16689211.

References

Begg, I. (2015), 'What Does the Five Presidents' Report Mean For The Future Of The Euro?', on *Social Europe*, 23 June, available at www.socialeurope.eu/2015/06/what-does-the-five-presidents-report-mean-for-the-future-of-the-euro.

Björn, E. and Terizakis, G. (eds) (2009), *Das Politische System Griechenlands: Strukturen, Akteure, Politikfelder*, Baden-Baden: Nomos Verlagsgesellschaft.

Crouch, C. (2004), *Postdemocracy*, Cambridge: Polity Press.

Dale, G. (2016), 'In Search of Karl Polanyi's International Relations Theory', *Review of International Studies*, March, doi:10.1017/S0260210515000273.

Dörre, K. (2015), 'Social Capitalism and Crisis: from the internal to the external Landnahme', in Dörre, K., Lessenich, S. and Rosa, H., *Sociology, Capitalism, Critique*, London: Verso Books.

Elliott, L. (2010), 'No EU bailout for Greece as PM promises to "put house in order"', *The Guardian*, 28 January, available at www.guardian.co.uk/business/2010/jan/28/greece-papandreou-eurozone.

Eurostat (2012), '"Government finance statistics" Statistics Explained', available at http://epp.eurostat.ec.europa.eu/statistics_explained/index.php/government_finance_statistics#database.

Fouskas, V. and Dimoulas, C. (2012), 'The Greek Workshop of Debt and the Failure of the European Project', in *Journal of Balkan and Near Eastern Studies* 14(1), March.

Fukuyama, F. (2012), 'The Two Europes', in *The American Interest*, 08 May, available at http://blogs.the-american-interest.com/2012/05/08/the-two-europes.

Fukuyama, F. (2015), *Political Order and Political Decay: From the Industrial Revolution to the Globalization of Democracy*, London: Profile Books.

Haken, N., Messner, J.J., Hendry, K., Taft, P., Kendall, L., Brisard, L. and Umaña, F. (2014), *Fragile States Index 2014*, Washington, DC: Fund for Peace.

Hayek, F. (1976), *Denationalisation of Money*, London: Institute of Economic Affairs.

Höpner, M., Petring, A., Seikel, D. and Werner, B. (2014) 'Liberalization policy: An empirical analysis of economic and social interventions in Western democracies', Discussion Paper 192, Wirtschafts- und Sozialwissenschaftliches Institut (WSI), Hans-Böckler Stiftung available at www.boeckler.de/pdf/p_wsi_disp_192.pdf.

International Labour Organization (2015), 'The Forthcoming Adjustment Shock Policy Brief', October, available at www.socialprotection.org/gimi/gess/RessourcePDF.action?ressource.ressourceId=53243.

Ioakimoglou, E. (2011), *Labour Costs, Profit Margins and Competitiveness in Greece 1995–2009*, Athens: Institute of Labour of the General Confederation of Greek Workers [In Greek].

Jessop, B. (2002), *The Future of the Capitalist State*, Cambridge: Polity Press.

Juncker, J.-C., Tusk, D., Dijsselbloem, J., Draghi, M. and Schulz, M. (2015) 'Completing Europe's Economic and Monetary Union', available at http://ec.europa.eu/priorities/economic-monetary-union/docs/5-presidents-report_en.pdf.

Karamessini, M. (2009), 'From a State-Led Familistic to a Liberal, Partly De-familialized Capitalism: The Difficult Transition of the Greek Model', in Bosch, G., Lehndorff, S. and Rubery, J. (eds), *European Employment Models in Flux*, London: Palgrave Macmillan.

Karamessini, M. (2012), 'Sovereign Debt Crisis: An Opportunity to complete the Neoliberal Project and Dismantle the Greek employment model', in Lehndorff, S. (ed.), *A triumph of failed ideas European models of capitalism in the crisis*, Brussels: European Trade Union Institute.

Katrougalos, G. (1996), 'The South European Welfare Model: The Greek Welfare State in Search of an Identity', *Journal of European Social Policy* 6(39).

Kazakos, P. (2011), *After the Memorandum: Economic Policy in Greece under International Control*, Athens: Papazisis [in Greek].

Lorey, I. (2015), *The Government of the Precarious*, London: Verso Books.

Louçã, F. (2012), 'Die Krise Europas: Elemente einer politischen Strategie', *transform: Europäische Zeitschrift für kritisches Denken und politischen Dialog*, October.

Louri, H. and Pepelasis-Minoglou, I. (2002), 'A Hesitant Evolution: Industrialization and Deindustrialization in Greece over the long run', *Journal of European Economic Studies* 31(2).

Markantonatou, M. (2013), 'Diagnosis, Treatment and Effects of the Crisis in Greece: A "Special Case" or a "Test Case"?', *Cologne, Max-Planck-Institut für Gesellschaftsforschung, Discussion Paper* no. 3/13.

Markantonatou, M. (2014), 'Social Resistance to Austerity: Polanyi's "Double Movement" in the Context of the Crisis in Greece', *Journal für Entwicklungspolitik*, 30(1).

McGinnis, J.O. (2015), 'The Euro Crisis and the Return of Culture', *Library of Law and Liberty*, 08 July, available at www.libertylawsite.org/2015/07/08/the-euro-crisis-and-the-return-of-culture.

European Commission (2015), Memorandum of Understanding between the European Commission acting on behalf of the European Stability Mechanism and the Hellenic Republic and the Bank of Greece, 19 August, available at https://ec.europa.eu/info/sites/info/files/01_mou_20150811_en1.pdf.

Münchau, W. (2015), 'Die Spur des Geldes: Daran wird der Euro zerbrechen', *Der Spiegel*, 25 December, available at www.spiegel.de/wirtschaft/soziales/euro-und-goldstandard-daran-wird-die-waehrungsunion-zerbrechen-a-1069474.html.

Organisation for Economic Co-operation and Development (2010), *Labour Force Statistics 2010*, Paris: OECD Publishing.

Önaran, Ö. (2012), 'From the crisis of distribution to the distribution of the costs of the crisis: the case of Europe', in Ramazzotti, P., Frigato, P. and Elsner, W. (eds), *Social Costs Today: Institutional Analyses of the Present Crises*, New York: Routledge.

Ott, K. (2011), 'Solidarität in Europa und der Fall Griechenland: Ein Argument für einen ökologischen Marshallplan', *Vorgänge* 4.

Papanikolaou, P. (2014), 'ActionAid Hellas Report on the Special Education of Students with Disabilities in Greece', Athens: ActionAid, December, available at www.actionaid.gr/media/452700/ekthesi-ereunas-actionaid-teliko.pdf [In Greek].

Pettifor, A. (2015), 'The Euro, Like The Gold Standard, Is Doomed To Fail', on Social Europe, 31 July, available at www.socialeurope.eu/2015/07/the-euro-like-the-gold-standard-is-doomed-to-fail.

Polanyi, K. (2001), *The Great Transformation: The Political and Economic Origins of Our Time*, Boston, MA: Beacon Press Books.

Radice, H. (2014), 'Enforcing austerity in Europe: The structural deficit as a policy target', *Journal of Contemporary European Studies* 22(3).

Rasmus, J. (2015), 'Greece as a Euro "Economic Protectorate"', *Counter Punch*, 15 June, available at www.counterpunch.org/2015/07/15/greece-as-a-euro-economic-protectorate.

Rosendahl, J. (2015), 'Finnish parliament will debate next year leaving euro zone', *Reuters*, 16 November, available at www.reuters.com/article/2015/11/16/us-eurozone-finland-exit-idUSKCN0T518O20151116#6MJhEFYESAoSOz5p.99.

Slaveski, T. and Nedanovski, P. (2002), "Foreign Direct Investment in the Balkans: The Case of Albania, FYROM, and Bulgaria", *Eastern European Economics* 40(4).

Straubhaar, T. (2012), 'Griechenland braucht Fachkräfte aus dem Norden', *Die Welt*, 4 March, available at www.welt.de/106041246.

Streeck, W. (2011), 'The Crises of Democratic Capitalism', *New Left Review*, vol. 71.

Streeck, W. (2015a), 'Es ist so weit – Raus aus dem Euro: Um die europäische Idee zu retten, muss das Monstrum der Währungsunion abgewickelt werden', *Die Zeit*, 5 February, available at www.zeit.de/2015/06/euro-waehrungsunion-europa-ende.

Streeck, W. (2015b), 'Why the Euro Divides Europe', *New Left Review*, September–October.

Task Force for Greece (2014), 'Seventh Activity Report', (Reporting Period: February–May 2014), July, available at http://ec.europa.eu/greece/pdf/7thtfgractivityreporten.pdf.

Tsoukalas, C. (2005), *State, Society, Labour in Post-War Greece*, Athens: Themelio [In Greek].

UNICEF (2014), 'Children of the Recession: The impact of the economic crisis on child well-being in rich countries', *Innocenti Report* 12, available at www.unicef-irc.org/publications/pdf/rc12-eng-web.pdf.

von Hold, K. (2012), 'Precarious society: the making and unmaking of social orders', Paper presented at the colloquium organized by the Society, Work and Development Institute (SWOP) on The politics of precarious society: comparative perspectives on the global South, Johannesburg, 4–6 September.

Winkler, H. (2000), *Der lange Weg nach Westen, Band I*, Munich: Verlag C.H. Beck.

Woodruff, D.M. (2014), 'Governing by panic: The politics of the Eurozone crisis', 'Europe in Question' *Discussion Paper Series*no. 81, London School of Economics and Political Science.

Zielonka, J. (2015), 'Greece has become the EU's third protectorate', on Open Democracy: Free Thinking for the World, 14 August, available at www.opendemocracy.net/can-europe-make-it/jan-zielonka/greece-has-become-eu%E2%80%99s-third-protectorate.

8 The Political Effects of the Greek Economic Crisis: The Collapse of the Old Two-Party System

Alexander Kazamias

From the establishment of the country's democracy in 1974 to the general election of 2009, Greece was under the hegemony of an omnipotent two-party system. In the 13 national elections fought during this period, the two main parties, the centre-right New Democracy (ND) and the centre-left Panhellenic Socialist Movement (PASOK), commanded a joint share of the vote averaging 82%. In the same period Greece was also ruled by single party governments, save for a 10-month crisis in 1989–90 over the investigation of ministerial corruption scandals. By contrast, in the four elections since the onset of the economic crisis,[1] the two largest parties saw their joint share of the vote plunge to an average of 55% and since November 2011 Greece has been continuously ruled by two- or three-party coalitions. Besides these structural alterations, the Greek party system also experienced significant qualitative changes. Of these, the most important was the electoral meltdown of the old party system's protagonist, PASOK, and its replacement by the once obscure Coalition of the Radical Left (Syriza); and the other was the emergence of the neo-Nazi Golden Dawn as the third largest party in the Greek Parliament.

To account for these momentous changes, several Greek commentators have coined the term 'minor two-partyism' to underline the contrasts with the old system were two 'major' parties dominated (Voulgaris, 2014; Marantzidis, 2014; Chrysochoidis, 2016). Others, like the psephologist Elias Nikolakopoulos (2016), have used the more nuanced term 'bipolar multipartyism' to emphasize the greater role of small parties in the post-2009 system. However, for reasons that will become apparent below, both concepts will be avoided here as insufficiently rigorous, while Greece's new party system will be conceptualized instead as a hybrid type combining elements of both a 'two-plus' and a 'multi-party' system simultaneously. In addition, the present analysis will historicize the transition from the old to the new party system to unveil the understated, yet important elements of continuity between them. Finally, the chapter will throw light on the close, but often overlooked connections between economic crisis and party system change, with the aim of highlighting how these impact on one another. In so doing, it will emphasize not only how economic crisis enacts the dynamics of party system change, but also how the party system itself, through its various incorporative mechanisms, can contribute to the deepening and prolongation of economic crisis.

If we place our analysis in a wider comparative framework, we shall find that Greece experienced many of the typical hallmarks of party system collapse precipitated by severe economic crises. Studies on Europe in the 1930s and Latin America in the 1980s have shown that the most common effects of economic crisis on party systems are: a sharp decline of support for establishment parties; high electoral volatility and a proliferation of smaller parties; the rise of far-right parties; and the erosion of democratic institutions (Remmer 1991: 777–79; Seawright 2012: 74, 80–2; Funke et al. 2016). Although all four phenomena exhibited themselves in Greece, what is particularly striking is their limited scale compared to the magnitude of the economic crisis. Since 2008, Greece has experienced an economic catastrophe comparable to the Great Depression of the 1930s. National income has shrunk by more than 25%, unemployment rose to 27%, suicide rates doubled and 4% of the population migrated abroad (Eurostat 2017; Imerisia 2016). Meanwhile, one of Greece's two establishment parties, ND, has stayed dominant throughout the economic crisis. Moreover, despite the initial shock of Golden Dawn's rise to 7% in the 2012 elections, after the arrest of its leadership in 2013, the party's popularity froze. Similarly, although the number of parties represented in Parliament has risen from an average of 4–5 in the years 1974–2009 to 7–8 in the crisis period, the Greek party system is still dominated, as before, by two large parties. Finally, despite some notable erosion in the period 2011–15 (United Nations General Assembly 2014: 21–22; Margaronis 2012; Margaronis 2013; Reporters Without Borders 2017), Greece's democratic institutions have not experienced a major decline compared to their far from perfect operation in the pre-crisis years. For all these reasons, therefore, it would be incorrect to accept the frequently expressed view that, after the economic crisis, Greece became a 'Weimar on the Aegean' (Krugman, 2015; Kazakos, 2012).

On this basis, the argument put forward in this chapter will develop around three main points. First, using an historicized approach, it will show that economic crises do not change party systems in a standardized fashion. Instead, through an analysis of the Greek case, the ensuing discussion will demonstrate that economic crises affect party systems chiefly through injecting a high degree of voter volatility, which magnifies anti-systemic trends that *were already under way before the outbreak of the economic crisis.* At the same time, however, emphasis will be placed on showing that *the political and institutional supports of the old party system react to the economic crisis in ways that seek to contain it*, either through absorbing and deflecting it or through suppressing its main effects. Second, drawing on the relational theories of the state, the argument will also underline the relative autonomy of politics and party systems from the economic sphere. As Nicos Poulantzas once remarked, 'political crisis is never reducible to economic crisis' (Poulantzas, 2000 [1978]: 206; see also Sherman, 1993: 108–13). Consequently, in the case of post-2009 Greece, political power and socio-cultural developments still retain a degree of relative autonomy from the economic sphere and contribute to shaping citizens' party choices as much as economic interests and needs. This approach contrasts sharply with the behaviourist tendency, which attributes limited agency to citizens and assumes that economic crises drive voters mechanically toward supporting small and 'extremist' parties. Third, insofar as economic crisis is, by definition, a transitional rather than a regular state of affairs, the party system that corresponds to it is also bound to have an indeterminate character. In this regard, the change of the party system in Greece since 2011 will be interpreted primarily as a transitional phenomenon that will not equilibrate around a stable model only when the economic crisis comes to an end. For this reason, Greece's current party system will be presented as a hybrid that combines elements of both a 'two-plus' party system and multi-party systems (Kazamias 2017).

The breakdown of the old two-party system, 2000–09

The crisis of the two-party system that dominated Greek politics from 1977 to 2009 was largely the outcome of its own 'success'. In the elections of April 2000, the two parties that defined Greek politics for a full generation, ND and PASOK, began to congest the middle ground in an unprecedented fashion. In 1957 Anthony Downs had famously argued that two-party systems with a non-polarized electorate tend to reward the parties that turn their politics to the centre (Downs 1957a: 143; Downs 1957b:114). Under the spell of the 'post-ideological' politics of the late 1990s, epitomized in British Prime Minister Tony Blair's 'third way', US President Bill Clinton's 'triangulation politics' and Spanish Prime Minister Jose-Maria Aznar's 'liberal centre', the leader of ND, Costas Karamanlis (1997–2009), declared his intention to shift his own party, too, to the 'middle ground' of Greek politics. PASOK's response, under the leadership of Costas Simitis (1996–2004), was to argue that Greece already had a traditional 'centre' and that, historically, its authentic representative, was PASOK, the party of Andreas Papandreou, whose career began in his father's Centre Union in the 1960s (Constantinos Simitis Foundation Archive 2000; Kazamias, 2000: 16–17).

From that point on, Greece's old two-party system began to turn hostage to a minority of floating centrist voters who denied the bulk of right-wing and left-wing citizens any real choice in elections. Meanwhile, the overcrowding of the middle ground became increasingly linked to a growing cross-party élite of media oligarchs, business people and senior technocrats, who often developed close (and suspect) relations with both parties simultaneously. While this élite encouraged and often engineered artificial disputes between the two main parties, its deeper loyalty was with the two-party system itself, whose reproduction required the regular alteration of PASOK and ND in power and the exclusion of the smaller parties. Yannis Loulis, the main theoretician of ND's shift to the 'middle ground', recently claimed in a book entitled *Road to the Abyss* that, somehow, the collapse of the Greek two-party system, was unconnected to the overcrowding of the middle ground (Loulis 2011: 30). However, even Downs himself warned that the strategy of appealing to centrist voters would not work if the electorate is ideologically polarized, which, to some extent, was the case in Greece (Downs 1957a: 143; Downs 1957b:114–41; Sartori 2005 [1976]: 170). However, what ultimately shook the Greek two-party system in the years 2000–09 was not so much the polarization of the electorate, but the fact that both PASOK and ND committed the same error as Downs' rational action model: all failed to realize that if every 'relevant party' in a competitive system pursued the optimum winning strategy at the same time, the very logic of the system itself, which is the promise of offering a true democratic choice between two competing alternatives, would be totally undermined. To be precise, the crisis of Greece's old two-party system since 2000 was chiefly the outcome of a growing sense of alienation among mainstream party voters, who began to sense that they were being robbed of their right to an authentic democratic choice.

The first signs of this crisis began to appear shortly after the 2000 election, when ND deputy George Karatzaferis left his party to found the Popular Orthodox Rally (LAOS), the first far right organization to enter Parliament since the fall the Dictatorship. Until the 1990s, studies on the far right in Europe either bypassed Greece or, on the rare occasions when they did not, sought to explain why that country displayed a 'virtual absence of an extreme right' (Dimitras 1992: 246–68). In September 2000, however, Karatzaferis (a media owner with links to fascist groups) launched an attack on the notion of the 'middle ground' and the moderate image constructed by the leadership of ND. According to Dimitris Psarras, author of the book *The Hidden Hand of Karatzaferis*:

> '…the electoral defeat of Karamanlis by Simitis in the elections of 2000 was a turning point in Karatzaferis's relationship with the party. He felt threatened by the turn to the 'middle ground' and waged a personal attack against the then party spokesman and close aide of the leader [Aris Spiliotopoulos]'.
>
> (Psarras et al. 2009; Psarras 2010: 96–101)

Although LAOS fell short of the 3% threshold for entering Parliament in 2004, in the 2007 elections it won 3.8% and 10 parliamentary seats. In 2009 its support increased further to 5.6% (and 15 seats) while its electoral rise was also marked in the European elections of the same year, where it received 7.2%.

The rise of LAOS' popularity continued into the early years of the economic crisis. Meanwhile, after signing the first bail-out agreement in May 2010, the popularity of the socialist PASOK Government of George Papandreou experienced a free fall and, after losing its parliamentary majority in November 2011, it started looking for coalition partners. The inclusion of Karatzaferis' far-right party in the tripartite government under former European Central Bank (ECB) Vice-President, Loukas Papademos, is still shrouded in mystery. In contrast to earlier practice, the minutes of the All-Party Leaders' Councils that led to the formation of that six-month transitional Government were never publicized. Leaked excerpts, however, suggest that, on the one hand, Karatzaferis was eager to enter a tripartite Government with ND, after Karamanlis was replaced by right-wing leader, Antonis Samaras, in an attempt to gain respectability among mainstream conservative voters. On the other hand, given Samaras' reluctance to join a bipartisan coalition with an increasingly unpopular PASOK to implement more austerity, the inclusion of LAOS became a non-negotiable pre-condition. As the centre-right newsaper *Kathimerini* reported at the time, 'according to sources, the inclusion of LAOS was sought after by the Syngrou-based party [ND], which did not wish to see Karatzaferis's party stay outside and thereby possess the capacity to "plunder" ND's electoral base' (Terzis 2011). Papandreou, in a desperate attempt to keep his party in government, accepted this condition.

In retrospect, it is clear that the short-lived Papademos Government left an indelible mark on Greek politics and, especially, the party system. Besides forcing Samaras to execute a U-turn from being a fierce critic of the Memorandum of Understanding (MOU) to one of its avid defenders, its other major effect was to destroy LAOS and give a breath of life to the neo-Nazi Golden Dawn. Opinion polls clearly show that support for LAOS in November 2011 was 8% (one point higher than the 2009 European elections), but after joining the Papademos Government, this plummeted to 2.9% in the May 2012 elections, thus denying the party any representation in Parliament. In the same six months, however, Golden Dawn's popularity soared, from around 1% in opinion polls in November 2011 to 7% in the May 2012 elections (Public Issue 2012a: 12; Mavris, 2013: Table 1). Athough Karatzaferis sensed the damage earlier and pulled out of the Papademos Government in February 2012, his brief association with the old two-party system and acceptance of the austerity proposed by the troika (the European Commission, the ECB and the International Monetary Fund) tarnished his anti-establishment image irreparably. Strictly speaking, Golden Dawn attracted about one-fifth of its own voters in May 2012 from Karatzaferis' party (Public Issue 2012a),[2] but the rise and fall of LAOS had a far greater effect on the neo-Nazi party's ascendance. As some commentators have observed, the rise of LAOS in 2000–11 and its inclusion in the Papademos Government had legitimized far-right politics in Greece in a manner unseen since the fall of the Dictatorship in 1974. Moreover, the institutionalization of anti-immigrant racism, chauvinism and anti-Semitism as 'eccentric', yet tolerated features of public life opened up a space in the Greek party system that was ready to accommodate a neo-Nazi party. Finally, another two-fifths of Golden Dawn voters in May 2012 came among disaffected ND supporters who, in all probability, would have turned to LAOS if Karatzaferis had not joined the Papademos Government (Public Issue 2012a).

The second aspect of the political crisis of the Greek party system before 2009 was the transformation of PASOK into an ossified 'state party' and the challenge it faced as a result from Syriza. In 2004, after spending 17 of the previous 21 years in power, for the first time in its history PASOK lost two consecutive elections (2004 and 2007). In the bitter leadership contest that followed, an unprecedented rise in Syriza's popularity was recorded in all opinion polls, from the party's traditional ratings of less than 5% to as much as 18% in 2007–08. Throughout the history of Greece's old two-party system since 1977, no other party had ever managed to make such inroads at the expense of either ND or PASOK. Although the causes of what the media called at the time 'the Spring of Syriza' are largely unexplored, it is clear from public opinion surveys that a serious representation gap had opened up because of PASOK's growing shift to the centre and its transformation into a 'state party' linked to a chain of major corruption scandals (Vernardakis 2008: 1–3; Kazamias 2015). Indeed, throughout 2006–07, opinion polls showed such high levels of alienation among PASOK supporters that nearly half believed that their party did not offer the best choice of government (Mavris-VPRC 2007). For many of these disaffected voters, PASOK's defeat in 2007 made Syriza appear a more attractive alternative. It should be noted, moreover, that part of the alienation among PASOK voters in 2006–07 was linked to the breakdown of the party's control over the state clientelistic networks, which had played a key part in consolidating its support during the Simitis era (Vernardakis 2008: 3–4; Kazamias 2008: 16–17).

The impact of the economic crisis

With the onset of the economic crisis in 2009, the underlying trends of the previous decade became magnified, often in a refracted form. The main reason for this non-linear change is that economic crises usually inject an intense degree of voter volatility that pours popular disaffection into the cracks of the old system *through smashing old loyalties*. To gain a clearer perspective on the scale and intensity of this volatility, it should be noted that between 1977 and 2009 Greek voters changed party from one election to the next (the Pedersen Volatility Index) on an average rate of 10.3%; in May 2012, however, voter volatility skyrocketed to 48.2% and within one month, in the June election, it rose again to 21.2%. Moreover, insofar as economic crisis is a liminal phase that brings about discontinuities through rapid and turbulent change (e.g. the Movement of the Indignant, civil disobedience campaigns, the sharp rise in suicides, etc.), the breakdown of old loyalties begins to involve an uncontrolled and disruptive element that makes change warped. For example, in the crucial months of June, July and November 2011, between 25% and 29% of all Greeks claimed to have taken part in some form of mass protest activity (Public Issue 2011b). At the same time, it is important to warn against the mechanistic hypothesis that economic crisis drives voters automatically to small and 'extremist' parties. If this were the case, ND would not have remained the dominant right-wing party throughout the crisis, with half of those years spent in government. Similarly, until its historic leap in

May 2012, Syriza was neither the only left-wing party nor the most radical among them. To its left stood the traditionally larger Communist Party (KKE), the anti-capitalist ANTARSYA and other small radical parties. Yet only Syriza saw its support soar from 4.6 % in 2009 to 27% in June 2012. If anything, the more left-wing KKE actually experienced some loss of support during the crisis, from 7.5% in 2009 to 4.5% in June 2012 and 5.5% and 5.6% in January and September 2015, respectively.

To understand why the impact of the economic depression on the old party system was limited, it is necessary to grasp the central role of incorporative mechanisms. The late Peter Mair stressed the importance of re-conceptualizing party systems to account for the fact that they do not simply reflect socio-economic cleavages in the way argued by Maurice Duverger and others, because parties embody intense power relations emanating from the state and the dominant political institutions. Mair (1997:11–17) highlighted specifically the capacity of parties and party systems to 'adapt' and 'control' social groups to engineer what Lipset and Rokkan famously called in the 1960s the 'freezing of party systems', that is a structural force that makes them stabilize and resist socio-economic change. In the case of semi-peripheral societies like Greece, the increased autonomy of politics and the state from socio-economic forces has been emphasized by several neo-Marxist (Wallerstein 1976: 468–72; Chase-Dunn 1980: 192) and Weberian theorists. The sociologist Nikos Mouzelis (1986: 43–48, 73–88) in particular, has shown how patrimonial power relations since the emergence of Greek mass parties in 1910 used extensive clientelistic and populist types of incorporation to admit and control new social groups in the political arena. A key distinction must be made, however, between the concept of the 'state party' (or 'cartel party'), which relies directly on bureaucratic incorporative mechanisms belonging to the state (Mair 1997: 105–16), and Mouzelis' notion of 'partitocracy', which refers to the indirect use of state resources by party 'bosses' whose authority is chiefly exercised through party clientelistic networks. While both 'state' and 'party' clientelism (together with the third type of incorporative mechanism, populism) all use institutional and state power to deter the impact of socio-economic change on the party system, state parties differ from clientelistic parties in crucial respects (Lyrintzis 2011: 6–8) that are essential to understanding why PASOK and ND had such contrasting fortunes since 2010–11.

From its foundation in 1974 to the death of its first leader, Andreas Papandreou, in 1996, PASOK functioned as a populist party. Under Andreas' successor, Simitis (1996–2004), the party was transformed into a 'state party', both because by 2004 it had spent 19 of the previous 23 years in power, and because Simitis' limited authority among PASOK's rank-and-file forced him to rule through the support of a bureaucratic/technocratic élite that was committed to his 'modernization' platform (Kazamias 2005: 68–9). In a gesture revealing of the bogus character of his 'modernization', at the end of his tenure in 2004, Simitis passed on the party leadership to Andreas' son, George Papandreou, in a prearranged leadership election where other candidates were strongly discouraged from taking part (Simitis, 2005: 592–94). In so doing, Simitis contributed greatly to the revival of PASOK's patrimonial character, which he had fought so hard against before his leadership. Hailed by the party faithful as 'the son of Andreas', George Papandreou led PASOK from 2004 to 2012 in the same personalistic and centralized manner as his father, but without Andreas' shrewdness and charisma. Consequently, after suffering two successive electoral defeats in 2004 and 2007, PASOK faced the biggest identity crisis in its history. On the one hand, it still resembled a state party, but without access to the instruments and resources of the state in order to win elections and, on the other hand, it was now in the hands of a patrimonial leader who seriously lacked vision and mass appeal. Following an acrimonious leadership challenge, which Papandreou narrowly survived, PASOK's standing in the polls plummeted to record low levels in 2007–08. Although a year later this recovered when news of the impending economic crisis forced ND to call an early election, PASOK's victory in 2009 was ephemeral and fragile. Despite winning that election with 44% of the vote, this time PASOK could not restore the state clientelistic structures of the Simitis period. The economic crisis forced Papandreou to cut services and budgets under the toughest austerity programme the country had known in peacetime, and after accepting the First MoU in May 2010, PASOK's popularity experienced a meltdown, falling from 44% in 2009 to 12 percent in June 2012.

To some extent, PASOK's electoral fate since 2010–11 reflects the broader crisis of European social democracy. Although the debate over the causes of this phenomenon remains obfuscated, with some even suggesting that social democracy is allegedly 'thriving' (Rothstein and Steinmo 2013: 91), PASOK's collapse can be linked to some of the well-known factors highlighted in the more serious scholarship a) overreliance on the expanded financial sector in the 1990s and 2000s; b) a poverty of ideas, especially after the post-ideological blurring of the left-right distinction by the Blairite/Giddensian 'Third Way'; and c) failure to properly redistribute growth to reduce social inequalities during the years of the economic boom (Keating and McCrone 2013: 10; Mény 2013: 184–98; Escalona and Vieira 2014: 30–33; Ryner 2014: 61–2, 67–72). At the same time, however, the demise of PASOK was also linked to factors peculiar to the Greek context. This is not to say that the party's worse predicament compared to other European social democratic parties is connected to the fact that Greece was hit harder by the global financial crisis. If this were the case, then one would expect other south European centre-left parties to have fared worse than their counterparts in northern Europe, because the economic crisis there was more severe there. Nevertheless, the record shows that since 2011, the Portuguese Socialist Party, the Italian Democratic Party and, to a lesser extent, the Spanish Socialist Workers' Party, have all done better electorally than most other social democratic parties in northern Europe (McCrone and Keating 2013: 42–45). PASOK's obliteration, however, must be linked primarily to other local factors. The first is the party's identification with what has been correctly described as a 'kleptocratic system' of governance, especially during the Simitis era (Pelagidis 2005: 136–42; Kazamias 2005: 75), a phenomenon whose full dimensions are only beginning to unfold today. Indeed, at an EU Summit in December 2009, Papandreou himself said that he was prime minister of 'a corrupt state', while soon afterwards he endorsed a Brookings Institution report claiming that Greece lost 8% of gross domestic product (GDP) every year through state-linked corruption (Barber and Hope, 2009; Papandreou, 2010; Kaufmann 2010). The second factor has been PASOK's failure since 2004 to substitute its state clientlistic networks with other effective forms of political incorporation. A third factor was Papandreou's own inept leadership, including his failure to comprehend the scale of the economic crisis and the troika's damaging policies before signing up to the harsh austerity of the first MoU (Sotiropoulos 2014: 196–204).

By contrast, ND managed to remain the dominant party of the centre-right throughout the economic crisis, partly because it avoided many of the pitfalls that George Papandreou fell into. Although ND always used state corporatist and populist methods as well, it has always remained, above all, a traditional clientelistic party. Its powerbase rests in a complex web of local party bosses, whose clients owe primary allegiance to the party and the influential family networks associated with it. Circumstances played a key role in preserving this partitocratic structure. From 1981 to 2004, ND was in government only for four years, while none of its leaders could remotely match the populist appeal of Andreas Papandreou. As a result, the party's only alternative (short of genuinely modernizing itself) was to compete for power through clinging onto the traditional clientelistic networks it inherited from the pre-Dictatorship era. Meanwhile, evidence shows that its traditional economic supporters in the country's entrepreneurial class continued to do well during the toughest crisis years, with more than 90% of the top 500 enterprises registering profits in the period 2012–14, especially in banking, tourism and manufacturing (Fouskas and Dimoulas 2017). In his 2005 memoirs, Simitis gave the following insightful description of ND's party structure, an organization he knew well as a chief rival in many elections.

> 'New Democracy encompasses diverse social groups with big differences among them regarding income, social power and education. On one hand, there are the high incomes, the economic and social ruling class, and on the other, the large masses of supporters who, for historical and local reasons and their dependence on clientelistic networks, but also because of their education standards, consider that the Right provides security.'
>
> (Simitis 2005: 581)

A corollary of this type of organization was ND's ability to retain its core base of supporters when the Greek state became insolvent and its incorporative mechanisms were totally paralyzed. Its greater autonomy from the state incorporative mechanisms, compared to PASOK, was a decisive factor in influencing the party's electoral tactics when the crisis set in. The most important decision emanating from this position was Karamanlis' determination in 2009 to call an early election that he knew he would lose, despite the fact that he was less than two years into his second four-year term. Nevertheless, Karamanlis correctly judged that a tactical retreat from power at that moment would guarantee ND's survival in the long term, a decision which he reached after a careful assessment of the scale of the economic crisis. In his televised address on 2 September 2009, he explained that 'the effects of the global financial crisis are visible. And the truth is that we have two very difficult years ahead of us' (Karamanlis 2009). This approach contrasted sharply with Papandreou's eagerness at that time to return to power on any terms and his promise to increase public spending under the populist slogan 'Where did the money go? There is money' (Sotiropoulos 2014: 197).

Later, ND again proved capable of shrewdly outflanking its rivals on the far right in a way PASOK could never match in its own dealings with its opponents on the left. In November 2011, as we saw, Samaras obtained PASOK's approval for LAOS's inclusion in the Papademos Government as a condition for ND's participation. This bold tactic instantly liquidated Karatzaferis' party after more than a decade of undermining ND's supremacy over the right half of the political spectrum. In addition, when Karatzaferis pulled out of the Papademos Government to salvage what was left of his damaged popularity, it emerged that in the previous weeks Samaras was audacious enough as to strike a deal with his two lieutenants, Adonis Georgiadis and former fascist youth leader, Makis Voridis, who defected from LAOS and instantly joined ND, with the latter also keeping his ministerial portfolio. Eighteen months later, Samaras moved equally shrewdly against his other far right rival, Golden Dawn, whose popularity in some opinion polls had risen to the shocking levels of 14%–16% in the summer of 2013,[3] leading senior ND politicians, like the former President of Parliament, Vyron Polydoras, to propose inviting the neo-Nazis to join a coalition with his own party (*Kathimerini* 2013). However, following the murder of anti-fascist singer Pavlos Fyssas during a gang attack by Golden Dawn members on 18 September 2013, ND Minister of Public Order and Citizen Protection, Nikos Dendias, presented the Public Prosecutor with hitherto withheld files of 32 cases implicating party members in a range of criminal activities. Two weeks later, the party leadership were arrested on charges of leading a criminal organization and have been under trial since. With Golden Dawn's image as the 'invincible' party badly tarnished, its popularity fell back to 6%–7% and has stabilized around this level in the January and September 2015 elections. Although Samaras later admitted that his Government 'lacked the political will' to move earlier against Golden Dawn, not least because his own all-mighty cabinet secretary, Panayiotis Baltakos, was later found to be an agent of the neo-Nazi party inside the Government (Samaras 2013; Savaricas 2014), ND still exhibited strong survival reflexes against its hitherto most formidable far right rival.

Against this background, the most striking change which the economic crisis brought to the Greek party system has been the meteoric rise of Syriza. This party, whose history goes back to the splits within the Greek communist movement over the Soviet invasion of Czechoslovakia in 1968, had never seen its share of the vote rise beyond 5% under the old party system. In May and June 2012, however, its popularity soared to 16.8% and 26.9%, respectively, making it Greece's official opposition. Although the electoral surge of Syriza had important roots in the crisis of the old party system in 2007–08, other factors played a major part. These, however, bear little connection to what Cas Mudde presents in his ill-informed account as the ostensibly 'populist' and 'illiberal' character of Syriza (Mudde 2017: 13, 48–9). Compared to its rivals, Syriza was always more sensitive over issues of social diversity and pluralism, as evidenced in its strong anti-racist record, defence of civil rights and minorities, including the legalization of same-sex marriage in 2015, which most deputies of the ostensibly 'liberal' ND vehemently opposed.

A more nuanced approach, however, must start by emphasizing Syriza's new left ideology and its roots in the Eurocommunist movement of the 1970s and 1980s. Far from embracing a populist agenda, a core element of the party's identity (including its marginalization under the old two-party system), was its staunch opposition to PASOK's populism until 1996. Indeed, it was Andreas Papandreou's populist discourse that famously derided Syriza in its earlier incarnations as *la gauche caviar* (the left of salons), a depiction keenly deployed by the otherwise anti-populist Mudde (2017: 16, 23). Underlying Syriza's standard portrayal as an 'élitist' party stood some clearly non-populist features, like its capacity to attract voters from the most educated and urbanized social strata until the elections of May 2012.[4] Indeed, this clichéd critique of Syriza as 'élitist' was used as late as February 2011, when PASOK's Deputy Prime Minister, Theodoros Pangalos, mocked Prime Minister Alexis Tsipras in a television debate for failing to obtain '3 percent' [of the vote] and behaving like 'the aristocracy of the country's political life' (Alter TV 2011). Indeed, a corollary of Syriza's anti-populism at the time was its support for a Federal Union of Europe along the lines advocated by the Italian Eurocommunist Altiero Spinelli, when PASOK advocated Grexit until the 1980s and a mild Euroscepticism until 1996.

These ideological credentials were all too familiar to the disaffected PASOK voters who turned to Syriza in 2007–08 and, again, in 2011–12. According to one opinion poll in 2011, five times more people than Syriza's own voters regarded it as 'the most modern party', while twice as many as its own voters singled out its 'European' character as its foremost characteristic. Consequently, when another opinion survey was carried out after the first year of harsh austerity under the first MoU, 59% of Syriza voters still had a positive view of the EU—compared with 66% of voters of the now ultra-Europhile PASOK, while 56% backed Greece's membership of the Euro—compared with 66% for PASOK and 64% for ND voters (Public Issue 2011a). In other words, the notion that Tsipras's party rose to prominence in 2011–12 because it championed a Eurosceptical populism is strongly refuted by the evidence. If anything, its electoral breakthrough in the early years of the economic crisis was made possible precisely because it managed to articulate a strong critique of the MoU's destructive measures with an anti-populist discourse that defended immigrants, pluralism and Greece's membership of the euro.

Although typical anti-Syriza propaganda distorted the party's Europeanism, calling it 'Eurosceptical' in order to then charge it with 'populism' (Spiegel and Carnegy 2014), Mudde has devised a more ingenious interpretation. According to him, what made Syriza populist was ostensibly this Europeanism, which led it to adopt what he calls 'a third way' position, promising both an end to austerity and continued membership of the eurozone (Mudde 2017: 19, 23, 32–33).[5] Although Mudde acknowledges that such a policy was 'economically possible' (and defends Nobel laureates Paul Krugman and Joseph Stieglitz for endorsing it) he still charges Syriza with 'populism' because, he says, the policy was politically 'unrealistic' (Mudde, 2017: 49). Besides stretching the meaning of populism to the absurd bounds of making it synonymous with any type of 'unrealistic' policies, Mudde also suggests, astoundingly, that if Syriza had opposed austerity through an anti-immigration/anti-EU platform (like the French National Front, for example), it would not have been a populist party. He says: 'SYRIZA could have tried to implement "radical politics", but only if it would have left the Eurozone (and, in the medium term, the EU altogether)'; elsewhere he insists that xenophobia should not be conflated with populism (Mudde 2017: 11, 32–3, 49, 50).

The above, of course, should not imply that Syriza was particularly immune to populist influences. Although its electoral breakthrough in 2011–12 was achieved mainly through a radical critique of neoliberalism from a new left perspective, after June 2012 the party began to blend its old ideology with growing elements of populism. Fearing a repetition of the 2007–08 experience, when it failed to retain the masses of disaffected PASOK voters, in its conference in July 2013 Syriza adopted the Manichean theory of 'the two blocs', which claimed that Greek politics was divided between the pro-austerity forces of the 'two-party system' and 'the anti-MoU forces'.[6] As Ernesto Laclau (2005: 38–9) pointed out, 'the dichotomization of the social space through the creation of an internal frontier', which leads to the 'discursive construction of an enemy', is an essential condition 'for the emergence of a populist rupture'. Moreover, in September 2014 Syriza launched its Thessaloniki Economic Platform, which even its own economic guru, Yanis Varoufakis, publicly denounced for its 'fake promises' (Varoufakis 2017: 88). However, populism must not be reduced to a single variable definition, in the way proposed by Mudde, as simply 'an ideology' that 'considers society to be separated into two homogeneous and antagonistic groups' (Mudde 2004: 543). Important theoretical contributions from scholars like Mouzelis, Kurt Weyland and others, have shown that populism must be also linked to a specific type of leadership and party organization, whereby 'a personalistic leader seeks or exercises government power through direct, unmediated, uninstitutionalized support from large numbers of followers' (Mouzelis 1986: 88–94; Weyland 2001: 1–22).

On the basis of this poststructuralist/Weberian definition, it is clear that Tsipras never commanded an unmediated/uninstitutionalized personal authority over Syriza, not even after becoming Prime Minister in January 2015. For this reason, during his tough negotiations with the troika in January–July 2015, his opponents began to declare that he could not be made to accept a third MoU unless he 'agrees to dismember his own party' (Smith 2015). This assessment was indeed confirmed when the party finally broke up as a result of Tsipras' dramatic U-turn and surrender to the troika on 12–13 July. Besides the Left Platform (which formed the new Popular Unity party under Panayiotis Lafazanis), Syriza also lost its dynamic Minister of Finance, Varoufakis (who went on to form the pan-European DiEM25 movement), the Leader of Parliament, Zoe Konstantopoulou (who formed the Course of Freedom party), and nearly a third of its Central Committee, including the party secretary, Tassos Koronaios. It was from that moment on that Syriza became Tsipras' own apparatus, approximating the structure of a populist party more than any other time in its history. Meanwhile, what the party lost in this transition was much of the Manichean discourse of period 2013–15, which divided Greek politics into 'two blocs' and any direct appeal Tsipras had established during his showdown with Greece's creditors in January–July 2015. Ironically, however, it was exactly at that point that his former opponents in the troika began to retract the accusation of 'populism', since Tsipras was now their major political ally in Greece. Consequently, in 2017, in reply to a question by a former PASOK minister, EU Commissioner Pierre Moscovici, refused to describe Syriza in such terms. 'I cannot consider Syriza today as a populist party…because they made the choice to remain in the Eurozone' (Michalopoulos 2017). These statements, of course, have more to do with the fact that Tsipras' Syriza has become a party of convenient semi-populists since accepting the third MoU, than with any serious assessment of the party's character or discourse.

Meanwhile, however, Tsipras seems unimpressed by such words of support and is anxious to portray himself at home as a true populist leader worthy of Andreas Papandreou's legacy. In September 2017, on the 43rd anniversary of PASOK's foundation, Tsipras published an astonishing article titled 'Was Andreas a Liar?', in which he implicitly likened his own volte-face over the third MoU in July 2015, to PASOK's U-turns in the 1980s over its promises to take Greece out of the North Atlantic Treaty Organization and the European Economic Community.

> 'Andreas Papandreou came under heavy fire from the "establishment" of his era, as he used to call it, for being a "populist", a "demagogue", a "liar"…. But the basic and dominant truth…is this: he possessed the political instinct to diagnose the historic moment of the transition to

> democracy.... Andreas understood that only with the momentum of this wave...was it possible for the country to make a leap forward.'
>
> (Tsipras 2017, translated by A. Kazamias)

With his tight grip on the party, clever tactics and compliance with the troika's neoliberal policies, Tsipras has managed to stay in power longer than any other Prime Minister since the beginning of the economic crisis. Meanwhile, however, he has turned Syriza into a political zombie, lacking any sense of identity or intellectual dynamism beyond a post-populist retro-nostalgia that yearns for Andreas' mass appeal.

'Two-plus' or 'pluralist'? A party system-in-crisis

A well-known blind spot in the theory of political parties is the area between two-party and multi-party systems (Siaroff 2003: 269). Giovanni Sartori's influential typology has no distinct category for systems where two parties are dominant, but are unable to form majority governments. In his argument, a two-party system is either one whose two 'relevant parties' regularly form majority governments (as was the case in Greece from 1977 to 2011) or we are straight into the category of 'moderate pluralism' (Sartori 2005 [1976]: 158). Jean Blondel, by contrast, has defined a distinct category, which he famously called the 'two-and-a-half' system, and used it for states like Belgium, Canada, West Germany and Ireland, whose two main parties could not form majority governments, but usually relied on a third small party (Blondel 1968: 185–6). An implicit assumption in this typology is that the two main parties are always relying on the same small party, e.g. the Liberals in Belgium, Labour in Ireland, and the Free Democratic Party in Germany (until 1998). For this reason, when the Greens emerged as the fourth 'relevant party' in Germany in the 1990s, Alan Ware spoke (perhaps with a tinge of irony) about an emerging 'two-and-two-halves' party system (Ware 1996: 178). In recent years, none the less, it has become more common to use the umbrella term 'two-plus' party system to refer to both 'two-and-a-half' and 'two-and-two-halves' party systems in states as diverse as Canada, Spain, Taiwan, the Netherlands and so forth (Aldrich 2012: 57; Gunther et al. 1988: 405; Cheng and Hsu 2015: 115). This term, however, which will be used below strictly for the sake of convenience, does not refer to a systematically devised category and remains seriously under-theorized.

With regard to the Greek party system, there is no question that since November 2011 it has ceased to be a conventional 'two-party' type. At the same time, its new configuration does not fall under either the 'two-plus' or the 'multi-party' system categories. To begin with, although the new Greek party system has operated as a 'two-plus-two-halves' system (with a ND-PASOK coalition in 2013–15, succeeded since January 2015 by a Syriza-Indeendent Greeks coalition), in 2011–13 it displayed all the typical hallmarks of a 'multi-party' system. To be more precise, in 2011–13 Greece had 'around five (or six)' parties that were 'relevant', a number defined by Sartori (2005 [1976]: 116–17, 154) as the optimum for a 'moderate pluralist' system. These produced, as is common in multiparty systems, two tripartite coalitions, one with PASOK-ND-LAOS under Papademos (November 2011–February 2012) and another with ND-PASOK-Democratic Left (DIMAR) under Samaras (June 2012–June 2013). Moreover, although the Greek party system since May 2012 was clearly dominated by two core parties, ND and Syriza, their joint share of the vote has been substantially lower than most established 'two-plus' systems. For example, when Germany was a 'two-plus-two-halves' system in 1998–2013, its two main parties received a joint average share of the vote of 69%, while the two main Irish parties since 1922 have received a joint average of 73% and in Portugal this average was even higher, approximating 75%. By contrast, since May 2012 Greece has produced a joint average share of the vote for ND and Syriza of just 55%. Even if we deduct their exceptionally poor performance in May 2012, this figure is still 61.5%, an average that Blondel (1968: 184, Table 1) considers low even for multiparty systems, let alone for 'two-plus' systems.

Based on these observations, one might be tempted to argue that during its emergence, the post-2011 Greek party system displayed strong multiparty tendencies, but after June 2013, this settled into a 'two-plus' system. Moreover, this argument could be couched in a political economy approach that would attribute early fragmentation to the years of severe crisis (Greek GDP fell by 25% in 2009–13), and a 'two-plus' system to the stabilization of the economy around zero growth (2014–16). Such an analysis, however, would have to contend with several problems. First, when Samaras reverted to a bipartisan coalition after DIMAR's withdrawal from his Government in June 2013, Greece was still in the depths of depression. It took one more year for GDP to stabilize around zero growth (and even that was artificially boosted by a negative rate of inflation).[7] Second, there is no established correlation in the scholarship between trends in economic growth and types of party system. Although economic crisis unleashes high political volatility and a degree of anti-systemic reaction, multiparty systems can be found in political systems that have experienced long-term sustainable growth (e.g. France, Italy and the Netherlands, 1948–1973) while two-partyism has proved capable of surviving periods of economic depression (e.g. Britain and the USA in the 1930s). Third, as already argued, the impression that party systems reflect changes in the economy in an immediate and mechanical way accords very little agency to voters and disregards the relative autonomy of culture and politics from productive relations. Finally, since the Greek elections of September 2015, opinion polls have shown a sharp decline in popularity for the Tsipras Government[8] and this has kept open the prospect of Greece's return to a multi-party system if Syriza loses badly in the next election.

Consequently, a more fruitful way of conceptualizing the post-2011 party system is required. This must start from the premise that the Greek party system was largely born out of the post-2008 economic crisis and, by implication, its dynamics are closely connected with it. Furthermore, if the economic crisis is by definition an exceptional state of affairs that does not conform to established patterns of regularity, then, equally, the party system that corresponds to it cannot be conceptualized as a stable type, coinciding with the established categories in the scholarship. On this basis, it is hereby proposed that we treat party systems-in-crisis as a distinct, hybrid form, that is by definition marked by a combination of diverse elements from more than one of the established categories. In the case of Greece, this approach would lead to the conclusion that the post-2011 party system is marked by an unusual mixture of elements from both 'two-plus' and 'multi-party' systems, blended together. A corollary of this conclusion is that, as long as two conditions remain in place, namely an ongoing economic crisis and the defensive political culture that has prevailed since 2011–12 (with a brief interval in 2014–15), the Greek party system will continue to manifest the hallmarks of a party system-in-crisis.

Besides its hybrid character, however, the second defining feature of a party system-in-crisis is its exceptionally high volatility. Mogens Pedersen, who devised the most widely used voter volatility index (the net percentage of those who vote for a different party between two elections), found that average volatility in 13 West European party systems from 1948 to 1977 was 8.1%, with the highest exhibiting itself in crisis-ridden France, at 16.8% (Pedersen 1979: 3, 7, 9, Table 1, Table 2). In accordance with this norm, the old Greek party system from 1977 to 2009 also sustained an aggregate volatility rate of 10.3%. By contrast, in the four Greek elections since May 2012, average voter volatility skyrocketed to an average of 25.3%, way above the most extreme case in Pedersen's study. What renders this feature all the more remarkable is that two of these four elections were contested within a few months of each other, but still displayed high volatility: 21.2% in June 2012 and 9.6% in September 2015. While a downward trend can be also detected across these four elections, from 48.2% in May 2012 to 9.6% in September 2015, any conclusions about the likelihood of party system stabilization at this stage would be premature. Without ruling out the possibility of future consolidation around a 'two-and-two-halves' system, with ND and Syriza acting as the core parties (Mouzelis 2016), opinion polls suggest that other outcomes are equally likely. These include a transition to either a moderate or polarized multi-party system or even to a dominant party system, with ND in that role. Moreover, the merger of the three centre-left parties in 2017 (PASOK, DIMAR and the Movement of Democratic Socialists) into the new Democratic Alignment coalition, and their potential alliance with the centrist party Potami (The River), could further limit Syriza's prospects of consolidating itself as the second largest party after the next election (expected in 2018 or 2019).

Overall, however, what is evident at the time of writing[9] is that the Greek party system remains in a high state of flux, both in terms of its non-conformity to any of the established types and its high voter volatility. Recent research has questioned the earlier view that high voter volatility should be considered as a trait of multi-party systems (Evans 2002: 160), a conclusion that makes it even harder to infer what party system Greece may be heading towards after the end of the current crisis. Meanwhile, Syriza's continued inability to openly proclaim itself a social democratic party (Mouzelis 2015) together with the growing consolidation of its centrist opponents in the new Democratic Alignment-Potami bloc, is building a new tension in the centre-left axis of the party system, with hitherto unpredictable consequences. Although Tsipras' entire venture now hinges on restoring some sort of short-term economic growth for 2017 and 2018 to claim that his capitulation to the Troika in July 2015 has supposedly paid off, the future of the Greek party system will ultimately be shaped partly by the voters' reaction to this message and partly by the ability of Syriza's opponents (on both the centre and the left) to offer more credible alternatives. However, even if Syriza emerges from the next election as the second largest party, depending on how big the gap with ND is, the possibility of its future relegation to the status of a small party remains an open question.

Conclusion

Most analyses of the political effects of economic crisis tend to rest on two implicit assumptions. First, they assume that developments in the economic field, i.e. the economic crisis itself, enjoy primacy over developments in the political field (including the party system) and treat the latter as essentially a function of the former. This tendency, which was ruthlessly attacked in the past as the black spot of Marxism, is now championed by some of its former neoliberal critics, who declare with the confidence of neophytes that 'political power follows economic power' or that economic crisis 'discredits politics',[10] i.e. all politics, not just establishment parties (The Economist 2016; Vasilopoulou and Halkiopoulou 2015). The second assumption, which largely emanates from the first, is to portray the notion of 'crisis' in purely negative terms as a homogenous wave of material destruction, with corresponding deleterious effects on the social, cultural and political spheres.

In the forgoing analysis, however, a sharply contrasting approach was adopted. Regarding the connections between economic crisis and party systems, the core assumption has been that both levels interact through an open-ended dialectic, whereby changes in one can influence changes in the other to a potentially equivalent degree. This Critical Political Economy approach also assumes that the direction of this dialectic is ultimately determined by the given historical circumstances of the society in question and the agency of its main social groups, with their corresponding ideas and cultural perceptions. As one recent study on party system collapse in Latin America put it, 'unlike more deterministic explanations that view collapse as a natural outcome of threats like economic crisis', what we need is a more nuanced approach which 'also analyzes the party system's response' to the economic crisis (Morgan 2011: 8).

In the Greek case, the importance of restoring the relative autonomy of the political lies, of course, not only in explaining how the party system responded to the economic recession, but also how it conditioned the recession as it was still coming in. In the previous paragraphs, in particular, it was argued that the breakdown of the old two-party system in 2011 cannot be understood without comprehending the political crisis of that system in the preceding decade. Of course, this does not mean that the decline of the Greek two-party system before 2008 was responsible for the global financial crisis nor that the collapse of that party system in 2011–12 was not chiefly the outcome of the economic crisis. What it does mean, however, is that the decline of the Greek party system before 2008 played a decisive part in aggravating the disastrous effects of the economic crisis in ways that could have been avoided. For instance, because of its rife nepotism, corruption and incompetence, the Greek party system faced the economic crisis of 2008 with two successive Prime Ministers who were, respectively, the nephew and son of their parties' founders and longest serving Prime Ministers.[11] Of those, the first withdrew from power almost instantly, and the second, until the Greek state went insolvent in April 2010, proclaimed that 'the money's there' and that 'the markets can wait' (Hope 2011). Similarly, understanding the old party system's bankruptcy before 2008 also explains why it had little chance of surviving the impact of the economic crisis. In contrast to what the economic determinists might imply, this outcome was by no means inevitable. The economic crisis crushed the old Greek party system because, for nearly a decade before, it had been politically feeble. Indeed, as a study on Venezuela and Peru has found, economic crisis is not a sufficient condition for bringing about a breakdown of the party system, but 'a substantial erosion of party identification is an almost essential precursor to party system collapse' (Seawright 2012: 89).

Equally, after the economic crisis set in, the Greek party system did not accept its demise passively. An important lesson from the Greek experience is that hegemonic party systems almost invariably interpret economic crises as structural challenges to their own authority (which, in many ways, they are) and are therefore quick to react to them in the same way they would in the case of mass uprisings with potentially revolutionary implications. This analogy is not theoretical, as the Greek crisis did unleash strong waves of popular unrest that were appropriately compared to the Arab Spring revolutions mushrooming at the time on the opposite side of the Mediterranean (Douzinas 2013: 8). This image, by implication, drives established systems to respond to economic crises through methods that are akin to a counter-revolutionary reaction. Ancient divisions between rival hegemonic parties (that is, ND and PASOK) suddenly vanish, broad pro-establishment coalition governments are quickly formed, and police repression reaches unprecedented heights. Amidst this polarized environment, intense battles are fought in the field of civil society, between social groups that suffer the brunt of the economic crisis and the forces backing the old party system and struggle for political survival. In the case of EU members, the latter can be occasionally backed by the bureaucracies of

Brussels and Frankfurt, either via interventions like the European Commission President's warning against a 'wrong result' in the January 2015 Greek elections and preference for 'known faces', or via disinformation campaigns sponsored through the international press. Ultimately, however, the survival or collapse of a party system during an economic crisis is determined by the social battles between the victims of the economic depression and the political alliance of the old hegemonic élites and their respective capacity to win over those in between.

As regards the notion of 'crisis' itself, the foregoing analysis has consistently avoided treating it as merely a synonym for destruction and loss of trust. While economic crises are certainly marked by material scarcity, social alienation and political instability, they constitute, above all, a limit: they divide historical time into a decaying past and a future that has not yet been born. As a liminal experience—for this is what they ultimately are—crises are chiefly marked by a heightened sense of volatility and uncertainty, in short, by a combination of intense pluralism and rapid changeability. Consequently, besides driving many incomes, jobs and institutions into sharp decline, crises also open up a new space for the growth of budding social movements and political actors in ways seldom encountered in normal times. For this reason, when we examine their impact on party systems, what we are effectively studying is just another form of party system change.

Notes

1 These were held in May and June 2012, and January and September 2015.

2 The data in this survey is somewhat inconsistent. Although Yannis Mavris (2013) claims that only one in 10 Golden Dawn voters came from LAOS, his own firm's *Pre-Election Barometer* (Public Issue, 2012a) shows more than two in 10 Golden Dawn voters coming from LAOS.

3 Pulse, *Editors' Newspaper*, 22 July 2013; Pulse: 'Poll of polls', *Avgi*, 21 December 2013.

4 Until May 2012, Syriza attracted 19% of university graduates and 20% of students, both above its national average (compared to 15% and 5%, respectively, for ND) and only 10% of voters with 'lower education' compared with 31% for ND, see Public Issue (2012c).

5 One is also at pains to understand how Mudde squares a 'third way' approach with his definition of populism as an ideology based on 'black and white views' and 'uncompromising stand[s]' that 'lead to a polarized political culture' (Mudde 2017: 12–13).

6 Commenting on Syriza's theory, I remarked at the time that 'it reveals the increased influence of populist elements in its discourse' (Kazamias 2013).

7 According to Eurostat data, Real GDP Growth Rate in Greece was recorded as follows: 2008 −0.3; 2009 −4.3; 2010 −5.5; 2011 −9.1; 2012 −7.3; 2013 −3.2; 2014 0.4; 2015 −0.2; 2016 0.0. Data available as http://ec.europa.eu/eurostat/tgm/table.do?tab=table&init=1&language=en&pcode=tec00115&plugin=1.

8 Most opinion polls since the summer of 2016 show Syriza's share of the vote around 20%, down from 35% in the September 2015 elections. (See MRB Hellas, 17 February 2017: 14.6%; Marc poll, 28 May 2017: 15.7%; Metron Analysis, 7 July 2017: 22.2%; Alco, 6 September 2017: 15.6%; Marc poll, 11 September 2017: 16.5%.)

9 September 2017.
10 Economic crises, of course, discredit some politics, but enhances the credibility of other types of politics.
11 Constantine Karamanlis (1955–63, 1974–80) and Andreas Papandreou (1981–89, 1993–96).

References

Aldrich, J. (2012), *Why Parties? A Second Look*, Chicago, IL and London: University of Chicago Press.

Alter TV (2011), Programme 'Face to Face' with Anchor Nikos Hatzinikolaou, 14 February, available at www.youtube.com/watch?v=bkjW1oawdyg.

Barber, T. and Hope, K. (2009), 'Papandreou says Greece is Corrupt', *Financial Times*, 12 December, available at www.ft.com/cms/s/0/6871e1e6-e6be-11de-98b1-00144feab49a.html?ft_site=falcon&desktop=true#axzz4nkSE6rBQ.

Blondel, J. (1968), 'Party Systems and Patterns of Government in Western Democracies', *Canadian Journal of Political Science* 1(2): 180–203.

Chase-Dunn, C. (1980), 'The Development of Core Capitalism in the Antebellum United States: Tariff Politics and Class Struggle in an Upwardly Mobile Semiperiphery' in , Bergersen, A. (ed.) *Studies of the Modern World System*, New York: Academic Press: 189–230.

Cheng, T.-J. and Hsu, Y.-M. (2015), 'Long in the Making: Taiwan's Institutionalized Party System', in Hicken, A. and Martinez Kuhonta, E. (eds) *Party System Institutionalization in Asia: Democracies, Autocracies, and the Shadows of the Past*, Cambridge: Cambridge University Press.

Chrysochoidis, M. (2016), 'Mikrós kai richós o dikommatismós Syriza-ND', Ta Nea, 11 June, available at www.tanea.gr/news/politics/article/5366178/mikros-kai-rhxos-o-dikommatismos-syriza-nd/.

Dimitras, P. (1992), 'Greece: The Virtual Absence of an Extreme Right', in Hainsworth, P. (ed.), *The Extreme Right in Western Europe*, London: Pinter, 246–268.

Douzinas, C. (2013), *Philosophy and Resistance in the Crisis: Greece and the Future of Europe*, Cambridge: Polity.

Downs, A. (1957a), 'An Economic Theory of Political Action in a Democracy', *Journal of Political Economy* 65(2): 135–150, April 1957.

Downs, A. (1957b), *An Economic Theory of Democracy*, New York: Harper Row.

Escalona, F. and Vieira, M. (2014), '"It does not happen here either": Why social democrats fail in the context of the great economic crisis', in Bailey, D. et al. (eds), *European Social Democracy During the Global Economic Crisis: Renovation or Resignation?*, Manchester: Manchester University Press: 19–41.

Eurostat (2017), 'Real GDP Growth Rate', available at http://ec.europa.eu/eurostat/tgm/table.do?tab=table&init=1&language=en&pcode=tec00115&plugin=1.

Evans, J. (2002), 'In Defence of Sartori: Party System Change, Voter Preference Distributions and Other Competitive Incentives', *Party Politics* 8(2): 155–174.

Funke, M., Schularick, M. and Trebesch, C. (2015), 'Going to Extremes: Politics after Financial Crises, 1870–2014', *European Economic Review* 88: 227–260, September, doi:10.1016/j.euroecorev.2016.03.006.

Fouskas, V. and Dimoulas, C. (2017) 'Imperial Bondage: Austerity in Greece, 2008–2018', in Sturm, R., Griebel, T. and Winkelmann, T. (eds), *Austerity in Europe: Social and Political Consequences.* Berlin: Nomos.

Gunther, R., Sani, G. and Shabad, G. (1988), *Spain After Franco: The Making of a Competitive Party System*, Berkeley, CA: University of California Press.

Hope, K. (2011), 'Humiliating End to Greece's Social Reformer', *Financial Times*, 6 November, available at www.ft.com/content/d0876ba8-08c6-11e1-9fe8-00144fea bdc0.

Imerisia (2016), 'Pósoi 'Ellines metanásteufsan sto exoterikó kai poú', 5 September, ava ilable at www.imerisia.gr/article.asp?catid=26510&subid=2&pubid=114121892.

Karamanlis, C. (2009), Prime Minister's Televised Statement to Ethnos, 2 September, available at www.ethnos.gr/politiki/arthro/diaggelma_me_dilimmata-5708815.

Kathimerini (2013), 'Veteran ND cadre's comments fuel storm after two MPs return to fold', 1 July, available at www.ekathimerini.com/132377/article/ekathimerini/news/ veteran-nd-cadres-comments-fuel-storm-after-two-mps-return-to-fold.

Kaufmann, D. (2010), 'National Disasters Teach Unorthodox Lesson on Governance', The Brookings Institution, 2 March, available at www.brookings.edu/opinions/na tional-disasters-teach-unorthodox-lessons-on-governance.

Kazakos, P. (2012), 'Eínai i Elláda Vaimári?', *Greek Political Review*, 18 December, available at http://politicalreviewgr.blogspot.co.uk/2012/12/blog-post_8698.html.

Kazamias, A. (2000), 'O synostismós tou "mesaíou chórou"', *Anti* 711, 14 April: 16–17.

Kazamias, A. (2005), 'I ánodos kai i ptósi tou kratikoú kommatismoú', in Pelagidis, T., Kazakos, P., Mouzelis, N. and Tsoukas, H. *I emblokí ton metarrythmíseon stin Elláda*, Athens: Papazisis: 59–82.

Kazamias, A. (2008), 'Se ti synístatai i krísi tou dikommatismoú?', *Anti* 919, 11 April: 16–17.

Kazamias, A. (2013), 'I esfalméni ektímisi tou fasistikoú kindúnou apo to Syriza', Editors' Newspaper, 29 August.

Kazamias, A. (2015), 'David Meets Goliath in the Greek Election', *Chronos*, 21 January, available at http://chronosmag.eu/index.php/a-kazamias-david-meets-goliath-in-the-greek-election.html.

Kazamias, A. (2017), 'Poió eínai to kommatikó sýstima tis krísis?', efsyn.gr, 4 May, available at www.efsyn.gr/arthro/poio-einai-kommatiko-systima-tis-krisis.

Keating, D. and McCrone, D. (2013), 'The Crisis of Social Democracy', in Keating, M. and McCrone, D. (eds), *The Crisis of Social Democracy in Europe*, Edinburgh: Edinburgh University Press, 1–13.

Krugman, P. (2015), 'Weimar on the Aegean', *New York Times*, 16 February, available at www.nytimes.com/2015/02/16/opinion/paul-krugman-weimar-on-the-aegean.html?mcubz=3.

Laclau, E. (2005), 'Populism: What's in a Name?', in Panizza, F. (ed.), *Populism and the Mirror of Democracy*, London and New York: Verso Books: 32–49.

Loulis, Y. (2011), *Road to the Abyss: The effects of the crisis of the party system (1981–2011)*, Athens: Kastaniotis Publications.

Lyrintzis, C. (2005), 'The Changing Party System: Stable Democracy, Contested "Modernization"', *West European Politics* 28(2), March: 242–259.

Lyrintzis, C. (2011), 'Greek Politics in the Era of Economic Crisis: Reassessing Causes and Effects', *GreeSE Paper 45, Hellenic Observatory*, London School of Economics, March, 1–11.

Mair, P. (ed.) (1990), *The West European Party System*, Oxford: Oxford University Press.

Mair, P. (1997), *Party System Change: Approaches and Interpretations*, Oxford: Oxford University Press.

Marantzidis, N. (2014), 'Pós fthásame stó apotélesma tis 25is Maíou', *Kathimerini*, 1 June, available at www.kathimerini.gr/769921/article/epikairothta/politikh/pws-f8a same-sto-apotelesma-ths-25hs-maioy.

Margaronis, M. (2012), 'Greek anti-fascist protesters "tortured by police" after Golden Dawn clash', *The Guardian*, 9 October, available at www.theguardian.com/ world/2012/oct/09/greek-antifascist-protesters-torture-police.

Margaronis, M. (2013), 'Greece at the Boiling Point', *New York Times*, 10 July, available at www.nytimes.com/2013/07/11/opinion/global/greece-at-the-boiling-point.htm l?_r=1.

Mavris, Y.-VPRC (2007), 'Apodynamónetai o dikommatismós', *Kathimerini*, 26 August.

Mavris, Y. (2013), 'Emergence and Stabilization of the Far-Right Phenomenon', Public Issue (First published in Greek in The Editors' Newspaper, 1 July), Athens, available at www.mavris.gr/en/298/snapshot-of-golden-dawn.

McCrone, D. and Keating, M. (2013), 'Social Democracy in Crisis: Outlining the trends in Western Europe', in Keating, M. and McCrone, D. (eds), *The Crisis of Social Democracy in Europe*, Edinburgh: Edinburgh University Press, 28–46.

Mény, Y. (2013), 'From Single Market to Social Market Economy: Is There Room for Solidarity?', in Keating, M. and McCrone, D. (eds), *The Crisis of Social Democracy in Europe*, Edinburgh: Edinburgh University Press, 184–198.

Michalopoulos, S. (2017), 'Moscovici: Leftist Syriza government is not populist', *Euractiv*, 30 June.

Morgan, J. (2011), *Bankrupt Representation and Party System Collapse*, University Park, PA: Pennsylvania State University Press.

Mouzelis, N. (1986), *Politics in the Semi-Periphery: Early Parliamentarism and Late Industrialization in the Balkans and Latin America*, London: Macmillan.

Mouzelis, N. (2015), 'Eínai o Tsípras sosialdimokrátis?', *To Vima*, 25 October, available at www.tovima.gr/opinions/article/?aid=748460.

Mouzelis, N. (2016), 'To méllon tou kommatikoú systímatos', *Ta Nea*, 28 May, available at www.tanea.gr/opinions/all-opinions/article/5362181/to-mellon-toy-kommatikoy-systhmatos.

Mudde, C. (2004), 'The Populist Zeitgeist', *Government and Opposition* 39(4): 541–563.

Mudde, C. (2017), *Syriza: The Failure of the Populist Promise*, London: Palgrave Macmillan.

Nikolakopoulos, I. (2016), 'I aísthisi mi apotelesmatikótitas tis kyvérnisis eínai to adúnató tis simeío, Epochi', interview to Klavdianos, P. and Georgoulas, C., 4 April, available at http://epohi.gr/ilias-nikolakopoulos-h-aisthsh-mh-apotelesma tikothtas-ths-kyvernhshs-einai-to-adynato-ths-shmeio.

Papandreou, G. (2010), Cross-Channel Televised Interview of Prime Minister George A. Papandreou, 25 October, http://papandreou.gr/διακαναλική-συνέντευξη-του-πρωθ υπου

Pappas, T. (2003), 'The transformation of the Greek party system since 1951', *West European Politics* 26(2): 90–114.

Pedersen, M. (1979), 'The Dynamics of European Party Systems: Changing Patterns of Electoral Volatility', *European Journal of Political Research* 7(1): 1–26.

Pelagidis, T. (2005), 'Oi Víkings stin Elláda: Prosodothíres enantíon eurúterou symférontos', in Kazakos, P., Kazamias, A., Mouzelis, N. and Tsoukas, H. *I emblokí ton metarrythmíseo stin Elláda*, Athens: Papazisis, 109–164.

Poulantzas, N. (2000) [1978], *State, Power, Socialism*, London: Verso Books.

Psarras, D. (2010), *To aórato chéri tou Karatzaféri (The Hidden Hand of Karatzaferis)*, Athens: Alexandria.

Psarras, D., Kostopoulos, T., Psarra, A. and Trimis, D. (2009), 'Pós stíthike to LAOS', *Eleftherotypia*, 21 September, available at www.enet.gr/?i=news.el.article&id=56282

Public Issue (2011a), MoU and Public Debt: A Year On, 18 May, available at www.publicissue.gr/1747/debt-afieroma.

Public Issue (2011b), Political Barometer 96, November 2011, Athens, available at www.publicissue.gr/1923/varometro-nov-2011.

Public Issue (2012a), Cumulative Archive of Pre-Election Barometer, February–May 2012, Athens, available at www.publicissue.gr/2011/koinwniko_profil-sunoxes.

Public Issue (2012b), Public Opinion Polls and Elections 2012: Review by Public Issue, Table 4: Political Barometer, January–June 2012, available at www.publicissue.gr/2046/greek-elections-2012-and-polls.

Public Issue (2012c), Parties' Political Profile, May, available at www.publicissue.gr/2011/koinwniko_profil-sunoxes.

Remmer, K. (1991), 'The Political Impact of Economic Crisis in Latin America in the 1980s', *The American Political Science Review*, 85(3): 777–800.

Reporters Without Borders (2017), 'Greece: Continued Disappointment', available at https://rsf.org/en/greece.

Rothstein, B. and Steinmo, S. (2013), 'Social Democracy in Crisis? What Crisis?' in Keating, M. and McCrone, D. (eds), *The Crisis of Social Democracy in Europe*, Edinburgh: Edinburgh University Press, 87–106.

Ryner, M. (2014), 'Why the financial crisis has not generated a social democratic alternative in Europe?', in Bailey D. et al. (eds), *European Social Democracy During the Global Economic Crisis: Renovation or Resignation?*, Manchester: Manchester University Press: 60–76.

Samaras, A. (2013), Speech to ND Central Committee, New Democracy Official Website, 11 October, available at https://nd.gr/omilia-toy-prothypoyrgoy-kai-proedroy-tis-nd-antoni-samara-stin-pe-toy-kommatos.

Sartori, G. (2005 [1976]), *Parties and Party Systems: A framework for analysis*, Colchester: European Consortium for Political Research.

Savaricas, N. (2014), 'Video Shows Aide to Greek Prime Minister Antonis Samaras admitting Golden Dawn arrests were "sought by government"', *The Independent*, 3 April.

Seawright, J. (2012), *Party-System Collapse: The Roots of Crisis in Peru and Venezuela*, Palo Alto, CA: Stanford University Press.

Sherman, H. (1993), 'The Relational Approach to Political Economy', *Rethinking Marxism* 6(4): 104–116.

Siaroff, A. (2003), 'Two-And-A-Half Party Systems and the Comparative Role of the "Half"', *Party Politics* 9(3): 267–290.

Simitis, C. (2005), *Politikí gia mia Dimiourgikí Elláda, 1996–2004*, Athens: Polis.

Smith, H. (2015), 'Varoufakis extends Washington DC charm offensive after talks with Lagarde', *The Guardian*, 6 April, available at www.theguardian.com/world/2015/apr/06/varoufakis-extends-washington-charm-offensive-after-talks-with-lagarde.

Sotiropoulos, D. (2014), 'Triumph and Collapse: PASOK in the wake of Crisis in Greece', in Bailey, D. et al. (eds) *European social democracy during the global economic crisis: Renovation or Resignation?*, Manchester: Manchester University Press, 193–212.

Spiegel, P. and Carnegy, H. (2014), 'Anti-EU parties celebrate election success', *Financial Times*, 26 May.

Terzis, G. (2011), 'Me kyvernitikés efthúnes pléon o LAOS', *Kathimerini*, 12 November, available at www.kathimerini.gr/442550/article/epikairothta/politikh/me-kyvernhtikes-ey8ynes-pleon-o-laos.

The Economist (2016), 'Political power follows economic power', 3 February, available at www.economist.com/blogs/buttonwood/2016/02/economics-and-democracy.

Tsipras, A. (2017), 'Ìtan o Andréas pséftis?', *Documento*, 3 September, available at www.documentonews.gr/article/to-arthro-toy-alexh-tsipra-sto-documento-htan-o-andreas-pseyths.

United Nations General Assembly (2014), Report of the Independent Expert on the effects of foreign debt and other related international financial obligations of States on the full enjoyment of all human rights, particularly economic, social and cultural rights, on his mission to Greece, A/HRC/25/50/Add.1, 23 March: 1–24.

Varoufakis, Y. (2017), *Adults in the Room: My Battle with Europe's Deep Establishment*. London: Bodley Head.

Vasilopoulou, S. and Halikiopoulou, D. (2015), 'Greek Politics: Economic Crisis or Crisis of Democracy?', *World Affairs*, Fall, available at www.worldaffairsjournal.org/article/greek-politics-economic-crisis-or-crisis-democracy.

Vernardakis, C. (2008), 'The Transition from a two-party to a multi-party system: deliberations and realignments in the Greek party system after the September 2007 elections', Occasional Paper, Athens.

Voulgaris, Y. (2014), 'I Ellàda autopagidévetai', *Ta Nea*, 18 December, available at www.tanea.gr/opinions/all-opinions/article/5170806/h-ellada-aytopagideyetai.

Wallerstein, I. (1976), 'Semi-Peripheral Countries and the Contemporary World Crisis', *Theory and Society* 3(4), Winter: 461–483.

Ware, A. (1996), *Political Parties and Party Systems*, Oxford: Oxford University Press.

Weyland, K. (2001), 'Clarifying a contested concept: Populism in the study of Latin American politics', *Comparative Politics* 34(1):1–22.

9 Blaming the Other: An Enquiry into the Cultural and Political Preconditions of the Greek crisis

Tolis Malakos

Introduction

This chapter is an attempt at understanding the 'cultural' significance of the Greek crisis. Its main concern is the ways modern Greeks endow life with meaning and the ways they critically reflect on those meanings. In critical reflection one must find a way to step back from one's beliefs—since to step outside is not possible—and subject them to critical scrutiny. Thinking requires some critical distance from the self. In modern Greece this has always been an almost impossible enterprise. If being modern means developing not just a critical quality, but also a self-critical ability, reflecting not only about the world but about the nature of the reflecting subject, being disenchanted not only from the world but also from the self, then we must admit that we have always found this prospect daunting. Knowing oneself has not been a priority of the modern Greek mind.

Today we are in dire straits, living for almost a decade through an acute crisis. We have reached a limit, we cannot go on being as we have been. In such a kind of crisis, reflection and distance become even more difficult but more necessary than ever. We are in a state of emergency and our predicament looks as bleak as ever, but it is now that we need to find the courage to take a step back and reflect on ourselves, because if we do not find this courage, we are bound once more to externalize, to look for the roots of the crisis anywhere else but ourselves. I am afraid that we are on our way to doing just that. The paradox of modern Greece is that as she remains obsessed with herself, she blames others for her fate. However, we need to find a way of being beyond fate. The range of issues facing us, of course, is huge, and now more than ever we live in an interdependent world, where the external and the internal tend to be inseparable. As Western liberal democracies find it difficult to sustain their distinctive forms of life in the face of globalization and hyper-modernity, as Europe finds herself at a crossroads that will either lead to new forms of deeper political and cultural integration or to new forms of catastrophic fragmentation, we find ourselves part of a wider crisis. Yet focusing on the wider picture tends to blur the focus on ourselves, and while such a wider picture is necessary, it tends, by itself, to obscure and lead to some kind of absolution of the self, which, however comforting, is extremely dangerous. The aim of this paper is to turn the lens inwards and try to substantiate three interdependent claims, namely, that having been obsessed with themselves, modern Greeks have not learned to think critically about themselves and the others, have not found ways to communicate meaningfully with each other and develop practices of communicative action, and have remained to a large extent unreconstructed, not being able to transform themselves into citizens of a modern polity. This paper is highly eclectic, touching on a wide but not, in any sense, exhaustive range of issues: philosophical, anthropological, sociological and political. However, its aim is not to provide an analysis of what went wrong. Its aim is to make a modest contribution towards provoking processes of thinking anew, of reconsidering, of reviewing and revising ourselves, of starting to listen to each other's voice as we search for ways to engage in a real debate; to contribute towards looking for ways to reflect on and perhaps reform our fantasies.

The elusive self-understanding

I take fantasies to be actual, real but ideal configurations of self-understanding that depend for their formation on imaginings of possible and actual self-transfigurations, and that can be but are not necessarily deceptive. In that sense, nations—as well as persons—never constitute a *brutum factum.* They represent interpretations of what counts as life but each such conception of life invokes what exactly a person—and a nation—thinks she is, as well as what she is.

> 'The interest of self-preservation cannot aim at the reproduction of the life of the species automatically and without thought, because under the conditions of the existence of culture this species must first interpret what counts as life. These interpretations, in turn, orient themselves according to ideas of the good life. The "good" is neither a convention nor an essence, but rather the result of fantasy.'
>
> (Habermas 1992: 288)

The most vital form of understanding is indeed self-understanding. It is on this foundation that all acts of fantasizing and transfiguring take place as the self opens to a world. However, self-understanding is impossible if it is self-referential, if it remains obsessed with the self; not only blind to its conditioning and to the world of others, but also caught up in the delusion of seeking the unconditional and normative in its own distinction from all others, in its particular essence. It is especially then that the presumed essence becomes 'pure fantasy', and it is this pure, transcendental fantasy that has haunted the self-understanding of modern Greeks from the inception of the modern Greek nation until today.

If it is true that Western European enlightenment thinkers fantasized in particular ways that the measure of all things was Greece, re-inventing a

Greece that never existed (and thus imposing a paradoxical tyranny of Greece over themselves), then it is not paradoxical that people, living in what used to be Greece and its periphery, took these fantasies to heart. As, particularly in the latter part of the 18th century, and especially in the nascent European romantic consciousness, Greece came alive, for Orthodox Christian intellectuals, having been born in what used to be Greece or its periphery and speaking a form of Greek, the attraction of the claim of being Greek became irresistible. If Europe owed so much to Greece, then it owed to them a Greek nation state. They started therefore a cultural proselytizing based on seeing the Europeans as debtors who were going to repay their debt to the ancients by supporting the claims of the modern Greeks for independence, since Greece was in the minds of those cultural missionaries the prototypical *Altneuland* (Old New Land). If the Europeans could claim some kind of cultural descent from Classical Greece, these 'modern Greeks' could do one better: they *were* Greeks. Greece became the only new European natin that did not use its spoken language as the prototype for the new official language, but a cleansed idiom that was created to serve two main purposes: to prove the links to the ancients and to allow the introduction of lexical and conceptual structures that were translated from French to Greek. The first constitutional document of the new state, the 1822 Constitution of Epidaurus, was written in a kind of language so 'cleansed' of modern elements that only very few Greeks could understand it. The continuous fantasizing had thus come full circle: the European fantasy of Classical Greece led to the self-fantasizing of modern Greeks via raw materials of European construction. The building block of the resultant fantasy was the identification of modern Greeks with the presumed ancient, and the building block of the new identity its 'hellenicity'. If only they could prove culturally and linguistically that they were Greeks, if they could prove their 'greekness', they would be granted what they were owed: it is here that the roots of the particular fascination of modern Greek intellectuals with 'greekness' lie. The preoccupation with defining this elusive 'greekness' and the assumption that the Europeans are not creditors—both literally and culturally—but debtors still plague modern Greek consciousness and continue to obstruct any attempt towards self understanding, which remains the condition *sine qua non* for the 'structural reformation' of Greek society. One would say, half-jokingly but in all seriousness, that the essence of being Greek is the obsessive, self-referential, almost autistic fascination with 'greekness'. The particular characteristic of this fascination is its intensity and literal conceptualization of cultural history, its questing for some kind of cultural transcendence in self-referential terms, its positing of a diffuse imagining of its essence as emanating solely from itself. Greece is:

> '… a country that quests for itself with intense passion, a country in search of bringing itself up to date… . The major illusion of modern Greek consciousness is what itself (with minimal modesty) calls greek-centredness. This conception presents Greece as a centre. *But a centre of*

> *what*? Nobody gives a clear answer to this question, but the representation of this centre posits the world as its periphery … . Greek-centredness is the sole *idea* that modern Greece was able to invoke … What was missing was the thinking that gives rise to any idea; it did not reflect any new opening to the world, it did not uncover its meaning."
>
> (Axelos 2010: 21–23)

Modern Greece's transcendence lies in its presumed immanence. The more it strives for transcendence the more it falls back unto itself, in the form of dead fragments for display in a museum. It is not that we are surrounded by ruins. It is rather that from the start we have imagined ourselves as ruins, falling prey to a peculiar aesthetization of life that perhaps is one of the keys to the modern Greek poetic consciousness. Amidst the hustle and bustle of modern life, there is a deadening silence that haunts. The quintessential Greek mood is a nostalgia of a particular kind, a longing for something forever lost, a crippling cultural melancholy, that resorts sometimes to a pathetic boastfulness and sometimes to an equally pathetic stoicism as well as to a sentimental monumentality, in order to conceal its feeling sorry for itself, its undeclared and repressed mourning. We carry too much dead weight because we took it upon ourselves to be the inheritors, the spoilt heirs who never engaged with and comprehended the spirit of their ancestors, because we thought we had some kind of privileged access. We misunderstood speaking some form of the same language with speaking (and thinking) the same. Our tradition is dead because we perceived it as a legacy to be claimed, as a monument to be preserved, as a cultural heritage to be offered to others as a spectacle. We have tried to be something we did not know and we did not try to learn; we were playing a part, we were imitating. We have never learned to listen to all these voices, pagan and Christian, philosophical and poetic, because we never tried to make them our own. We have been constantly talking about them and not of them. Every meeting with them was not a meeting, because it never was a meeting with an *other* but a meeting with our selves. We have become incapable of perceiving the other in his or her otherness, because we projected ourselves into our own others, we perceived the ancient Greeks as an incarnation of ourselves. *They existed for us to claim them as our own.* We transfigured them into cultural capital to live on, historical spoils to brag about, dead commodities to be consumed. Our relationship to them has been a fetishistic relationship in the Marxian sense. We took them for granted, we could not become truly obsessed with them because in reality we were obsessed with ourselves. If they were some kind of fathers, we have killed them. We are blind and furious, pitiful modern Oedipuses, besides ourselves in rage but our rage is hollow. This tragedy takes place neither in the splendour of Thebes, nor in the fragrant Athenian countryside that used to be Colonus, but in the modern, barren wasteland that lies between modern Thebes and the sprawling, ugly, cemented capital of the modern Hellenes. We have become incapable of relating because we have lost our capacity to remember. Our remembering is not a gathering, rather it is in essence an act of forgetting, a burial ceremony of deception where everybody sheds crocodile tears but is insensitive to the grave loss and hurls abuse and threats to anybody who is not one of us. We live in a graveyard, we are in denial, we wallow but we still need to learn to weep; to learn living in absence. That would be some kind of a start.

The elusive communication

We have never gone through the mourning of adolescence. We have never grown up at least in three senses. We have not gone through a decentring process, which could lead us away from primitive egocentrism towards the differentiation of our cognitive capacities, towards the differentiation of the capacities for coping with the external world, the social world, and the world of inner subjectivity. Of course, since we have not differentiated, we now are in no position to mediate among them in order to develop some kind of integrated personality. Second, we have never deposed the ego from its sovereignty in the sense of deposing a king; we have never entered a 'being-for-the other'. Both at a personal level and at a collective level we have not developed the conception of not only being responsible *to* the other, but also being responsible *for* the other, every concrete other we come to face.

> 'Responsibility in fact is not a simple attribute of subjectivity, as if the latter already existed in itself, before the ethical relationship. Subjectivity is not for itself; it is once again initially for another … . The Other is not simply close to me in space, or close like a parent, but he approaches me essentially insofar as I feel myself—insofar as I am responsible for him … . I am responsible for the Other without waiting for reciprocity, were I to die for it. Reciprocity is his affair … . The I always has one responsibility *more* than all the others.'
>
> (Levinas 1985: 96–99)

Third, we have not developed a public personality capable of communicative action, engaging in a critically reflective way with traditional life forms, with pre-interpreted, taken for granted, non-reflective ways of conduct, as well as with modern subsystems of instrumental rationality, which are necessary for, but at the same time undermining processes of communicative rationality and the pursuit of personal, common and public goods. Until today we strive to be modern without facing the disquieting disembeddedness of modernity. We want freedom without the angst. We want the best of both worlds: a taken-for-granted universe of social activity based on personal ties, i.e. a relatively secure traditional *Lebenswelt* (lifeworld) where pre-established beliefs and codes of behaviour are not to be challenged; and an instrumentally rational, efficient accumulation of money and power. As a result we have ended up with the worst of both worlds. Unreformed practices that retain their external shell by striving for external goods but lose their soul because they are not supported by the communicative pursuit of internal goods to the practice, goods pursued for their own sake rather than for money or power, and corrupted institutions that instead of providing resources for the achievement of common and public goods, provide resources for their nomenclatures.

We are very fond of our 'rights' but we still mistake privileges for rights. We prefer not to think about our actions in terms of their *telos*, in terms of a substantive rationality that ensures that, as we enter common practices, accepting but also challenging their standards of excellence and the inadequacy of our own individual performances, we engage in communicative, reflective, critical action regarding those standards, the means towards achieving the ends as well as the meaningfulness of the ends themselves. We have never learned to think in terms of goods, common goods internal to our practices as reasons for our actions, because we find it easier to justify our actions in terms of interests, which we tend to baptize 'rights'. However, even having a positive right, for example, the constitutional right to form a political community, does not fully solve the problem of what kind of *polis* we want to be part of, what kind of goods this *polis* will pursue and by what kind of means. Having the right, certainly is a necessary, but is not a sufficient, condition for forming a specific kind of *polis*. Processes of procedurally rational communication do not take place in a void, but within specific social and cultural contexts where ethically substantive questions, differing conceptions of the human good, are debated. And while some kind of neutral standard is never available within the essentially hermeneutic human condition, the search for a standard that, if not eternally true is at least sound and better than others, and aspires to transcending the particular and to having some ecumenical value, is also part of the human condition and, normally, is and should be part of any communicative activity. That is why both the formal rules of a functional rationality and the substantiality of a communicative rationality of ends are necessary but individually not sufficient. Unless we enter some kind of communicative activity where the force of the better argument is procedurally guaranteed, and that will discursively pursue particular goods while continuously debating the common and the human good, the resulting community will either be a compartmentalized non-community, in which universally prescribed rights have been transformed into selectively distributed privileges, or a totalizing community based on personal ties of exclusion.

We have not grown accustomed 'to living with dissent in the realm of questions that admit of truth' (Bernstein 1985: 194), we do not know how to listen to the claims of others. The other seems to be an abstract, undifferentiated, generic other, a foreigner, rather than a concrete other, an *autre* rather than an *Autrui*. We are blind to the person of the other and her ethical claim. We moved from an inferiority complex towards the Western European other directly to a superiority complex towards the East European other. We have been the original, prototypical migrants and immigrants. Thessaloniki has been justifiably called 'the capital of immigrants' in its pre-war guise, yet we have never truly accepted immigrants during the last 25 years. We are not travellers anymore and we do not accept travellers. We travel as tourists and we accept only tourists. Our land has been closed.

> 'Modern Greece does not aim at all at the distant, she loves the limited ... She hides in fear behind her rocky shores, afraid of the lengths and the heights. Her fear is not at all physical, it is a metaphysical fear.'
>
> (Axelos 2010: 45)

A metaphysical fear: a fear for anything that transcends a non-eventful 'there is', a rumbling cacophony of the '*il y a*' that happens despite us, a voice returning after the negation of every voice, a comforting but deadening fatalism of living towards a 'fate'. A fear for being with the other, that is a fear for thinking and willing reasons for being for the other, because being can never be a reason for itself: 'a person exists' is not the same as 'it rains', because existing does not possess the fatality of raining. A dread for the incarnation of a human subjectivity, in other words, a dread for the spirituality of a human being that, in its natality and creativity, lives towards the unacceptability of fate as death and of death as fate. We have not only mistaken the past as fate but also the present as such. While everything around us points towards a continuous rebirth, while the world to which we were thrown presents itself as a kosmos, a jewel, and discloses its poetic nature, unconceals a transcendence that is immanent, a beyond being that resides in being, we capture only the mundane and the prosaic. Our living has been a continuous evasion, an impotent recoil gripped by a dread before every other that is perceived as a threat. Our spirit is closed, it does not admit of questing, it is a mere shadow, a ghost. We mistake our pathetic, weak passion for spirit, we mistake our wilfulness for will, our dogmatism and wishful thinking for thought. Our minds have been closed, they do not admit of questioning, they do not know how to postpone, or better to suspend, answering in order to stay with the questioning. We promise but we do not deliver. We are fond of 'Great Ideas', but we mistake our pretensions for ideas and they are seldom great; they very rarely signify an opening to the world, they disclose nothing new, besides the delusion of redemption for lost grandeur. We do not think what deserves thinking, 'our thoughts like bats are circling in the shadow' (Sikelianos 1995: 73), while pretending to scorn death, we lead a life constantly rehearsing for death and we are mistaking this continuous rehearsing for death for a life. We have been living towards death for a long time because our life did not mean something, it was *temps perdu*, never gained, lost in an everydayness, an ordinariness that pointed to nothing extraordinary, a banality pointing only to itself. Within this banality of nothingness that never understood being as an event, the only flowers that could flourish were flowers of evil. Amidst a nihilistic amoral indifference, that has blotted any creative impulse, any opening to the other, and scorned any showing of true character, it is not totally incomprehensible how a good percentage of Greek citizens now yearn for a 'Golden Dawn', albeit Nazi. We are not waiting for the barbarians, they are already here and they look uncannily like us. We have forgotten that 'barbarian' was, in classical Greece and continues to be today, a primarily political concept.

> 'What is a barbarian? Not merely a non-Greek (whose language sounds to Hellenic ears like 'ba, ba, ba') but someone who lacks a *polis* and thereby shows—on Aristotle's view—that he is incapable of political relationships. What are political relationships? The relationships of free men to each other, that is the relationships between those members of a community who both rule and are ruled over. The free self is simultaneously political subject and political sovereign.'
>
> (MacIntyre 2007: 158–59)

But we were never able and virtuous enough to create such a kind of political community because the members of our *polis* thought always themselves only as sovereign and never as political subjects, as ruling and never as being ruled. We have mistaken modern representative democracy for a kind of direct, plebiscitary democracy in which the 'people' rule without any rules. As we were celebrating our new-found liberties and longed-for democratic freedoms and we started constituting new democratic institutions, we never discussed what kind of a society we want to be and we did not take care to develop the practices that would make us flourish. In the words of Alasdair MacIntyre, a 'practice' means:

> '... any coherent and complex form of socially established cooperative human activity through which goods internal to that form of activity are realized in the course of trying to achieve those standards of excellence which are appropriate to, and partially definitive of, that form of activity, with the result that human powers to achieve excellence, and human conceptions of the ends and goods involved, are systematically extended.'
>
> (MacIntyre 2007: 187)

We forgot the warning that democratic institutions need to be sustained by practices, which pursue specific common goods and enable citizens to develop excellences and virtues and a shared conception of the human good. It is within such practices that rational communication and characters could be formed. In their absence ethical discourse and judgements found no room to develop and vicious rather than virtuous characters predominated, and it was these that were recruited by institutions who in their turn were bound to fail. Thus, we fell prey to many vices, including the quintessential modern Greek vices of arrogance and *pleonexia* (avarice). For at least the last 40 years we were like Herman Broch's sleepwalkers, impervious to a world that was opening up, to its grave dangers and opportunities, and we have had a very rough awakening. Yet this threatens to be a long day of deep woes and unimaginable sorrows.

The elusive reform

We have opted for 'a strategy of hibernation, whose obvious weakness lies in its defensive character' (Habermas 1979: 43). The important and puzzling question about the rise of 'Golden Dawn' is not why an extreme right-wing party has risen to being the third largest party, polling around 10% and rising, in such a country that, besides its cultural malaise described above, experienced a severe economic crisis. The real question is how and why the rise of a distinctly and unashamedly Nazi party was made possible. There are still many, both in Greece and abroad, that have not fully realized that this is not some kind of extreme, right-wing, nationalistic party. It is a Nazi party that has copied and pasted its strategy and tactics from the Nazis in the Weimar Republic. It is the first time since the Holocaust that precisely such a party has risen to such unimaginable heights in a European country. However, in Greece the holocaust, the gulags, and the other horrors of the 20th century have been barely discussed in schools, universities and public spaces. Until 1974 a post-civil war, undemocratic state, monopolized by the right wing, built and operated its own *lage* of exile for the defeated communists in some Aegean islands and legitimized itself on the basis of a fiercely nationalistic discourse that transmogrified the phronesis of the ancients into 'ethnicophrosini', i.e. national mindedness, which even when officially rejected after 1974, it had done long-term damage in cultural terms.

After 1974 and the fall of the military junta, an idiosyncratic left-wing radical activism, based on a shallow politicization and over-determined by Marxist stereotypes, dominated political and cultural life and in its socialist guise gained power in 1981 and ruled with two right-wing breaks until recently. Its cultural and ideological poverty, underscored by nationalistic overtones since the nation was not abandoned but democratized in populist terms, coupled with an extension of 'clientelistic' privileges to wide sections of society ('the underprivileged' as they were called by Andreas Papandreou) and wrapped in the rhetoric of 'rights', did not allow the creation of a real public sphere of communicative action and discussion. The better argument seldom won because there was no room for it to be heard and listened to, and therefore it was doomed to marginalization. The force of the better argument was gravely devalued. Universities, old and new, became the antechambers for recruiting political personnel, not only among students but also among teachers. In order to become a member of the academic staff you invariably needed party connections, and after one was 'elected', with few notable exceptions, he or she was *en route* to becoming a member of Parliament, or some kind of political consultant. Even very important, well-known Greek intellectuals from abroad like Cornelius Castoriadis were, literally, not allowed to give a talk because they were considered reformist, never mind have their work read. What happened in Greek education in the last 35 years barely falls short of a crime. The internal good of education as a practice was totally forgotten. What was never realized was that in order for teaching to take place, learning should take place. The internal good of teaching is transforming through genuine learning, through opening ways to thinking the most thought provoking, the unthought and the unthinkable, by enabling the student to open up to the world through creating her own openings. Teaching is an uncovering of a density, a disclosure of a hidden opening, a pointing towards the loftier, a gracious giving. It is placing a student on her own way towards thinking, on her way within thinking. The Socratic maieutic method consisted exactly of that: genuine knowledge is a form of opening to a world that becomes our own, directed to what is other but springing from our within. However, in Greek education teaching and learning did not take place, and to be a teacher meant transferring pretensions of half-truths and enforcing what Heidegger called one-track thinking.

> 'In one-track thinking, thinking means as much as 'having views'. One might say for instance: "I think it will snow tonight". But he who speaks that way is not thinking … . [Thinking] is what inherently gathers and keeps within itself the greatest riches of what is thought-worthy and memorable.'
>
> (Heidegger 1968: 35)

At the same time, 'mild forms' of violence were prevalent in all forms of public debate and subsystems of selection were created in all forms of public life that not only advantaged those who were unworthy in intellect and character, but literally were selecting the worst or, at least, the less capable, than those in charge of the selection process. These mechanisms were diffused almost in every aspect of political, social, cultural and even economic life. Even in the private sector employment was dependent upon party affiliations and connections. Privileges trickled down to most sections of the population, but political, cultural and economic élites benefitted most and were leading by example in shallowness, corruption, tax evasion, nepotism and smugness in a society mesmerized by its own image. Max Weber famously defined élites as 'culture carriers'. However, the Greek élite was not an élite but a coalition of nomenclatures that were non-accountable, politically and socially irresponsible, and fiercely protective of their privileges to the point of organizing their reproduction on the hereditary principle. It was not only politicians' children that were taking their place as heirs. By almost miraculous intervention, which seemed to defy all exam systems of entry into higher education and all existing systems of evaluation, the child of the doctor was becoming a doctor, the child of the lawyer a lawyer, the child of a pharmacist a pharmacist, the child of a journalist a journalist, the child of an actor an actor, inheriting the clientele and the privileges of the parents. The argument that such a doctor will fail patients, that such a lawyer will fail wrongly accused citizens, such a politician his or her political community, did not seem to cross anybody's mind. The result of these processes of élite articulation and reproduction, which were reproduced throughout the social order, was the fragmentation of the political community into closed shops minding their particularistic interests, and the inability to think in terms of common goods. Practices were corrupted internally, because by definition they were serving only interests, not goods. The cultural implications were devastating because they were sowing the seeds for anti-social mentalities, that justified the means if they were serving particular interests, and disregarded the interests of others, which were perceived only in antagonistic terms.

> 'Why him and not me became the necessary stereotype … . It meant the relapse of a cultural deficit of self-consciousness, the heavy price paid for the void of an image of the self we do not receive from within and a desire which, instead of having its own object, mimics the desires of others. As we do not really care about the distant and unknown other, we do not know to love in the abstract and we stick desperately and jealously to what is close and 'ours'.'
>
> (Ramfos 2012: 47)

Attitudes of conformism, the refusal to subject to any kind of impersonal, formal rules, to accept a set of rights and obligations, the particularity of interests based only on personal and interpersonal ties, the deactivation of the pursuit of any common goods and the corruption of practices and institutions, resulted in undermining any form of genuine public sphere of common practices based on real virtues, the striving for excellence and communicative, reflective action. The universal, the particular and the individual were losing their specificity, being conflated as moments bound within a given particularistic totality. They were not allowed any room to constitute themselves radially, enabling thus the individual members of the political community to understand themselves and others as rational agents operating within multiple and fragile inter-subjectivities, which should not be conflated with each other since they call for different attitudes as individual citizens, family members, professionals, etc. Due to the conflation of different social roles in which each individual in a modern society is called to act in different ways, and their integration in a 'totality of sameness', and to the leftist as well as traditionalist right-wing scorn towards traditional liberal freedoms, the practice of these freedoms was not only disparaged but also disconnected from the activities of an extremely weak public sphere, which deteriorated into a vehicle for the promotion of particularistic interests. Under such conditions, communicative practices broke down and forms of discourse and communication that were not oriented towards reaching some form of genuine, if limited, understanding, but were masking strategies for manipulative preservation and extension of privileges, became dominant.

The democratic consensus reached from 1974 onwards was, of course, a great improvement to the pre-1974 autocratically constituted body politic, but it was partly deceptive, because it appeared as liberal democratic, but it was far from being genuinely liberal, and formally and substantively democratic.

With the fall of the military junta, Greece managed to establish stable democratic institutions and the rule of law was maintained, perhaps for the first time since the end of the civil war in 1949 and this was a seminal achievement. However, institutional progress, and the protection of the new European Communities framework, only managed to bring about painfully slow political and cultural growth and were not able by themselves to transform long-established practices of a basically traditional, organic *Gemeinschaft* into the practices of a modern *Gesellschaft*. Structural features like the preponderance of the nation understood in ethnic terms over the state and the subsequent understanding of citizenship in cultural and not in political terms, the hypertrophy of the bureaucracy in numerical terms but its weakness in terms of its modernizing effectiveness persisted. The various tensions exerted on traditional social ties by new processes of economic and social development and the resistance of more traditional as well as new privileged coalitions of interests, coupled with the rearticulation of political and economic networks of patronage along new party lines, reaffirmed patterns of cultural and political underdevelopment and did not allow the articulation of a consistent and self-reflexive modernist project. In the words of Jay M. Bernstein, when inconsistencies in 'traditions' become habitual, social agents:

> '... attach to [the symbolic field] a comprehensibility it does not really possess (e.g. by rationalizing the inconsistency in question). Secondly, as a result of the habitualized inconsistency communication becomes inhibited: Non-verbal expressions, motives, desires, even doubts, uncertainties and "felt" failures of understanding become incapable of being made verbal and thus communicated. As a result there are "meanings" which are excluded from public discourse. Finally, if communication is inhibited, then the consensus about beliefs and norms which is operative in public discourse must be deceptive or false.'
>
> (Bernstein 1995: 46)

It is still puzzling and disturbing to note how Greeks tend to not listen, and seem to not care to listen, to their co-discussants in a debate. They seem to fortify themselves into a position of absolute conviction, which perceives any criticism as a personal attack and requires an indignant justification of the truth of their conviction. Within such circumstances, communication is inhibited and distorted. Not only has the consensus been deceptive, constituted under conditions of pseudo-communication, since for all the above reasons the better argument could rarely win, but also there were no real possibilities and public space available for detecting the false consensus underlying this pseudo-communication. In other words, the extremely weak public sphere and the corrupted forms of communicative action were not detected as such, and the political and cultural establishment continued to operate under the illusion of a genuine liberal democratic consensus. Widespread nationalistic discourse, xenophobic and barely disguised racist attitudes, the multiplication of 'soft' and 'hard' violent attitudes by both right-wing and leftist groups, neo-traditional cultural phenomena and anti-European tendencies were gravely underestimated when not encouraged during the 1990s and 2000s. While new, mostly economic, immigrants from eastern European but also Asian and African countries, came to Greece during those two decades and were used as cheap labour in construction, tourism and agriculture, a debate about their cultural and political integration and the issues surrounding multiculturalism, which was taking place in other European countries for decades and had important repercussions on social policy, did not even begin in Greece. The immigrants were employed, exploited, consigned to the margins, ghettoized and ignored, while politicians were congratulating themselves for the absence of racism in Greek society. However, characteristically, when immigrants' children were becoming the best students of their classes in primary and secondary schools and the responsibility to carry the Greek flag in national festivities fell on them, xenophobia and racism was showing its teeth.

While a cultural paradigm characterized by nationalistic, xenophobic, populistic and anti-democratic discourses was becoming predominant, the more enlightened segment of the political élite, led by Kostas Simitis, the social-democratic Prime Minister (1996–2004), was arguing and pushing for modernization and reforms, but his valiant efforts faced stern resistance from a variety of privileged groups. More than that, however, he represented a technocratic, functionalist and economistic outlook, which on the whole disregarded the cultural preconditions for reform, and embraced a form of modernization from above, that prioritized economic development, institutional reform, and the speedy integration to the newly emerging eurozone. The strategic decision to push for admission to the eurozone at the earliest possible opportunity, while arguably correct, since ultimately it ensured that Greece was at the core of the European Union when the crisis struck, also resulted in a hasty fiscal consolidation without any long-overdue reforms to the productive model, which was based on unproductive and over-priced services and was heavily dependent on imports even for agricultural products. The overestimation of the cultural and political effects of institutional change from above, and the underestimation of the importance of social and cultural practices, meant a shallow 'modernization' that did challenge but was not able to defeat the clientelistic ethos. Once admitted to the eurozone the Government prioritized big infrastructural projects that were presumed to bring prosperity and usher Greece once and for all into 'modernity'. Although some of these projects, like the Athens underground, the new ring road around Athens and the new airport, were completed successfully and were indeed long-overdue, a lot of projects were undertaken for 'one use', for the 'successful' staging of the 2004 Olympic games; they cost much more than originally planned and were mostly assigned to a few oligopolistic construction and media concerns, reinforcing clientelistic ties and practices of corruption.

Although some vital reforms were implemented like the crucial introduction of a new, impersonal system of selection for employment in the public sector, others were neglected, i.e. the long-overdue reforms in education and immigration, where an urgently needed new law on citizenship was never introduced. Some others were attempted but not seen through in the face of resistance, as with the law introduced to reform the National Insurance System (NIS). This was an absolutely vital reform, which if successful, would have saved the NIS from the disaster experienced today. However, the new law was withdrawn because of the reaction by a coalition of clientelistic networks and the inability of the Government to challenge those networks, which comprised to a large extent its own voters and by both right-wing and left-wing opposition parties. On the whole, reforms were tried only in a scrappy, timid, fragmented way, without the necessary cultural depth. With few notable exceptions, the old political personnel was put in charge of the reforms, comprising mainly people belonging to the corrupted political nomenclature who were both unwilling and incapable of planning and introducing real reforms. The collapse of the Government's popularity in the polls, its attempt to justify its actions in the face of mounting criticism, and the hasty change of leadership limited any opportunity for critical evaluation and debate. This is perhaps the real Achilles' heel of the 'modernizing' block, from its formation until today, i.e. the absence of self-reflexivity and critical debate about its shortcomings, its timidity in the face of expected reactions, and its inability to reflect critically about the problematic nature of 'modernization'. Part of the paradox of reform is that all those that want to reform society, only rarely reflect on and reform themselves. At the root of the problem lies a social positivism that, inspired by a mono-dimensional, functional and linear view of progress, thematizes social change as nomological and underestimates its hermeneutical dimension and cultural preconditions. It accepts axiomatically that meanings, ways of thinking, mentalities and communicative practices change more or less automatically, if some fundamental economic and institutional structures are reformed from above; at its roots lie supposedly value neutral conceptions of the human, public and common goods, which are assumed to be provided unproblematically by scientific knowledge and technocratic expertise. Reform is understood only as an institutional and not also as a cultural event. The 'good' is identified with what is considered as the proven, given 'true', and therefore the search for an always limited and provisional truth as a critical quest atrophies. The issues surrounding the problematic nature of the 'modern' and the 'progressive' as contentious, controversial, debatable and uncertain stakings within particular social and cultural settings, far from being simple adjustments to the currently 'modern', and not exhausted by the application of an ideal type, are not addressed.

The new right-wing Government of the New Democracy party that gained power just before the Olympic games in 2004 and ruled until 2009 abandoned all reformist attempts and policies of the previous Government and almost doubled the already high national debt, proving catastrophic for subsequent developments. New and old clientelistic networks were reinvigorated and hundreds of thousands of new public sector employees were appointed in ways that managed to bypass the independent exam system by legislating among others for oral interviews. Greece was walking blindly towards the abyss, impervious to its fate, amidst a generalized euphoria and ignorance.

At the same time, a particular voluntaristic radicalism had beset social and political forces to the left of the political spectrum. This left radicalism espousing a generalizing, denunciatory, unreformed, eclectic Marxist discourse was nothing more than a dangerous decisionism: a voluntaristic discourse that, being convinced of the validity claims of its own dogmatic conception of the 'good', being defined not in its own terms, but in contradistinction to an 'evil' represented by the exploiting creditors, the European allies and many other invisible forces covered studiously its ideological and cultural poverty, behind a naïve but extremely dangerous hyper-activism and populist clichés, which denounced and opposed any kind of real reform. Here an arbitrary, ideological (in the sense of false consciousness) conception of the 'good' was taken for granted as indisputably 'true'. This ever-present, in its essence deeply conservative, crypto-nationalistic and to an extent Eurosceptic undercurrent in Greek society, which is one of the major causes of its current state, has been reinvigorated by the severity of the economic crisis and, amidst the weakness of a serious reformist political and cultural project, managed to set the agenda both on the left and the right, and claim some form of hegemony. Repeating unreformed ideological platitudes, resisting the reform of the clientelistic state in the name of the 'people', prioritizing a statist, generalizing, abstract and vague opposition to the 'market forces' and to the European Union, this uncritical and unreflective current, with its newly found popularity, emerged as a primary obstacle to the long-overdue cultural, political and social reform, and drew together forces from both ends of the political spectrum.

Today we are faced with a coalition Government between Syriza (espousing leftist, unreformed, unreflective and, in many cases undemocratic, policies that tend to reproduce the old left's ideological certainties) the Independent Greeks (a right-wing nationalistic party), a coalition with disastrous effects for the economy, culture and education. We are also facing the discrediting of the reformist project, partly due to its own weaknesses and the absence of critical debate about its various flawed assumptions and practices. This urgent and long-overdue debate and communicative practice could, under certain conditions, mobilize reformist-minded social forces to the centre-left, centre and centre-right of the political spectrum, only if its political agents adopt a self-critical and reflective attitude and succeed in forging new political and social subjects. It might also, in due course, inspire and mobilize younger voters who have been exposed to the beneficial cultural effects of processes of European integration and this mobilization could prove crucial for developments in the decades to come.

As Greek society, paralyzed by fear, remains in denial, unable and unwilling to recognize its fundamental flaws and to reach some kind of intelligible self-understanding, increasingly being radicalized and looking for the scapegoat to designate as 'foe', our 'fate' still looks bleak. In the world of advanced modernity, faced with multiple crises largely of her own making, as well as by the threats and opportunities of globalization that she was not prepared for, Greece looks like a weak link in the European chain. Will she manage, despite all this, to redefine her position within Europe and the world and overcome her 'fate', both as past and as present? Will she reach a new understanding of her past and a vision of her future that will lead to a real opening to the world? Will she stop talking dangerous platitudes, will she resist its nationalistic, xenophobic self? Will she desire and think something worth being? Will she face her propensity to being towards fate, to being without a reason for being, to being absorbed in herself? Will she overcome her metaphysical fear, her physical fear and her dread of the other? What is apparent, as we live through the later stages of this tragedy, is that there will be no *deus ex machina* to save us. It is only we who can save ourselves.

Bibliography

Axelos, K. (2010), *The Fate of Modern Greece*, Athens: Nefeli Publications.

Bernstein, J.M. (1995), *Recovering Ethical Life: Jurgen Habermas and the Future of Critical Theory*, London: Routledge.

Bernstein, R.J. (ed.) (1985), *Habermas and Modernity*, Cambridge: Polity Press.

Gerth, H.H. and Wright Mills, C. (eds) (1948), *From Max Weber: Essays in Sociology*, London: Routledge.

Habermas, J. (1979), 'Consciousness-Raising or Redemptive Criticism: The Contemporaneity of Walter Benjamin', *New German Critique*, 17(1).

Habermas, J. (1992), *Knowledge and Human Interests*, London: Heinemann.

Heidegger, M. (1968), *What is Called Thinking*, New York: Harper and Row.

Kazamias, A. (2010), 'Pseudo-Hegelian contrivances: the uses of German Idealism in the discourse of the post-Civil War Greek state', Κăμπος, *Cambridge Papers in Modern Greek* 19: 47–73.

Kondylis, P. (2011), *The Causes of Decline in Modern Greece: the Weakness of the Bourgeois Element in Modern Greek Society and Ideology*, Athens: Themelio.

Levinas, E. (1985), *Ethics and Infinity*, Pittsburgh, PA: Duquesne University Press.

MacIntyre, A. (2007), *After Virtue*, London: Duckworth.

Sevastakis, N. (2016), *Ghosts of our Times: Left, Critique and Liberal Democracy*, Athens: Polis.

Sikelianos, A. (1995), *Selected Poems*, by Keeley, E. and Sherrard, P. (trans.), Evia: Denise Harvey.

Ramfos, S. (2012), *Time Out: The Greek sense of Time*, Athens: Armos Publishers.

Tsoukas, H. (2015), *The Tragedy of the Commons: Political Corruption, Institutional Decline and Bankruptcy*, Athens: Ikaros.

Index

1929 global financial crisis 3, 15
1973 profitability crisis 112–13, 116
2007–08 global financial crisis 5, 7, 26, 65, 78–9; as asymmetric shock 64, 67–9; banking 5, 8, 29–30, 57–8, 65; causes of 26; commodities and 76; costs inflicted on the weakest countries 79; eurozone crisis and 8, 29, 41, 44, 73–4, 105; Germany 5, 8; Greece and 6, 65, 147, 170, 172; Greek crisis and 105, 108, 112; as mere financial crisis 110, 111; redefining the crash 29–32; securitization of assets 26; sovereign debt crisis and 74–5; structural nature of 105; US subprime mortgage market, collapse of 65
2009–10 global economic crisis 68, 78

Acheson, Dean 4
Aegean Sea 1
aerospace sector 25
Afghanistan 25, 151
Andreotti, Giulio 21
ANTARSYA (Front of the Greek Anticapitalist Left) 169
Arghyrou, Michael G. 78–9
Argitis, Georgios 109
Asian crisis (1997) 26, 89, 100
asymmetry: asymmetric shock 68; asymmetrical structure of the EU 8, 77; asymmetrical structure of the eurozone 8, 68; asymmetry in European monetary relations 50, 60, 77; common currency and core/periphery asymmetry 41, 60; EMU, structural asymmetry of 64, 66, 79, 88; symmetrical adjustment structure in the eurozone 58
austerity 6, 9, 29, 31–2, 58, 145; deflationist austerity measures 5; eurozone 13, 36; eurozone crisis 40, 41, 55, 56–8, 59, 60, 78, 80, 86, 87; *expansionary austerity* doctrine 115; France 32; Greek crisis 107; Greek socio-economic model 144, 147–8, 149, 156, 157; normalization of 80; oligarchy and 35; party system and 167, 170; social reproduction crisis 128; social resistance against 147; southern eurozone 32; SYRIZA and 13, 173–4
Austria 90, 97, 99, 100, 101
Austro-Hungarian Empire 3
authoritarianism 10, 26, 36; authoritarianism-neoliberalism/ordoliberalim link 8; authoritarianism/neoliberalism similarities and links 11, 14, 35; critique of 11; Europe 10; eurozone project and 1; France 32–6; Greece 144; money-dealing capital and 27; oligarchic authoritarianism 31; southern eurozone and 32; Turkey 3
Axelos, Kostas 189–90, 193
Aznar, Jose-Maria 165

bail-out 5, 26, 30, 40, 65, 143; eurozone crisis 31, 50, 58, 59, 60; Greece 136–7n3, 159n2; Maastricht Treaty, no-bail-out clause 52, 58, 61n2; no bail-out/no exit/no default trilemma 52, 58, 59, 60
balance-of-payments crisis 54; eurozone crisis as balance-of-payments crisis 8, 40–1, 44, 52, 54–9, 60, 84, 88; Greek crisis 8–9, 61n5; policy implications 41, 54, 55
Balibar, Étienne 131–2

the Balkans 2, 3, 5, 7, 146, 148
banking 3, 5; 2007–08 global financial crisis and 5, 8, 29–30, 57–8, 65; bank crisis 30, 32; bankruptcy 66; *Bundesbank* 50, 60, 76; European banking 29, 31; eurozone crisis 8, 29, 57–8; France 8, 29, 58; Germany 5, 8, 29, 58, 59; inter-bank lending 26; liberalization 142; shadow banking 27; socialization of bank debts 30; Spain 66
bankruptcy 2, 3, 5, 29, 180; banking 66; household bankruptcy 126; industry 145; *see also* economy
Beck, Thorsten 86
beggar-thy-neighbour policies 27, 46, 54, 60, 86
Bernstein, Jay M. 198
Bernstein, Richard J. 192
Bilderberg Conferences 19, 21
bio-power 126, 137n7
Blair, Tony: 'Third Way' 165, 170
Blondel, Jean 176, 177
bond market 23, 41, 65; bond yields 29, 66; EMU bond yields **42**; eurobond 58; German bonds 76; government bond 23–4, 41, 79; Greece 41; US government bonds 76
Bosnia-Herzegovina 153, 159n8
bourgeoisie 1, 2, 13, 15, 108, 115, 116, 145; bourgeois state machine 10; democracy and 4, 16–17; petty bourgeoisie 126, 127, 134, 135, 137n8, 138n.20, 144; private sector 127; 'unfit to rule' 131
Bourgeot, Rémi 71, 72
Brenner, Robert 9
Bretton Woods Conference 17
Bretton Woods System 18
Brzezinski, Zbigniew 19
Burke, Edmund 14

capital: capital/labour relationship 6, 53; capital market 136; capital mobility 43–4, 146; democracy and 24; industrial capital 2, 6, 16; *see also* money capital; money-dealing capital
capitalism 10, 106; capitalist class power 19; capitalist economy 16, 26, 50, 118; capitalist imperialism 24; corporate liberal capitalism 15, 18, 19; corporate neoliberal capitalism 33; democracy and 10, 16, 26, 159n3; 'divergent capitalism' 142–3; Golden Age of 4, 144; Greek capitalism 112, 113, 114, 115–16, 136n3, 142–3; Greek crisis and 106, 109; state capitalism 24–5; workers' discipline device 130, 136; *see also* internal devaluation
Carter, James 20, 22
Castoriadis, Cornelius 195
'catching up with the West' discourse 1, 2, 4
CDO (collateral debt obligation) 26, 29, 30, 31
CDS (credit default swap) 26, 30–1
Chang, Michele 79
China 7, 28, 96, 97, 99, 100; People's Republic of China 24–5, 57, 89
CIA (Central Intelligence Agency) 4, 20, 21
City of London 7, 24, 29
Civil War (1944–49) 3, 4, 144, 198
class compromise 14, 19, 36; erosion of 35; neoliberal class compromise 22; organized labour and 16, 17, 20, 21, 22, 24, 33; social cohesion and 14–17, 35
class formation 14, 19, 24
clientelism 107, 142, 143, 148–9, 156, 158n1, 195, 199, 200; party system and 168, 169, 170, 171
Clinton, Bill 25, 165
Cold War 4, 23, 25; New Cold War 22, 25
collective bargaining 16, 124, 150
colonialism 3, 153
common currency 154; balance-of-payments crisis and 40, 44, 60; core/periphery asymmetry and 41, 60; eurozone crisis 40, 41, 43, 50, 52, 54, 55–6, 60; International Currency Union 17; macroeconomic adjustment and 55; *see also* currency; EMU; euro; eurozone crisis; exchange rate
communism 4, 21, 34, 169, 173; *see also* left-wing politics
competitiveness 53; balance-of-payments crises and 55; competitive devaluation 50, 78, 117; competitive disinflation 122, 136n2; crisis of 69; eurozone crisis 40, 43, 46, 53–4, 55, 64, 76, 79, 86, 99; eurozone crisis as crisis of competitiveness 69–73, 77–8, 88; eurozone periphery 40, 43, 57; Germany 46, 54–5, 72, 78; internal devaluation and 9, 121, 122, 147
Comunale, Mariarosaria 86
consumption 57; CPI/Consumer Price Index 43, **44**, 72, 77; domestic consumption 43, 87; internal

devaluation and 121, 122–3, 128; reduction of 112, 121; wages/consumption relation 122–3; working class 128, 137n11
corporate 20, 22, 56, 142; corporate liberal capitalism 15, 18, 19; corporate liberal class compromise 28; corporate liberal class configuration 32; corporate neoliberal capitalism 33; profits 29; USA 15, 22
corruption 3, 142, 148, 171, 180; Greek crisis and culture 196–7, 198, 199; PASOK 168
Costa-Gavras 13, 33
CPI (consumer price index) 72, 77
credit 23, 74, 152; cheap/easy credit 5, 31, 57, 69; credit crunch 65, 66; credit liberalization 143, 146
crisis: class compromise and 14; negative notion of 179, 181; as opportunity 10–11, 181
Crisis of Democracy report (1975) 20
Critical Political Economy 179
Crozier, Michel 20
culture 148, 179; political culture 35, 178, 181n5; *see also* Greek crisis and culture
currency: devaluation 5, 46, 55–6, 61n7; Germany 28, 50, 76, 78; monetary sovereignty 5, 6, 13; optimal currency area 88; return to national currencies 55–6, 61n7; *see also* common currency; dollar; euro
current account balance **49**, **51**, *70*, 90, *91*, 100, 123; CAD/current account deficit 5, 92, 101, 107, 109, 110, 113, 114, 117; euro, impact over current account disequilibrium 85, 88, 89; eurozone 84; eurozone core, current account surpluses 84, 85, 87, 88; eurozone crisis as current account disequilibrium 84, 86, 87, 88; eurozone crisis as part of a wider current account disequilibrium crisis 85, 89, 100; eurozone periphery 69, *93–4*; eurozone periphery, current account deficits 84, 85, 87, 88; eurozone periphery and current account disequilibrium 86, 87, 89–92, **95**, 96; Germany, current account surpluses 46, **49**, **51**, 84, 86, 89, 90, 96, 97, 99, 100, 101; Income Balance 90, 91, 92, 96, 100, 101n9–10; trade and financial sector deregulation and current account disequilibrium 88–9; trade as main source of current account disequilibrium 99–101, **100**; Unilateral Transfers 85, 90–1, 92, 96, 100, 101n10; *see also* eurozone core/periphery dichotomy
Cyprus 3, 4, 7

De Gaulle, Charles 35
De Grauwe, Paul 69, 81n16
debt: debt and guilt as synonymous 56; high debt to GDP ratios 5–6; private debt 86, 143–4; *see also* Greek debt; sovereign debt
deficit 66–7; budget deficit 5; CAD/current account deficit 5, 92, 101, 107, 109, 110, 113, 114, 117; deficit in periphery countries as caused by world trade 9; FD/fiscal deficit 107, 109, 113, 114; general government deficit/surplus **47**; TDH 107, 113; USA 18, 19, 29, 66
deflation 5, 6, 154
Delors, Jacques 28
democracy 21, 56, 61n7; bourgeoisie and 4, 16–17; capital and 24; capitalism and 10, 16, 26, 159n3; de-democratization 155–6; democratic capitalism 159n3; democratization 6, 158, 195; economy and 20; equality and 20; eurozone and 158; Greece and 148–9, 194, 197–8; liberal democracy 187, 197, 198; 'market-conforming democracy' 156; neoliberal economics and 22; political democracy 16–17, 19; social democracy 8–9, 170; socialist democracy 6; terrorism and 35; undemocratic nature 1, 61n7, 195, 201; voting 16, 17; *see also* party system
Democratic Alignment-Potami bloc 178, 179
Dendias, Nikos 172
depoliticization 11n1, 155, 159n10
derivatives 26, 31
devaluation 5, 30, 50; competitive devaluation 50, 78, 117; currency devaluation 5, 46, 55–6, 61n7; exchange rate devaluation 46, 50, 78, 110, 111; *see also* internal devaluation
Diaz Sanchez, Jose Luis 86, 89
dictatorship 21; Greek military dictatorship 4, 20, 112, 138n20, 145, 195
Dijsselbloem, Jeroen 149–50
Diliyiannis, Theodore 2

DIMAR (Democratic Left) 177, 178
Dimoulas, Constantine 1–12, 61n5
'divergence thesis' 142–3, 144, 147, 150, 152, 156, 157, 158; 'divergence thesis'/policies link 144; *see also* Greek socio-economic model
the Dodecanese 3–4
dollar (US dollar) 18, 20, 22, 29
Dörre, Klaus 155
Downs, Anthony 165, 166
Draghi, Mario 58, 79, 149–50
Duménil, Gérard 22, 131
Duverger, Maurice 169

EAP (Economic Adjustment Programme) 108, 114, 115–17
ECB (European Central Bank) 28, 155, 156; eurozone crisis and 65–6, 80; interest rate 20, 41, 43, 54; as lender of last resort 58, 59, 64, 79; *see also* the troika
economy 7; capitalist economy 16, 26, 50, 118; demand-led policies 4, 15; democracy and 20; economic convergence 88, 149, 150; economic nationalism 111; globalization of 142; Greece 2–6, 121, 123; separation of economy and politics 155; separation of economy and society 144, 156; wage-led economy 121, 123; *see also* bankruptcy; debt; Greek debt; Greek socio-economic model
EEC (European Economic Community) 4, 5, 18
EFSF (European Financial Stability Facility) 30–1, 65
Eichengreen, Barry 69
El Khomri, Myriam 33
El Khomri labour law 35
employment 17, 33, 78, 121, 122, 143, 155, 199–200; capital/labour cleavage 6; party affiliation and 196; self-employment 129
EMS (European Monetary System) 5, 40, 44, 60, 72, 76, 77; exchange rate 50, 52, 69
EMU (Economic and Monetary Union) 40, 59, 64, 107, 111, 146; anti-inflationary caps 28; asymmetry in European monetary relations 50, 68; EMU bond yields **42**; eurozone crisis 64, 66, 79; Germany and 52; Greece's exiting from the EMU while remaining in the EU 115, 117; internal contradictions of 64; as Optimal Currency Area 87, 111; structural asymmetry of 64, 66, 79, 88; *see also* common currency
ESM (European Stability Mechanism) 50, 59, 65
EU (European Union) 35; anti-European stance 199, 201; asymmetrical structure of 8, 77; budget 53; democratization of institutions 6; Greek disengagement from 6, 7, 9, 106, 111, 117–19; Greek transitional programme 118; pro-European stance 9, 10, 35, 145, 173–4; *see also* Europe; the troika
EU Association Treaty 36
euro 27, 53, 158; 1999 introduction of 9, 41, 43; as causal agent of the eurozone crisis 85, 86, 88, 89, 100, 101n2; euro crisis 41, 50, 52, 56, 57–8, 59, 60; eurozone periphery and 43, 53–4; exchange rate 28, 40, 43, 44, 46; exiting the euro 88, 101n2; imbalances after the introduction of 84; money-dealing capital and 28; *see also* common currency; eurozone crisis; exchange rate
Europe 189; authoritarianism 10; Central and Eastern Europe 25–6; Germany and 26; neoliberalism 10; sovereign debt crisis 29; *see also* EU
European Commission 153, 156, 159n10, 167, 181; *see also* the troika
European Constitution 35–6
European integration 28, 56, 58–9; Germany and 58, 59; Greece and 112, 113, 114, 115, 116, 117, 201
Euroscepticism 9–10, 173, 201
eurozone: assumptions of eurozone architecture 52, 60; asymmetrical structure of 8, 68; austerity 13, 36; authoritarianism 1; break-up/exit of 55–6, 59, 61–2n8, 110, 142; 'conservative exit'/'progressive exit' from the eurozone 61–2n8; democracy and 158; fascism and 13, 14, 32; Germany and 27–9; gold standard and 154; Greece's entry in 5, 199; Greece's exit from 6, 7, 9; as 'monetary system' 157; neoliberalism and 29, 32, 35, 157; as playground for hot money 27–9; *see also the entries below for* eurozone
eurozone core 41, 43, 50, 101n1; 2007–08 global financial crisis 41; eurozone break-up and 56, 61–2n8; fiscal issues

44, 46; *see also* eurozone core/periphery dichotomy; eurozone crisis; Germany
eurozone core/periphery dichotomy 84, 85, 100, 101; common currency and core/periphery asymmetry 41, 60; eurozone core/periphery trade links 96–7; eurozone core/periphery's trade disequilibrium 97, **98**, 99–100, **100**; *see also* current account balance; eurozone core; eurozone crisis; eurozone periphery
eurozone crisis 41–50, 64, 84; 2007–08 global financial crisis and 8, 29, 41, 44, 73–4, 105; 2007–08 global financial crisis as asymmetric shock 64, 67–9; alternative explanations of 86–9; austerity measures 40, 41, 55, 56–8, 59, 60, 78, 80, 86, 87; bail-out 31, 50, 58, 59, 60; as balance-of-payments crisis 8, 40–1, 44, 52, 54–9, 60, 84, 88; banking 8, 29, 57–8; competitiveness and 40, 43, 46, 53–4, 55, 64, 76, 79, 86, 99; as competitiveness crisis 69–73, 77–8, 88; as *crisis in the eurozone* 101; crisis within a common currency 40, 41, 43, 50, 52, 54, 55–6, 60; as current account disequilibrium 84, 85, 86, 87, 88, 89, 100; ECB 65–6, 80; EMU, structural imbalances of 64, 66, 79; euro as causal agent of the crisis 85, 86, 88, 89, 100, 101n2; euro crisis 41, 50, 52, 56, 57–8, 59, 60; *eurozone crisis* thesis, validity of 89–101; fiscal issues 40, 44, 46, 53, 55, 56, 57, 60, 66–7, 74–5; Germany 40, 44, 46, 50, 56, 58–9, 60, 61n5, 73–6; Greece 64, 65, 79; 'n-1' country problem 73, 76–7; sovereign debt and 64, 65, 66–7, 79–80; as sovereign debt crisis 40, 55, 56, 59, 60; sovereign debt crisis is a symptom of 41; structural logic of adjustment in the eurozone 50–4; unfolding of the crisis 65–6; *see also* eurozone core/periphery dichotomy; eurozone periphery; PIIGS
eurozone periphery 41, 55–6, 59, 60, 101n1; 2007–08 global financial crisis 41; competitiveness 40, 43, 57; current account balance 69, *93–4*; current account deficits 84, 85, 87, 88; current account disequilibrium 86, 87, 89–92, **95**, 96; economic growth 43; euro and 43, 53–4; eurozone break-up and 55–6, 59, 61–2n8; fiscal issues 40, 44; inflation 43, 69, 71–2; interest rates 44, 89; modernization of 57; southern eurozone 14, 27, 32; *see also* eurozone core/periphery dichotomy; eurozone crisis; Greece; Ireland; PIIGS; Portugal; Spain
exchange rate: EMS 50, 52, 69; euro 28, 40, 43, 44, 46; European Exchange Rate Mechanism 28; exchange rate crisis 44; exchange rate devaluation 46, 50, 78, 110, 111; flexible exchange rate 46, 52; Germany 46, 50, 54–5, 76; monetary union 52; nominal exchange rate 40, 43, 46, 50, 52–3, 54, 55, 60, 76, 81n17; pegged exchange rate 44, 46, 50, 52; PIIGS real exchange rates *77*; real exchange rate 46, 50, 53–4, 55, 56, 57, 58, 60, *77*, 81n17, 88, 89; *see also* common currency; euro

fascism 15, 16, 31; eurozone and 13, 14, 32; neo-fascism 21, 31, 32, 33; neoliberalism 14, 32
Feulner, Edwin, Jr. 20, 21
financial integration 43–4, 86
financial services 5, 10, 16
financialization 88, 112, 146; crisis of 9; 'financial deepening' 26; Greek crisis, *financialization* thesis 109–10, 111; neoliberal globalization/financialization 4, 5, 7
Fine, Ben 9
fiscal issues: eurozone crisis 40, 44, 46, 53, 55, 56, 57, 60, 66–7, 74–5; FD/fiscal deficit 107, 109, 113, 114; federalist fiscal system 80; fiscal policy 53, 55, 57, 88, 119, 150, 159n10
'Five Presidents' Report' 149–50
Fordism 15, 16, 17, 19, 30
Foucault, Michel 11n1; bio-power 126, 137n7
Fouskas, Vassilis K. 1–12, 61n5
Fragile States Index 151
France 5, 14, 44, 46; 2007–08 global financial crisis and 8; austerity 32; authoritarianism 32–6; banking 8, 29, 58; *Charlie Hebdo* attack 33–4; eurozone crisis 44, 46; labour 28, 33, 35; *loi Macron* 33–5, 36; media 34; monetary union 50; NATO 28; neo-fascism 32, 33; predatory neoliberalism 32, 35; social contract

33; social protection 33; Socialist Party 33; terrorism 33–5
Frankel, Jeffrey A. 68
free market 8, 11n1
Friedman, Milton 20
Fukuyama, Francis 143, 144, 148–9, 150, 153, 156, 158; *The End of History and the Last Man* 148; foreign intervention 149, 151; *Political Order and Political Decay* 143
Fyssas, Pavlos 172

al-Gaddafi, Muammar 31
Gamble, Andrew 11n1
Gaulier, Guillaume 86
Gelli, Licio 21
geopolitics 2, 3, 7
Georgiadis, Adonis 172
Germany 15, 50, 177; 2007–08 global financial crisis and 5, 8; banking 5, 8, 29, 58, 59; competitiveness 46, 54–5, 72, 78; current account surpluses 46, **49**, **51**, 84, 86, 89, 90, 96, 97, 99, 100, 101; deutschemark/currency 28, 50, 76, 78; economic growth 46, 50; EMU 52; euro 28; Europe and 26; European integration and 58, 59; eurozone and 27–9; eurozone crisis 40, 44, 46, 50, 56, 58–9, 60, 61n5, 73–6; exchange rate 46, 50, 54–5, 76; interest rate 50, 60; international affairs 27–8; labour 27, 60; 'n-1' problem 76; ordoliberalism 7; unemployment 29; wages 18, 27, 28, 110; *see also* eurozone core
Glass-Steagall Act (1933) 15–16, 24
the Global Minotaur 19, 27, 29; architects of the Minotaur's labyrinth 19–22; combating inflation 22; the many-headed Hydra of money capital 22–4; *see also* Varoufakis, Yianis
the 'Global Plan' 17–19, 21, 22
globalization 71, 115, 187, 202; globalization of the economy 142; neoliberal globalization 4, 7, 8, 25
gold standard 15, 18, 19, 152, 154, 158
Golden Dawn 167, 172, 181n2; neo-Nazism 163, 167, 172, 195; third largest party in the Greek Parliament 163, 195; *see also* party system
governance 146; corporate governance reforms 142; 'kleptocratic system' of 170–1; lack of financial market governance 57
Gowan, Peter 24
Gramsci, Antonio 16, 132
Great Depression (1930s) 15, 23, 121, 123, 164
Greece 67, 92; 1822 Constitution of Epidaurus 189; 1830 foundation of the Greek state 1, 2; 2007–08 global financial crisis 6, 65, 147, 170, 172; authoritarianism 144; democracy 148–9, 194, 197–8; economy 2–6, 121, 123; European integration and 112, 113, 114, 115, 116, 117, 201; eurozone crisis 64, 65, 79; Greek state 2, 189; state modernization 57, 144, 146, 148, 149, 150, 152, 158, 199; trade deficit 97, 99, 101; *see also the entries below related to Greece*; eurozone periphery; PIIGS
Greek crisis 1–2, 7, 40, 105, 109, 111, 147, 164; 2007–08 global financial crisis and 105, 108, 112; austerity 107; as balance-of-payments crisis 8–9, 61n5; capitalism and 106, 109; causes of 8–9, 157; circulation sphere and 105, 108, 110; as debt crisis 105, 109, 111; disengagement from the EU 106, 111, 117–19; domestic origins of 61n5; EAPs, redesigning with anti-cyclical and debt-relieving measures 114–15, 116–17; EAPs' strategy 114, 115–16; exiting from the EMU while remaining in the EU 115, 117; *financialization* thesis 109–10, 111; Greek capitalism 112, 113, 114, 115–16; 'Greek disease' 107; heterodox approach 7, 106, 109–11, 116; Keynesianism 106, 109, 112–13; mainstream/orthodox approach 106–108, 110, 115, 116; marxist approach 106, 112–14, 117; neoliberalism 106, 109, 112, 113; production sphere and 105, 107, 110; strategies for overcoming the crisis 114–19; *see also* Greek crisis and culture; Greek debt; Greek production model
Greek crisis and culture 1, 158, 187; ancient Greeks 190; blaming others 187, 201; Classical Greece 189, 194; corruption 196–7, 198, 199; critical reflection 187, 200; cultural deficit of self-consciousness 197; cultural poverty 195, 201; elusive communication 191–4, 198; elusive reform

195–202; elusive self-understanding 188–91, 201; greek-centredness 189–90; Greek education 195–6; Greek élite 196–7; 'greekness' 189; modernity 188, 189, 190, 191, 193, 194, 197, 198, 199, 200; modernization 199; the other 190, 191, 192, 197; *polis* 192, 194
Greek debt 2–5, 41, 143; cancelation of 6, 9; external borrowing 2, 4, 5, 145; geopolitics and 2, 4, 5, 7; high debt to GDP ratios 5–6; interest rates demanded by financial markets 46; internal borrowing 2, 3, 4, 5; internal devaluation and 124–5, 127; sovereign debt 46, 54, 67, 123, 143–4, 145, 146, 159n6, 200; USA and 4; welfare state and 4
Greek Depression 121, 122, 123, 126, 128, 129, 130, 135; *see also* internal devaluation
Greek production model 105, 199; deindustrialization 105, 108, 113; failure of 105, 108; primary sector, shrinkage of 105, 108, 113; productive restructuring 105, 108, 111, 114, 116, 117, 118; services bubble 105; tertiary sector, oversizing of 108; *see also* Greek crisis
Greek socio-economic model 142, 143, 157; 2007–08 global financial crisis 147; austerity 144, 147–8, 149, 156, 157; convergences and divergences in 144–7; democratic capitalism 159n3; four phases of post-war Greece 143–4; 'good money' project 144, 156; Greek 'precarious state' 144, 148, 151, 153, 154–6; market liberalism 144, 154, 155; Memoranda 143, 144, 147–9, 153, 156, 157; neoliberalism 152, 153, 157; 'politics of fulfilment'/ *Erfüllungspolitik* 144, 151–4, 157; separation of economy and politics 155; separation of economy and society 144, 156; social resistance 147; state modernization 144, 146, 148, 149, 150, 152, 158, 199; *see also* 'divergence thesis'; Keynesianism; neoliberalism
Greenspan, Alan 24, 26
GUAM (Georgia, Ukraine, Azerbaijan and Moldova) regional security bloc 26

Habermas, Jürgen 188, 195
Harvey, David 14
Hayek, Friedrich 20, 144, 156
Heath, Edward 18
hedge fund 26, 27, 30, 31
hegemony 132; double function of 132; new hegemonic formula 21; USA 4, 19; *see also* political hegemony crisis
Heidegger, Martin 196
Heritage Foundation 20
Hessel, Jeroen 86
Holbrooke, Richard 25
hot money 26, 27, 30; eurozone as playground for hot money 27–9
Hume, David 14
Hungary 15
Huntington, Samuel 20
Hussein, Saddam 31

IMF (International Monetary Fund) 17, 129, 150, 153, 156; SAPs/Structural Adjustment Programmes 115; *see also* the troika
imperialism 3, 7, 24, 112, 113, 136n3
Indignados, Spain 27
industrial sector 3, 46, 57, 68; import substitution industrialization policy 3; industrial backwardness 5; industrial capital 2, 6, 16; industrial policy 108, 111, 116, 117
industrialization 3, 22, 148; deindustrialization 105, 108, 113
inflation: anti-inflation measures 21, 28; combating inflation 22; divergent inflation 72, 77; dollar inflation 20; eurozone periphery 43, 69, 71–2; harmonized inflation rates 69, *70*; inflation convergence 43; PIIGS countries 69
Institutionalism 109
interest rate 20, 31; ECB 20, 41, 43, 54; eurozone periphery 44, 89; Germany 50, 60; Greece 46, 54
internal devaluation 5, 9, 80, 115, 133–4; 2010 Memorandum of Understanding 121, 122, 136n1; competitive disinflation 122, 136n2; competitiveness and 9, 121, 122, 147; consumption and 121, 122–3, 128; debt 124–5, 127; economic depression and 121, 122–5, 134; labour and 9, 121, 122, 125; labour market structural reform 121, 122, 124, 128, 133; a macroeconomic disaster 122–4; negative impact of 121, 122, 123–5, 147; objectives of 121, 122, 133–4; political hegemony crisis 9, 121, 133–5; poverty and material

deprivation 9, 122, 123, 127, 128, 130; social reproduction crisis and 9, 121, 122, 125–31, 136; tax increase 124, 126, 147; uncertainty and social conflict 135–6; unemployment 9, 121, 122, 123, 129, 130, 147; wage flexibility/ reduction 9, 121, 122–3, 124, 125, 126, 133, 147; *see also* Greek Depression; political hegemony crisis; social reproduction crisis; wage labour in Greece, segments of
International Labour Organization 150
Ioakimoglou, Elias 8, 9, 121–41
Iraq 28
Ireland 40, 46, 96, 101n1, 177; sovereign debt 67; trade surplus 99, 100, 101; *see also* eurozone periphery; PIIGS
Italy 15, 21, 34; sovereign debt 66, 67; *see also* eurozone periphery; PIIGS

Japan 18, 23, 66
JBNES (*Journal of Balkan and Near Eastern Studies*) 11
Juncker, Jean-Claude 33, 116, 149–50

Kaelberer, Matthias 8, 40–63
Kaldor, Nicholas 108
Karamanlis, Constantine 4, 10, 165, 166, 167; 2009 early election 172; *see also* ND
Karatzaferis, George 166–7, 172; *see also* LAOS
Katrakilidis, Constantinos 107
Kazakos, Panos 159n2
Kazamias, Alexander 7, 10, 163–86
Keynes, John Maynard 17, 18, 20, 23, 29
Keynes Plan 17, 18
Keynesianism 19, 20, 101n3, 109, 143, 144, 145; Keynesian income distribution policies 112–13; New Keynesianism 106; post-Keynesianism 8, 106, 109, 110
Kindleberger, Charles 19, 30
Kissinger, Henry 19
KKE (Communist Party of Greece) 169
Klein, Naomi 32
Kontonikas, Alexandros 78–9
Kosovo 28, 153, 159n8
Krugman, Paul 84, 174
Kupchan, Charles 24, 35

labour 54; capital/labour relationship 6, 53; France 28, 33, 35; Germany 27, 60; internal devaluation 9, 121, 122, 125; internal devaluation and labour market structural reform 121, 122, 124, 128, 133; labour flexibilization and flexicurity 146, 150; labour migration 53, 61n4, 129, 130, 199; labour power 126, 128, 129, 130, 132, 137n13, 137n14; labour precarization 146, 149; organized labour 16, 17, 20, 21, 22, 24, 27, 33; *see also* ULC
Laclau, Ernesto 174
Lagarde, Christine 96, 158
LAOS (Popular Orthodox Rally) 166–7, 172, 181n2; tripartite government 166–7, 172, 177; *see also* Karatzaferis, George; party system
Lapavitsas, Costas 8, 11n2, 50, 96, 109, 110–11; CAD 109, 110; eurozone crisis 84, 86, 88, 96; exit from the eurozone 61n8, 110
Layard, Richard: *Unemployment. Macroeconomic Performance and the Labour Market* 133
LCTM (Long-Term Credit Management) 26
LeBaron, Genevieve 131
Leblond, Patrick 79
left-wing politics 9–10, 20, 32, 169, 195, 197, 199, 200; left radicalism 201; populism 201; *see also* communism; socialism
Lehman Brothers 25, 65, 74
Lenin, Vladimir I. 15
Levinas, Emmanuel 191
Lévy, Dominique 22
liberalism 16; corporate liberal capitalism 15, 18, 19; economic liberalism 159n11; liberal democracy 187, 197, 198; liberal internationalism 15; market liberalism 144, 154, 155, 159n11; 'sado-liberalism' 156
liberalization 142, 146, 147, 150, 153, 158; banking sector 142; credit liberalization 143, 146
Libya 28, 97, 99, 151
Lorey, Isabell 159n9
Loulis, Yannis: *Road to the Abyss* 165–6
Lynteris, Chrystos 31

Maastricht Treaty 52, 53, 57, 58, 59, 61n2, 77
Machiavelli, Niccolò: *The Prince* 132
MacIntyre, Alasdair 194
Macroeconomics of the New Consensus 106

Macron, Emmanuel 33
Mair, Peter 169
Makarios III, Archbishop of Cyprus 4
Malakos, Tolis 1, 7, 187–202
Maniatis, Thanasis 112
Markantonatou, Maria 10, 142–62
Marshall Plan 4, 17, 145
Marx, Karl 128, 130, 131–2, 137n14; *The Communist Manifesto* 131; *encounter* 131, 138n19; *tendency* 131, 138n18
Marxism 8, 9, 109, 179, 201; Greek crisis, marxist approach to 106, 112–14, 117; neo-Marxism 169; *see also* internal devaluation
Marxist Political Economy 106, 107
Mavroudeas, Stavros 6, 8–9, 87, 105–20
McCarthy, Joseph 17
McGinnis, John 158
McNally, David: *Global Slump* 136
Memoranda 121, 122, 136n1, 143, 144, 147–9, 153, 156, 157, 167, 170, 171, 173, 174, 175; *see also* the troika
Merkel, Angela 33, 156
Metaxas, Ioannis 3
Mexican crisis (1994) 26
middle class 16, 35; asset-owning middle class 18, 22, 23, 24, 26, 27; upper middle class 22, 24
Middle/Near East 2, 3, 7, 25, 148, 151
migration 174, 192–3, 199; immigration reform 200; labour migration 53, 61n4, 129, 130, 199
the military: military coup 22; military dictatorship, Greece 4, 20, 112, 138n20, 145, 195; military industry 25
Milios, John 53, 61n5, 88, 109, 110, 111
Milosevic, Slobodan 31
Minotaur *see* the Global Minotaur
Mitterrand, François 5
modernization 22; Achilles' heel of the 'modernizing' block 200; Greek state modernization 57, 144, 146, 148, 149, 150, 152, 158, 199; shallow 'modernization' 199; Trikoupis, Charilaos 2
money capital 16, 22, 23, 26, 109–10; the many-headed Hydra of money capital 22–4; *see also* capital
money-dealing capital 23, 24–7, 29, 30, 31; 1933 Glass-Steagall Act 15–16; authoritarianism and 27; euro and 28; oligarchy and 27; predatory neoliberalism and 35; *see also* capital
Moro, Aldo 21
mortgage 26, 65, 143
Mouzelis, Nikos 169, 174–5
MPS (Mont Pèlerin Society) 20
Mudde, Cas 173, 174, 181n5

nationalism 10, 195, 198–9, 201; economic nationalism 111; nationalist populism 31
nationalization 4, 5, 118, 145
NATO (North Atlantic Treaty Organization) 4, 5, 22, 25, 28; 'strategy of tension' 21
Naylor, R.T. 23
ND (New Democracy) 10, 178, 180, 200–201; Greek economic crisis and 164, 168, 171–2; Greek two-party system 163, 165–6, 177; populism 171; shift to the 'middle ground' 165, 166; tripartite government 166–7, 172, 177; *see also* Karamanlis, Constantine; party system
neo-Gramscianism 8, 10
neo-Nazi movement 9, 163, 167, 172; *see also* Golden Dawn
neoliberalism 20, 106, 130–1, 152; authoritarianism-neoliberalism/ordoliberalim link 8; authoritarianism/neoliberalism similarities and links 11, 14, 35; City of London 7; corporate neoliberal capitalism 33; critique of 11; democracy and 22; disciplinary neoliberal regime 136; fascism 14, 32; Greece 4, 5, 144, 146; Greek crisis and 106, 109, 112, 113; Greek socio-economic model 152, 153, 157; Europe 10; European 'neoliberal colonialism' 153; eurozone and 29, 32, 35, 157; money-dealing capital and 35; neoliberal class compromise 22; neoliberal financialization 4, 5; neoliberal globalization 4, 7, 8, 25; ordoliberalism/neoliberalism comparison 11n1; ordoliberalism/neoliberalism connection 7–8; precarization and 154; predatory neoliberalism 10, 24, 27, 30, 32, 35; systemic neoliberalism 22, 24, 28; taxation 29; Volcker-style neoliberalism 22; wages and 10; Wall Street 7; welfare state and 10, 146
the Netherlands 35–6, 90, 97, 99, 100, 101, 176, 177
New Deal 15, 16, 17, 19, 30
New International Economic Order 20, 22
Nietzsche, Friedrich 62n9

Nikolakopoulos, Elias 163
NIS (National Insurance System) 200
Nixon, Richard 18, 19
Nobel prize 20, 26, 174
NSRF (National Strategic Reference Framework, EU) 116

Obama, Barack 66
Occupy Wall Street movement 27
OECD (Organisation for Economic Co-operation and Development) 153; *Jobs Study* 133
oligarchy 24, 29; austerity and 35; money-dealing capital and 27; oligarchic authoritarianism 31, 35
Olympic games (2004) 199
ordoliberalism 11n1; Germany and 7; main tenets 11n1; neoliberalism/ordoliberalism comparison 11n1; ordoliberal project 7; ordoliberal rigidity 6, 8; ordoliberalism/neoliberalism connection 7–8; wage and 10; welfare state and 10
Ott, Konrad 159n2
Ottoman Empire 2–3
over-accumulation crisis 9, 112–13, 116

Paitaridis, Dimitris 112
Papademos, Lucas 149, 166–7, 172, 177
Papandreou, Andreas 4, 5, 165, 169, 170, 173, 175, 195; *see also* PASOK
Papandreou, George 46, 142, 158n1, 166, 167, 169–70, 171; *see also* PASOK
party system 10, 163, 177–8; austerity 167, 170; 'bipolar multi-partyism' 163; breakdown of the old two-party system 163, 165–8, 180; clientelism 168, 169, 170, 171; democratic choice 166; elections 163, 165, 166, 168, 177, 178, 181n1; far-right politics 164, 166, 167; hybrid party system 163, 165, 178; 'minor two-partyism' 163; 'multi-party' system 163, 165, 176–7, 178, 179; 'partitocracy' 169, 171; party affiliation 195, 196; party coalition 163, 166–7, 176, 177, 178, 180, 201; party system-in-crisis 178; 'two-and-a-half' party system 176; 'two-and-two-halves' party system 176, 178; two-party system 163, 174, 176; 'two-plus' 163, 165, 176, 177, 178; *see also* democracy; Golden Dawn; LAOS; ND; party system/economic crisis relationship; PASOK; SYRIZA
party system/economic crisis relationship 10, 163–4, 168–76, 177–8, 179–81; autonomy of politics/party systems from the economic sphere 164–5, 177, 180; change of party system as transitional phenomenon 165; dialectic relationship 179; 'freezing of party systems' 169; Memorandum of Understanding 167, 170, 171, 173, 174, 175; voter volatility 164, 168, 178–9; *see also* party system
PASOK (Panellínio Socialistiko Kinima/Panhellenic Socialist Movement) 10, 145, 155, 165, 178, 180; corruption 168; decline and demise of 163, 166, 168, 170–1; Greek two-party system 163, 165–6; 'kleptocratic system' of governance 170–1; populism 169, 172, 173; pro-European stance 145; state modernization 146; as 'state party' 167–8, 169, 170; tripartite government 166–7, 172, 177; *see also* Papandreou, Andreas; Papandreou, George; party system
Passas, Costas 112
Pedersen, Mogens 168, 178
pension system 6, 9, 56, 142, 150
Pesenti, Carlo 21
Pettifor, Ann 154
Peydró, José-Luis 86
PIIGS (Portugal, Ireland, Italy, Greece and Spain) 13; eurozone crisis 64, 66; fiscal issues 66; real exchange rates *77*; *see also* eurozone crisis
Pijl, Kees van der 8, 10, 13–39
Piketty, Thomas 131
Pinay Circle (*Cercle Violet*) 21
Le Point 34
Polanyi, Karl 10, 144, 152, 155, 158, 159n11; 'double movement' 147; 'precarious foundations' 154
political economy: global political economy 6, 17, 27
political hegemony crisis 9, 121, 131–5; counter-tendency to passivity 9, 122, 133, 134, 136, 138n20; Greece and 133; hegemonic crisis 121–2, 136; internal devaluation/hegemonic crisis link 9, 122; political destabilisation 121, 132, 133; tendency to hegemonic crisis as structural feature of disciplinary neoliberal regime 136; *see also* hegemony; internal devaluation; social reproduction crisis

politics: aestheticization by fascism 16; political culture 35, 178, 181n5; political democracy 16–17, 19; separation of economy and politics 155; *see also* political hegemony crisis
politicization 9, 136, 195
Polydoras, Vyron 172
Pompidou, Georges 18
populism 2, 26, 169, 174–5, 195, 199; Diliyiannis, Theodore 2; left-wing politics 201; nationalist populism 31; ND 171; PASOK 169, 172, 173; SYRIZA 173–5, 181n6
Portugal 40, 92, 96, 177; sovereign debt 67; trade deficit 97, 99, 100, 101; *see also* eurozone periphery; PIIGS
Poulantzas, Nicos 8, 10, 121, 133, 164; new petty bourgeoisie 137n8; *Political Power and Social Classes* 132
poverty 6; child poverty 152; cultural poverty 195, 201; internal devaluation and 9, 122, 123, 127, 128, 130; population of paupers 125, 129–30; trap of self-sustained misery 130
power: capitalist class power 19; labour power 126, 128, 129, 130, 132, 137n13, 137n14; power-shift 7; ruling class power 17; trade union and 20, 71, 78
precarization 154–6, 159n9; Greek 'precarious state' 144, 148, 151, 153, 154–6; labour precarization 146, 149; neo-colonial dimension of the precarious state 156
private sector 21, 107, 115, 118, 127, 142, 147, 196
privatization 5, 22, 142, 146, 147, 153, 159–60n12
Propaganda Due 21
Psarras, Dimitris: *The Hidden Hand of Karatzaferis* 166
public debt *see* sovereign debt
Putin, Vladimir 31, 32

racism 10, 32, 167, 198–9
Radical Political Economy 106, 109, 111, 117
Ramfos, Stelios 197
Reagan, Ronald 19, 21, 22, 23
referendum (July 2015) 13, 80, 135, 155
refugee 3, 7, 13, 137n17
rent-seeking 143, 156, 157, 159n2
rentier 16, 23, 134
right-wing politics 4, 197, 199, 200; far-right politics 10, 164, 166, 167, 195; USA 22
Roberts, Adrienne 131
Rockefeller, David 19
Roosevelt, Franklin D. 15, 17; *see also* New Deal
Rose, Andrew K. 68
Rubin, Robert 25
Russia 2, 3, 15, 28, 96, 97; rise of 7; *see also* USSR

Samaras, Antonis 167, 172, 177
Sapir, J. 36
Sarkozy, Nicolas 33, 34
Sartori, Giovanni 176, 177
Schröder, Gerhard 27, 46, 71
Schulz, Martin 149–50
Schumpeter, Joseph 17
security issues 7, 53
Shultz, George 19
Sikelianos, Angelos 193
Simitis, Costas 165, 166, 168, 169–70, 171, 199
Single European Act 57
Single Market 28, 43, 56
Smith, Adam 156–7
social cohesion 35, 144; class compromise and 14–17
social contract 31, 33, 36
social protection 31, 32, 33, 150, 159n7
social reproduction crisis 125, 128–31, 132, 135, 136; additional-worker trap 128; austerity 128; internal devaluation and 9, 121, 122, 125–31, 136; internal devaluation/hegemonic crisis link 9, 122; internal social exile 130, 137n17; segments of wage labour in Greece 125–30; unemployment and 125, 126, 128–9, 136; *see also* internal devaluation; political hegemony crisis; poverty
social resistance 147, 168, 180
social security 15, 27, 124, 125, 145
social services 9, 126
socialism 4, 5, 9, 22, 33, 145, 195; socialist democracy 6; USSR 23; *see also* left-wing politics
socio-economic model 142, 143; eurozone 157; *see also* Greek socio-economic model
Sotiropoulos, Dimitris P. 53, 61n5, 88, 109, 110, 111, 137n4

sovereign debt 30, **48**, 66–7, *67*; 2007–08 global financial crisis and 74–5; 2007–2010 GDP loss 67, *68*; CDOs/ CDO-like debt instruments 30; Europe 29; eurozone crisis and 41, 64, 65, 66–7, 79–80; eurozone crisis as sovereign debt crisis 40, 55, 56, 59, 60; Greece 46, 54, 67, 123, 143–4, 145, 146, 159n6, 200; Ireland 67; Italy 66, 67; Portugal 67; post-2010 sovereign debt crisis 29, 31, 32; Spain 66, 67; speculation and 79; *see also* debt
Spain 40, 46, 92; sovereign debt 66, 67; trade deficit 97, 99–100, 101; *see also* eurozone periphery; PIIGS
speculation 5, 30, 32, 52, 64, 66, 67; Greece and 65; sovereign debt and 79
speculative arbitrage 24, 26, 30, 31
SPV (Special Purpose Vehicle) 30
Stability and Growth Pact 44
state: fragile state 151, 154; Greek 'precarious state' 144, 148, 151, 153, 154–6; Greek state modernization 57, 144, 146, 148, 149, 150, 152, 158, 199; state capitalism 24–5; Weberian notion of 148–9, 151, 153; Western state as highest stage of political development 151
Stathakis, George 109
Stockhammer, Engelbert 137n4
'strategy of tension' 21, 34–5
Strauss, Franz-Josef 21
Strauss-Kahn, Dominique 17
Streeck, Wolfgang 10, 143, 144, 154, 156–7, 159n3
Subasat, Turan 8, 9, 84–104
subsidy 36, 144
Sun Tsu 132
Syria 7, 151
SYRIZA (Synaspismos Rizospastikis Aristeras/Coalition of the Radical Left) 5, 9, 10, 36, 134, 135, 147, 176, 178, 179; austerity 13, 173–4; brake up of 175; as 'élitist' party 173; Greek two-party system 177; populism 173–5, 181n6; pro-European stance 173–4; rise of 163, 168, 169, 173–4; Syriza-ANEL Government 147, 201; Thessaloniki Economic Platform 174; *see also* party system; Tsipras, Alexis

Talani, Leila Simona 8, 64–83
taxation 4, 6, 24, 143, 146, 151; internal devaluation and tax increase 124, 126, 147; neoliberalism 29; tax avoidance/ tax evasion 146, 159n5
TC (Trilateral Commission) 19–20, 21, 22
TDH (Twin Deficit Hypothesis) 107, 113
terrorism 8; democracy and 35; France 33–5; predatory neoliberalism and 35
Thatcher, Margaret 19, 23; Thatcherism 133
there-is-no-alternative doctrine 133, 136, 147–8, 157
Trachanas, Emmanouil 107
trade 88–9, 96–7; eurozone core/ periphery's trade disequilibrium 97, **98**, 99–100, **100**
trade union 34, 134, 145; power of 20, 71, 78; strike 134, 147
Triffin, Robert 19
Trikoupis, Charilaos 2, 3
the troika 36, 56, 167; authoritarianism-neoliberalism/ordoliberalim link 8; deflationist policies and 6; EAP 108; Memoranda 121, 122, 136n1, 143, 144, 147–9, 153, 156, 157, 167, 170, 171, 173, 174, 175; non-sustainability of troika economic programme 6; undemocratic nature of restructuring process driven by 61n7; *see also* ECB; EU; European Commission; IMF
TRPF (tendency of the rate of profit to fall) 112, 113
Trubowitz, Peter 24, 35
Tsipras, Alexis 32, 173, 175–6, 177; capitulation to 13, 135, 175, 179; 'Was Andreas a Liar?' 175–6; *see also* SYRIZA
Turkey 3, 4, 26, 90
Tusk, Donald 149–50

UK (United Kingdom) 14, 66; Brexit 6
Ukraine 7, 25, 26, 27, 28
ULC (Unit Labour Cost) 70–2, *73*, *74*, *75*, 80n14; NULC/nominal unit labour cost 107, 110; RULC/real unit labour cost 108; *see also* labour
UN (United Nations) Security Council 28
unemployment 6, 53, 152; Germany 29; internal devaluation 9, 121, 122, 123, 129, 130, 147; long-term unemployment trap 128–9, 130; social reproduction crisis 125, 126, 128–9, 136
UNICEF (United Nations Children's Fund) 152

USA (United States of America) 115, 153; 1933 Glass-Steagall Act 15–16; Civil War 6–7; as deficit country 18, 19, 29, 66; foreign investment 22, 23; Greece and 4, 5; hegemony 4, 19; right-wing politics 22; subprime mortgage market, collapse of 65; USA Embassy in Athens 4; wages 22, 23
USSR (Union of Soviet Socialist Republics) 17, 23; collapse of 24–5, 26; *see also* Russia
Uxó, Jorge 86

Valls, Manuel 34
Varoudakis, Aristomene 86, 89
Varoufakis, Yianis 10, 23, 28, 29, 30, 62n10, 174, 175; *The Global Minotaur* 13; the 'Global Plan' 17, 21; *see also* the Global Minotaur
Venizelos, Eleftherios 3
Vietnam War 18, 20
Volcker, Paul 19–21, 24; 1979 Volcker Shock 21–2, 23; Volcker-style neoliberalism 22
Von Holdt, Karl 155
Voridis, Makis 172

wage labour in Greece, segments of 125–31; employees 125–8; population of paupers 125, 129–30; relative surplus population 125, 128–9, 130, 135, 136; working-class employees and young workers 127–8, 130; *see also* internal devaluation; social reproduction crisis; wages
wages: collective bargaining and 16; 'Five Presidents' Report' and 149–50; Germany 18, 27, 28, 110; Greece as wage-led economy 121, 123; internal devaluation and wage flexibility/reduction 9, 121, 122–3, 124, 125, 126, 133, 147; Japan 18; minimum wage 6, 124, 125, 150; neoliberalism and 10; ordoliberalism and 10; reduction of 10, 18, 33, 108, 150; USA 22, 23; wage-labour trap 128; wage share 71, *72*; wage repression 28, 112; wages/consumption relation 122–3; *see also* wage labour in Greece, segments of
Wall Street 7, 25, 29; 1929 Wall Street Crash 15
Walters, Alan Arthur 69, 72; 'Walters critique' 68–9
Ware, Alan 176
Warsaw Pact 22, 26
Washington Consensus 115
Watanuki, Joji 20
wealth 24; distribution/redistribution of 18, 125, 135
Weber, Max 10, 143, 147, 169, 196; notion of the state 148–9, 151, 153; perspective on money 156–7
welfare state 19, 32; Greece 4, 121, 126, 144, 145; neoliberalism and 10, 146; ordoliberalism and 10; shrinking of 144
the West 24, 25, 32, 35, 112–13, 118; geopolitics and 2, 3; Western state as highest stage of political development 151
West Germany 23, 176
Weyland, Kurt 174–5
Wolf, Martin 8
Woodruff, David M. 155
working class 20; assault on 22; consumption 128, 137n11; social reproduction crisis and 127–8, 130
World War I 3, 14–15
World War II 3, 15, 23
Worstall, Tim 88

xenophobia 174, 198–9, 202

Zielonka, Jan 159n8
Zolotas, Xenophon 4

For Product Safety Concerns and Information please contact our EU representative GPSR@taylorandfrancis.com
Taylor & Francis Verlag GmbH, Kaufingerstraße 24, 80331 München, Germany

www.ingramcontent.com/pod-product-compliance
Lightning Source LLC
LaVergne TN
LVHW021727021026
849161LV00004BA/753
9781857438673